The Demon and the Damozel

Dynamics of Desire in the

Works of Christina Rossetti and

The Demon & the Damozel

Dante Gabriel Rossetti

SUZANNE WALDMAN

Ohio University Press • Athens

Ohio University Press, Athens, Ohio 45701
www.ohioswallow.com
© 2008 by Ohio University Press
All rights reserved

To obtain permission to quote, reprint, or otherwise reproduce or distribute material from Ohio University Press publications, please contact our rights and permissions department at (740) 593-1154 or (740) 593-4536 (fax).

Printed in the United States of America
Ohio University Press books are printed on acid-free paper ⊗ ™

15 14 13 12 11 10 09 08   5 4 3 2 1

Library of Congress Cataloging-in-Publication Data

Waldman, Suzanne.
 The demon and the damozel : dynamics of desire in the works of Christina Rossetti and Dante Gabriel Rossetti / Suzanne Waldman.
  p. cm.
 Includes bibliographical references and index.
 ISBN 978-0-8214-1816-1 (cloth : alk. paper)
  1. Rossetti, Christina Georgina, 1830–1894—Criticism and interpretation. 2. Rossetti, Dante Gabriel, 1828–1882—Criticism and interpretation. 3. Art and literature—England—History—19th century. 4. Literature and society—England—History—19th century. 5. Aesthetics, Modern—19th century. I. Title.
 PR5238.W35 2008
 821'.8—dc22
                                                                2008017863

Contents

	List of Illustrations	vii
	Acknowledgments	ix
	Introduction	1
one	The Transcendental Tendency in Christina Rossetti's Poetry of Love and Devotion	10
two	The Superegoic Demon in Christina Rossetti's Gothic and Fantasy Writings	38
three	Imaginary Oscillation in Dante Gabriel Rossetti's Illustrations of Dante	69
four	The Symbolic Perfection of the Imaginary in Dante Gabriel Rossetti's *The House of Life*	93
five	Hysterical Desire in Dante Gabriel Rossetti's Narrative Poems and Portraiture	118
	Conclusion	155
	Notes	165
	Bibliography	187
	Index	197

Illustrations

1. D. G. Rossetti, Paolo and Francesca da Rimini — 75
2. D. G. Rossetti, Beatrice Meeting Dante at a Marriage Feast, Denies Him Her Salutation — 78
3. D. G. Rossetti, The Salutation of Beatrice — 79
4. D. G. Rossetti, The First Anniversary of the Death of Beatrice (1849) — 82
5. D. G. Rossetti, The First Anniversary of the Death of Beatrice (1853) — 83
6. D. G. Rossetti, Dante's Dream at the Time of the Death of Beatrice (1856) — 85
7. D. G. Rossetti, Dante's Dream at the Time of the Death of Beatrice (1871) — 86
8. Jacques Lacan's optical schema for the theory of narcissism — 107
9. D. G. Rossetti, Beata Beatrix — 119
10. D. G. Rossetti, Design for Genevieve — 136
11. D. G. Rossetti, The Girlhood of Mary Virgin — 139
12. D. G. Rossetti, Ecce Ancilla Domini! — 141
13. D. G. Rossetti, Fazio's Mistress — 143
14. D. G. Rossetti, Bocca Baciata — 148
15. D. G. Rossetti, Mary Magdalene at the Door of Simon the Pharisee — 153

Acknowledgments

I would like to thank the colleagues who have generously advised me on the manuscript in the various stages: Antony H. Harrison, Steven Bruhm, Patricia Rigg, Mary Arseneau, and especially Marjorie Stone, who has been an invaluable guide. I would also like to thank both of the anonymous readers for their careful and helpful comments on the manuscript and the editorial staff of Ohio University Press, particularly David Sanders, for their friendly support. In addition, Jerome McGann and the staff of the Rossetti Archive have very graciously provided some of the images of Dante Gabriel Rossetti's work.

I am grateful to the Social Science and Humanities Research Council of Canada and the Killam Foundation for their fellowship support during the writing of this book at the dissertation stage. In addition, I would like to acknowledge *Victorian Poetry* for publishing an early version of the first chapter of this book in a special issue, "Victorian Sexualities and Desires" (edited by Donald E. Hall), in 2000.

Thank you to colleagues at Carleton University for your friendship and to my family for your love.

My deepest gratitude is to Brian, who has encouraged me in this project.

Introduction

OH FOOLISHEST FOND folly of a heart
  Divided, neither here nor there at rest!
    That hankers after Heaven, but clings to earth;
    That neither here nor there knows thorough mirth,
Half-choosing, wholly missing, the good part[.]
        (Christina Rossetti, *Later Life*, 24.9–13)

A sonnet is a coin: its face reveals
  The soul,—its converse, to what Power 'tis due.
      (Dante Gabriel Rossetti, *The House of Life*, 1.9–10)[1]

The common factor structuring both Christina Rossetti's and Dante Gabriel Rossetti's presentation of human experience and the psychoanalytic presentation of the subject is that of an integral duality. In the above excerpts from their most comprehensive poetic statements—the virtually contemporaneous sonnet sequences *Later Life* (1881) and *The House of Life* (1881)[2]—the two poets consider the divisions that structure their oeuvres and plague their biographies. Christina Rossetti's speaker describes the conflict within herself in traditional Christian terms, depicting the conflicting appeals of heaven, where as a "wise" and scrupulous woman she aims to "send [her] heart[ ]," and of earth, where her heart contrarily clings.

Dante Gabriel Rossetti's *House of Life* sonneteer presents a somewhat different split, giving an account in the introductory sonnet of the fissured nature of an ideal poetic expression, which must not only attend to the needs of one's individual loving soul but also supplicate power, paying "tribute to the august appeals / [o]f life" in order to attain social goods such as money and fame (11–12). Thus, in contrast with the Christian framework in which Christina's speaker describes duality as a conflict of world against heaven, Dante Gabriel's speaker represents the fundamental conflict as one of self against world, expressing what Loy Martin has described as the typical Victorian split between a "desire for autonomy" and a "desire for coherence in the system of social . . . ties."[3] Not merely isolated expressions, the speakers' testimonies in these sonnets portray the divisions that underlie Christina Rossetti's and Dante Gabriel Rossetti's oeuvres as wholes. Christina's writings divide starkly between her lyrics, in which speakers disavow earthy sensuality and cultivate an austere ideal in pure language, and her Romantically tinged fantasy and gothic poems that make use of sensually appealing imagery to dramatize scenes of demonic temptation; this radical division makes it difficult to decide whether, as an author, she ultimately celebrates austerity and obedience or pleasure and subversion. Dante Gabriel's works, in contrast, split between works that glamorize private amorous ecstasies and works that indulge in dispassionate fantasies that display how symbolic iconographies and hierarchies mediate desire. These two alternating thrusts, toward autonomous intimacy and toward social ratification, also produce duality within Dante Gabriel's individual works such as "Jenny" (1848–59/1870), in which tones of tenderness interweave with tones of exploitation.

But while Christina's and Dante Gabriel's modes of representing the duality of subjectivity are sharply distinct from each other, both are circumscribed within psychoanalytic theories of divided subjectivity, particularly within the theories of Jacques Lacan, who observes that "essential dualism [is] constitutive of the subject."[4] Lacan's theories, which he describes as a "return to the origin of the Freudian experience," revise Sigmund Freud's economic split between death instincts and life instincts to imagine the subject (as well as his speech) as split between the effects of the symbolic order and the imaginary order.[5] The symbolic order of the subject is that of culture, through which the subject becomes linked through the sharing of discourse into a community that offers "recognition and transcendence" while demanding submission to "the order of a law" (SI, 177). The imaginary order comprises the vestiges of the subject that were created before he came to understand himself in these symbolic terms, that is, while he subsisted within a "specular state" of mirrored relations with others (SI, 177). As Lacan insists, "The line of cleavage [in the subject] doesn't pass between the unconscious and the conscious but between . . . something which is repressed and tends simply to repeat itself, that is to say speech which insists . . . and something which is an obstacle to it, and which is organised in another manner, namely the ego . . . the imaginary" (SII, 321). Thus, in the mature subject, an insistent symbolic order impels the subject toward social belonging and a share of immortal meaning through a relationship with what Lacan calls "the Other"—the abstract position often held by a God who supervenes these values. Meanwhile, the subject's imaginary attachments continue to underlie pressing and potentially obstructive libidinal attractions toward "others," or other particular subjects.

Julia Kristeva, a semiotician and student of Lacan, further relates how a split in the subject is constitutive of the dynamics of art and literature. The networks of signification in works of art from the late Victorian period onward are, she finds, bifurcated between the effects of the symbolic order and the effects of desire.[6] Kristeva's account of art as a network of symbolic regulations and the libidinal impulses that oppose them helps to map the conflict in Christina's writing in psychoanalytic terms, as between a dominant symbolic order of Christian devotion and the imaginary desires that persist despite all of the subject's attempts to sublimate them. Kristeva's model of the opposition of desire and symbolic law also sets out a way to read the struggle in Dante Gabriel's work. According to this model, we may see his work as divided between the cultivation of a state of libidinal fusion characterized in Freudian theory as narcissistic and associated by Lacan with the imaginary order, and the compulsion to sacrifice the imaginary connection to an other in order to be inserted into what Juliet Flower MacCannell calls a "function within the symbolic order" in the pursuit of fame, social acceptance, and aesthetic or spiritual redemption.[7]

In this book, I argue that the psychoanalytical account of a subject divided against himself that was formalized by Freud and further developed by Lacan and Kristeva is more capable than most other interpretive models of characterizing the Victorian formations of the Rossettis. I further propose that a congruence between nineteenth-century art and twentieth-century theory in this case is neither ahistorical nor coincidental, given the range of formative contexts shared between the Rossettis and psychoanalytic theory. Most obviously, psychoanalytic criticism can be understood to account for dynamics in the Rossettis' works because these works were created amid the same nineteenth-century conflicts and frustrations that Freudian theory was originally devised to explain. James Eli Adams has pointed out that Freud's skepticism about the possibility of reconciling one's sexuality with the demands of one's culture expresses the Victorian sense of an insoluble division within the self.[8] In particular, the works of Christina and Dante Gabriel foreground an opposition between individualistic and regulated desires that Wendell Stacy Johnson has described as the Victorian question as to why the sexuality exhibited by subjects frequently obstructs them from social harmonization.[9] Thus, in several of her gothic poems, Christina depicts brides who are torn between taking a place within ordinary society and surrendering to deeper, more-occult sexual pressures, while Dante Gabriel typically portrays, and inhabits, the position of the romantic rogue whose desire leads him beyond the bounds of social acceptability.

Furthermore, the experience of inner disharmony that underlies both the works of the Rossettis and the theories of psychoanalysis can be analyzed in relation to the legacies within Christian metaphysics and Romantic literature. Both the Rossettis' art and Freudian theory display vestiges of the Christian model of the subject occupied by forces of evil and goodness, as well as vestiges of the Romantic model of the subject imagined by writers such as William Blake and George Gordon Byron, who inverted Christian values to reclaim the individual desire that Christianity labeled demonic. Indeed, psychoanalytic theory and the Victorian art of the Rossettis can each be said to share the burden of preserving dualist conceptions of the subject from the monistic rationalizations of post-Enlightenment humanism. As Joan Copjec explains, psychoanalytic theory arose in resistance to nineteenth-century utilitarians who conceived of the subject as a pure ego singularly in pursuit of desire, and it has persisted in resistance to twentieth-century cultural materialists such as Louis Althusser and Michel Foucault who have envisioned the subject in reverse, as totally susceptible to the symbolic order of ideology.[10] In contrast with these monistic treatments of the subject, psychoanalytic theory identifies the subject neither with his desire nor with a higher symbolic will but as relentlessly split between these thrusts (Copjec, 23). According to psychoanalytic theory, as Copjec elaborates, the psychoanalytic subject does not "purely and simply follow his inclination," in Lacan's words (SII, 326), because he also expresses ethical potential: the ability to participate in a symbolic order that has evolved to regulate human relationships (Copjec, 92). Lacan thus equally preserves the Christian intuition that a subject's libidinal desire is not necessarily well motivated or even authentic; if "desire is not self-originating" but "is first grasped in the other and in the most confused form," it consequently retains a fatal thrust (SI, 147, 225). This fatal thrust of desire is registered throughout the Rossettis' oeuvres, especially in the Christian terms in which their subjects—who frequently resemble the Rossettis[11]—are accused of indulgence and distraction from higher aims.

But while insisting that the subject must be wary of his desire, Lacan also displays how psychoanalytic theory has preserved the Romantic intuition that a life that excludes one's deepest impulses is barren,[12] insisting that "the only thing one can be guilty of is [of] giving ground relative to one's desire."[13] The writings of both Christina and Dante Gabriel, notwithstanding the former's severe Christian commitments, are each likewise inhabited by a Romantic compulsion to excavate and release hidden psychic elements and thereby give full scope to emotional life. Both, of course, read widely in the Romantic literature that preceded them and—as with many Victorian writers—continued to explore issues raised during the Romantic period, such as the claims of one's passion when it is at odds with one's morality. Dante Gabriel identifies himself as an explorer of hidden desire in the sonnet "Dantis Tenebrae" (1861 / 1870), in which he describes how he is drawn to the "magical dark mysteries" of the infernal valley (6). Christina experimented with the Romantic gothic genre particularly during the mid-1850s, when she imagined many scenarios in which demon lovers promise, at least initially, to save women from sterile lives. In the same way that in Freud's writing desire that becomes unrepressed can emerge as a "thing of terror,"[14] Victorian poets such as the Rossettis articulated their deepest desire as a demonic reflection of the self, as Ekbert Faas observes.[15] The Rossetti family context was especially suited to engendering in these artist siblings the sense of the duality of the human subject that psychoanalytic theory would later excavate in clinical terms. Whereas their mother, Frances Rossetti, was a member of a fervently antisensual brand of Anglo-Catholicism, their Italian father was a culturally free skeptic, and the Rossetti children enjoyed free rein in a library full of gothic writings by such authors as their maternal uncle, John Polidori.[16] This clash between religion and romanticism shows up throughout Christina's and Dante Gabriel's works, in which the glamorization of desire contests with the condemnation of it. In the most famous example, Christina's narrator of *Goblin Market* seems undeniably to relish the landscape of desire that she structurally determines as demonic. And while Dante Gabriel's writing is famous for its inveterate "fleshl[iness],"[17] it is also laden with signs of sexual guilt, as in "Jenny," in which the scholarly young speaker expresses the abjectness of the male physiological response in the face of an alluring female body (366–69).

In this regard, Faas has discussed how Victorian poetry is distinctive insofar as it began to reflect the psyche in a highly analytical manner, echoing contemporaneous developments in the fields of scientific psychiatry and philosophical psychology, in which an intuition that the rational life was overshadowed by unconscious elements was burgeoning, preparing the ground for Freud's discoveries.[18] We can see this kind of analytical rigor in the Rossettis' sketches of the architecture of anxious and depressive states and the archaeology of childhood delights and traumas, to a degree that the Rossettis can be said to have "often anticipated the new science," according to their general characterization by Faas (31). Christina's *Goblin Market* thus itemizes with disturbing precision a traumatized response to a precocious sexual encounter in its account of how Laura came to "dwindle[ ], as the fair full moon doth turn / [t]o swift decay and burn / [h]er fire away" after her submission to the goblins' invitation (278–80). Dante Gabriel displays striking insight into the displacement of sexual guilt in "Jenny" where the speaker admits to regarding Jenny in a dismissive and mocking manner because he is "ashamed of [his] own shame" (380–83). Given the convergence of the reference points of psychoanalytic theory and Victorian literature, one should not be surprised by the parallel courses taken by each to illuminate the depths of human experience.

Another reason for the intersection of art and theory in the case of the Rossettis can be drawn from the conditions of the production of Freudian theory. In an interview conducted late in his life, Freud attributed his discovery of the unconscious not primarily to his research in earlier forms of mental science but to the products of the poets and philosophers who had preceded him, claiming that what he added to this heritage was the "discover[y of] . . . the scientific method by which the unconscious can be studied."[19] While Freud was presumably in large part referring to the backdrop of Romantic culture upon which he extensively draws in his formulations, Victorian literature is even more broadly a site in which complex psychic formations suggested by the artistic and mythical structures of the past were opened up. In the terms of Jerome McGann, Dante Gabriel Rossetti's works map out "forms of desire" by elaborating in a self-conscious and aesthetic manner on a legacy of highly suggestive medieval, renaissance, and Romantic imagery.[20] Christina Rossetti, for her part, interweaves rich biblical and Byronic backdrops to dramatize the kind of "intimate . . . apocalypses" that Kristeva observes in horror novels and nightmares, in which subjects are torn wrenchingly between libido and law.[21] The same kinds of classical, biblical, literary, and visual backdrops are frequently referenced by Freud, Lacan, and Kristeva, who admit through their eclectic means to owing a great debt to this heritage, through which Western subjectivity was broadly formulated. The Rossettis might therefore be included among the great number of Victorian writers and artists who foraged in the clearinghouse of past arts and, by doing so, lent interpretative depth to the same literary formulations that would stimulate Freud and his followers.

Despite the historical convergence between the Rossettis' art and protopsychoanalytic thought, very little of their work has been subject to the kind of detailed psychoanalytical treatment it would seem to merit. A few articles have offered subtle post-Freudian interpretations of the Rossettis.[22] Often, however, psychoanalytical criticisms of the Rossettis' works have been analytically reductive and prone to pathologizing generalizations, portraying Dante Gabriel as an out-and-out narcissist or fetishist, for instance, or taking Christina's religious dedication as a sign of masochism.[23] Out of frustration with damaging treatments of Christina Rossetti in particular, critics such as Antony H. Harrison have come to assert that her poetry is "hardly best served by . . . neo-Freudian interpretations."[24] In this book, I have added a new dimension to psychoanalytic criticism of Victorian poetry by emphasizing Christina's and Dante Gabriel's analyses and discoveries about the psyche, showing how their works exhibit ingenious analyses that augment, as well as qualify, existing theory. I have meanwhile followed Ellen Handler Spitz's guidelines for treating artistic works as cultural objects, interpreting the Rossettis' artistic preoccupations and habits not only in relation to biographical events and trends but also in relation to matters of genre, technique, historical context, reception, and requirements of commercialization.[25]

In *The Demon and the Damozel*, I have also tried to surmount another limiting aspect of more-recent psychoanalytical readings of both Christina's and Dante Gabriel's works: the way in which such readings tend to polarize the gender politics of these writers' works in predictable ways. Typically, recent psychoanalytic criticism of Christina Rossetti draws on theories of Hélène Cixous, Luce Irigaray, and Judith Butler to find that she subverts patriarchy,[26] while recent psychoanalytical criticism of Dante Gabriel Rossetti tends to draw on the writings of film theorist Laura Mulvey to find that Dante Gabriel traps women in destructive masculinist fantasies.[27] A careful reading of the Rossettis' works, such as I have done, suggests that these post-Freudian frameworks are, in themselves, too single-faceted to encompass these artists' sexualities, of which "no [singular] drive presents [a] totality," in the words of Lacan (Four, 184). Apart from those works in which Dante Gabriel portrays a norm-determined idea of masculine desire, there are also works in which he is willfully unmanly. Likewise, whereas Christina sometimes exposes the particular perils of women's lives, as in her critical sonnet "A Triad" (1856/1862), she also frequently eludes such concerns through the pursuit of a Christian redemption that promises to lead her into a realm beyond gender. I have therefore attempted to present a more nuanced treatment of how these artists' works embody and depict gender, dealing especially with struggles inherent in their sexualities as well as contradictions in their gender politics.

Meanwhile, the collection of interpretations of the Rossettis' works into a single volume perhaps goes some way toward overcoming the gender segregation that has kept the Rossettis from being read in relation to each other, with Christina Rossetti tending most often in recent decades to be critically grouped with women writers and Dante Gabriel Rossetti with other members of the Pre-Raphaelite Brotherhood. *The Demon and the Damozel* continues in the line of more recent efforts to treat in tandem[28] two artists whom the record shows were mutually influential, companionate, and collaborative (if not in the writing process, then in the process of editing and illustrating each others' works).[29] In this book, I augment this growing effort to understand the Rossettis as a distinctive Victorian phenomenon, using a methodology that investigates how their intricate visions of the paradoxes of selfhood were born out of a singular, highly charged context and consequently intersect as well as collide in fascinating ways.

The critical methodology of this volume emphasizes recent psychoanalytical theory that is faithful to the original Freudian concept of the economically divided subject, which is largely found in Lacan's writings, as well as in interpretations of these writings by critics such as Julia Kristeva, Joan Copjec, and Slavoj Žižek. Kristeva's writings likewise open up the literary and artistic implications of Freudian and Lacanian concepts, while contributing additional useful concepts such as "the abject."[30] In addition, culturally and historically situated uses of Lacanian ideas by Copjec and readings of courtly love, horror, medieval art, and mystical devotion by Kristeva in this book elicit psychoanalytic readings of the Rossettis that are responsive not only to the logic of their works but also to the cultural traditions in which they lived and the influences on which they drew.

The book's content generally reflects the aim of distinguishing discursive and formal divisions in Christina's and Dante Gabriel's texts that anticipate Lacan's opposition between the symbolic and imaginary orders. In keeping with Lacan's description of the symbolic order as a system of regulation (SII, 254), the dominance of the symbolic order can be observed in those instances of Christina's and Dante Gabriel's art that are dominated by teleologies and other overriding structures of meaning. In contrast, the imaginary order is found in the pleasure—what Lacan calls the jouissance[31]—of a scopic dynamic in which the self is discovered though reflection in mirrors constituted by others.[32] Thus, imaginary effects are observed in works that feature passionate glances, for instance, Dante Gabriel's paintings of Dante meeting Beatrice and Christina's sonnet sequence *Later Life*, in which her speaker longs to set "the eyes of [her] desire" upon Jesus (11.9). Furthermore, because the imaginary order is the compulsion in the subject that disrupts symbolic meaning—"sowing discord in the discourse," as Lacan puts it (SII, 306)—its pressures are indicated in jumbled and surreal poetic and visual imagery. As a complement to these confusing imaginary suggestions are hints, meanwhile, of the elusive expression of "the real," Lacan's formulation for the terrifying and sublime experiences that "resists all symbolization absolutely" (SI, 66). At the same time, no perfect division between the the three orders can ever be found in the texts, since, as Lacan claims, these "two different dimensions . . . never cease getting caught up with one another" and "crisscross" in multitudinous ways (SII, 105). Indeed, the places where Christina's and Dante Gabriel's evocations of the symbolic, imaginary, and real orders crisscross—where Christina's quest for Christian transcendence is permeated by an imaginary desire for companionship and where Dante Gabriel's expressions of narcissism in *The House of Life* are elevated through invocations of the sacred—are where we find the most striking effects.

one

The Transcendental Tendency in Christina Rossetti's Poetry of Love and Devotion

> What is this transcendental tendency towards sublimation? . . . This is the point where we open out into the symbolic order, which isn't the libidinal order in which the ego is inscribed, along with all the drives. It tends beyond the pleasure principle, beyond the limits of life, and that is why Freud identifies it with the death instinct. . . . And the death instinct is only the mask of the symbolic order, in so far . . . as it hasn't been realised.
> —Jacques Lacan, *Seminar I*

THE DISCOURSES OF SEXUAL LOVE and of religious devotion have not always been sharply distinguished from one another. In twelfth-century Europe, for instance, there was not a great difference between religious and secular theories of love, according to Julia Kristeva, who describes how twelfth-century mystics characterized the basis of religious love, like amorous love, as a mutual yearning between two beings "for what one does not have."[1] Kristeva explains that, after the twelfth century, this theology of desire gave way to the rational distinction of God as being above all desire by theorists such as Kant, but she also notes that some later devotional writers dared to sustain this mystical tradition, including the seventeenth-century Jeanne Guyon, who addressed God in prayers that sounded like love letters and was consequently condemned as a heretic. Christina Rossetti is another postmedieval writer who transgresses the boundary between religious and sexual love; critics including Antony H. Harrison and Colleen Hobbs have noted the influence on her poetry of religious devotion of medieval mystics such as Thomas à Kempis, Margery Kempe, and Julian of Norwich.[2] We can see mystical-amorous overtones in poems such as "A Better Resurrection" (1857/1862), in which Rossetti describes her experience of a grave dryness that she seeks to water through love: "My life is like a faded leaf, / My harvest dwindled to a husk" (9–10). Her invitations to Jesus to fulfill her express a strong phallic component, as when she hopes for him to essentially fertilize her with a spiritual equivalent of the "sap of spring," begging "O Jesus, rise in me" (15–16). Finally, having asked Jesus to "remould" her broken self into a holy cup, she emphasizes her feminine nature as a vessel, reversing Jesus's adjuration in John 7:37 to "come unto me and drink" into the invitation "O Jesus, drink of me" (24).

Even more common—and more crafty—than these suggestively sexual forms of solicitation of the divine is the oblique strategy adopted by Rossetti in "Confluents" (1865/1876), in which she makes use of syntactic ambiguity to yoke together amorous and religious discourses.³ For much of this poem, the object of the speaker's desire cannot be determined to be either human or divine, as, for instance, when she declares,

> As the delicate rose
> To the sun's sweet strength,
> Doth herself unclose,
> Breadth and length;
>> So spreads my heart to thee
>> Unveiled utterly.
>>> (9–14)

Her comparison of the unveiling of her heart with the spreading of a rose's petals is erotic, given the rose's association with the theme of love and its function as a plant's sexual organ. But the image of the rose also has a legacy of portraying spiritual reception, as when an Old Testament writer describes how "the desert shall rejoice, and blossom as the rose" when it experiences "the glory of the Lord" (Isaiah 35:1). Likewise, at the terminus of Dante Alighieri's *Paradiso*, the sacred "eternal rose" is said to "unfold[ ], fragrantly" when Dante sees it, extolling the "Splendour of God" that is immanent in it (30:124, 97).⁴

Similarly ambiguous is the exultation of Rossetti's speaker:

> As dew leaves not a trace
> On the green earth's face;
> I, no trace
> On thy face.
>> (21–25)

Her invocation of a relationship with an other seems like a sentiment of tenderness between human lovers, particularly because of how it refers to the lover's face, thus invoking the vestiges of imaginary desire in the subject. As Lacan explains, although the imaginary attachments developed by the subject in the mirror stage are eventually overwritten by the symbolic order, they continue to exert pressure on the "discourse of the subject" in the forms of "first symbols" stemming from "image[s] of the human body" (SII, 306). The speaker's description of her gentle touch of the other's face accordingly evokes a sense of identification with the beloved other through this contact. However, the trope of the face is also traditionally devotional, as we see in the biblical account by King David that God instructed him, "Seek ye my face" (Psalm 27:8–9).[5] In each of these cases, the poem's imagery is teasingly indeterminate about its addressee.

Toward the end of the poem, however, the tone of "Confluents" becomes distinctly religious, "modulat[ing] upward," to borrow a phrase from Harrison (Context, 102). The speaker compares her desire with the river that "its goal . . . knows" (26), invoking an image of sublime self-transcendence as well as the oceanic sensation that Freud associates with religious feeling.[6] Lacan glosses such oceanic desire as the subject's pursuit of the "point where we open out into the symbolic order" through a process of "sublimation" (SII, 326), a term defined by Freud as a means of redirecting libido toward "an aim other than, and remote from, that of sexual gratification."[7] Drawing on a similar hydraulic metaphor, Freud describes Leonardo da Vinci's process of sublimation as one in which Leonardo dammed up his desire through intense artistic and scholarly concentration until the desire broke "loose and flow[ed] away freely" in the form of spiritual ecstasy, "as a stream of water drawn from a river is allowed to flow away when the work is done."[8] Lacan further explains that the oceanic thrust toward such spiritual dissolution does not issue from "the libidinal order in which the ego is inscribed, along with all the drives" but is instead a case of desire that been subjected to "the transcendent tendency," in which ultimate meaning is pursued through religious, artistic, and philosophical quests (SII, 326, 307). Through such quests, the imaginary drive for connection with a distinct human other is converted into a symbolic pursuit of absorption into the sublime presence of "the Thing":[9] that elusive entity or being that occupies for one the position of supreme value.[10]

The idealizing subtext of "Confluents" is declared overtly in the final sentence, where the speaker asks,

> Shall I, lone sorrow past,
> Find thee at last?
> Sorrow past,
> Thee at last?
> (29–32)

The speaker's modulation from the lowercase pronoun *thee* of the second line to the reverent, capitalized form of the beginning of the final line warrants acts like the ascendant motion of her metaphors, as it subtly leads the reader to envision a divine object beyond the realm of personal attraction. The title "Confluents" ultimately shows itself to be metatextual, with the poem not only depicting forms in which the self flows into the Other but also dramatizing how amorous libido can flow into the cause of religious quest.

Because the carefully wrought ambiguities of Christina Rossetti's poems, such as "Confluents," produce a irresolvable experience of tension, some critics have proposed that her motive for writing such poems was aesthetic—that is, geared to exploring art's potential for oscillation.[11] However, the aesthetic reading does not fully capture the sense that a poem such as "Confluents" actually makes use of its ambiguities, drawing on the subtle powers of language to approach the very goal it describes. Such a poem, in other words, becomes a means whereby the speaker, and perhaps also the reader, can progress in one's sublimation, in keeping with Lacan's understanding of language as the vehicle by which one transforms desires by submitting them to a universal symbolic principle in the "field of the [O]ther" (*SI*, 157; *Four*, 188). Kristeva has adapted this Lacanian analysis of language to poetry, which she characterizes as a "minimal signifying structure" with "boundaries admitting of [the] upheaval, dissolution and transformation" of desire (*Desire*, 25). While Kristeva focuses on the politically radical destabilizing poetics of avant-garde poets, Christina Rossetti's poetry pursues no-less-radical dissolutions of subjectivity as it dismantles boundaries between the isolated individual and its spiritual source and so produces sites of sublimation where desire can, in Freud's words, fuel "an ecstatic language praising the splendour of . . . creation" ("Da Vinci," 164).

Christina Rossetti's literary practices of sublimation took several forms over the course of her literary oeuvre. Her poems about love, for example, characterize erotic love as a false path that always leads to disappointment, thus warranting the sublimation of desire into a quest for a higher goal. In these poems, she simultaneously encapsulates the ideology of

Christianity and anticipates the theoretical critique that Lacan would perform of "imaginary passion," a form of relating to the Other that is precarious because it is based in the illusory, narcissistic structure of the ego (SI, 276). In the middle of her career, Rossetti undertook even-more-powerful strategies of sublimation, both those that reorient the imaginary libidinal drives toward ideal objects and those that more-specifically recruit the resources of the symbolic order, including linguistic repetition and the invocation of death. A comparison of the relative success of two extended narratives of sublimation, Monna Innominata (1880) and Later Life (1881), yields an index of viable practices within Christina Rossetti's developing oeuvre. Finally, there are several indications in Rossetti's later devotional tract, The Face of the Deep (1892), that her pursuit of sublimation allowed her to cultivate an indifference to gender constraints in keeping with her growing conviction of an apocalyptic context to being. It concludes that Christina Rossetti's vision of an end to gender repels critical applications to her of theories of écriture féminine that hold that her femininity ran deeper than her symbolic commitments, observing that she was deeply committed to the patriarchal discourses that she believed would help her to transcend her worldly bond.

Taking Death for Life

Christina Rossetti's decision to undertake a course of sublimation was doubtlessly overdetermined, impelled as it was by both biographical experiences and underlying philosophical attitudes that preceded and subtended the biographical events that are considered to have informed it. She appears to have resolved on her path of renunciation and transformation after the demise of her hopes with Charles Cayley in the mid-1860s confirmed for her that love was bound to be disappointing; as biographer Jan Marsh finds, Rossetti "henceforth conveyed the recognition that the happiness she craved could not be attained in real life, but only in 'nell' altro mondo'" (CR, 375). Rossetti frames such a retreat from interpersonal love in the poem "Twice" (1864/1866), which was written around the time of that disillusionment. Here the speaker overtly pronounces that if one gives one's heart to a man to "scan," he will misjudge it, but if one gives one's heart to God, he will judge it truly, refine it, and hold it forever (11). This conviction conforms with what Kristeva has described as the mystical idealization of divine love as a perfect and viable substitute for human erotic love and is consistent with Christina's ideology of transcendence as a whole (Tales, 205).[12] "Twice" thus provides a biographical reference point to Christina's ongoing poetic critique of erotic love as attended by inevitable alienation and loss.

However, the critique of interpersonal love in Christina Rossetti's work precedes any concrete disappointments, with even her earliest poetry testifying that erotic love is unsatisfying and abrading to individuals, leading them into the forms of corruption that Lacan likewise associates with imaginary desire. Christina's juvenile "Death's Chill Between" (1847/1848), for instance, draws on gothic conventions that she likely came across in the Rossetti library to create a relatively sophisticated allegory of how lovers are perpetually haunted and tormented by their erotic desire, finding it to express "an element necessarily lacking, unsatisfied, impossible, misconstrued"—as Lacan likewise contends (Four, 154). This lyric is spoken by the widow of the Prince of Wales, who finds after her husband's death that everywhere she goes, she feels her departed husband's presence as a "love-cord" that ties her to him (4). Tranquility is lost forever to her because there remains "something at [her] heart / [g]nawing" after her husband's death, turning the legacy of a happy love into an eternity of suffering (38–39). The widow repeatedly senses that her husband has returned to her as a ghost and then realizes that the revenant is merely an illusion; she is thus suffering from a version of what Lacan describes as the "specular mirage" of love, whereby a conviction of correspondence and contact with the other that is felt to be external is actually internally generated (Four, 268). According to Lacan, such mirages occur because one's image of the other is anticipated in the psyche as a lost "imago" on which the self was founded and goes on to be carried as a template within the self; an intense bond is thus felt with an other who seems to match that template ("Mirror," 4). The imaginary correspondences with an other that seem authentic and vital are described by Lacan in one place as "phantoms that dominate" the subject, further reinforcing the parallel with the ghost lover that dominates Christina Rossetti's bereft princess ("Mirror," 3). The sum effect of Rossetti's poem is to convey through the sad story of a woman deluded with grief the essentially bereft and haunting condition of imaginary love, which is founded in the same illusions of presence.

This sense of love as a haunting is extended in "Echo" (1854/1862), a poem whose title evokes Ovid's myth of the woman paired with Narcissus who fell in love with a voice indistinguishable from her own. Christina Rossetti's "Echo" seems equally to be a poem about narcissistic confusion, as the speaker recalls a deeply fulfilling "love of finished years" that has left behind a sense of incompleteness parallel to the void in the self, which the subject seeks to fill with imaginary love (6). These hopes of imaginary intimacy are never fulfillable in reality but "can only ever be partial, wishful, anticipated, put off into the future, delayed," in the words of Lacanian critic Elizabeth Grosz.[13] Rossetti's speaker similarly describes the sensation of her love as "too sweet, too bitter sweet" to ever have been fully manifested in real life, and she proposes that its "wakening should have been in Paradise" (7–8). She asks of her lover, "Come to me in the speaking silence of a dream" (2), in which love's manifestation could be closer to what the emotion promises, thereby embodying Lacan's observation that the dream is the ultimate site for revisiting libidinal fixations, because "in the field of the dream" is where the imaginary ego is most "at home" (SII, 167; Four, 44). When the speaker finally tells her lover, "Speak low, lean low, / As long ago, my love, how long ago" (17–18), her echoing lines replicate the sound of a hollow that evokes Lacan's fundamental "rupture" in the dim and remote origins of the subject that is the cause of her sense of lack and that imaginary love is an effort to mend (Four, 26).

Christina Rossetti provides a more detailed critique of imaginary love in "An Echo from Willowwood" (1870/1896), an obvious retort to Dante Gabriel Rossetti's four *Willowwood* sonnets of 1869. These sonnets, discussed fully in chapter 4, constitute Dante Gabriel's most elaborate affirmation of the attraction of imaginary passion. They unfold a brief narrative in which an appearance of a beloved other is constituted out of a reflection in a pond but drowns back into it, leaving the speaker alone, as when he began. Even though the tone of the sequence is melancholy, it ultimately portrays narcissistic love in a mystifying light, showing the speaker finally gathered within the angel Love's "aureole" ("Willowwood IV," 14). By contrast, in "An Echo from Willowwood," Christina refuses to glorify imaginary attraction. Her lovers do not experience etherealization at their pond. Instead, she depicts a psychologically realistic deprivation in concrete images related to the materiality of pond life; they have "hungering heart[s]" like fish that "leap up and sink" and experience "bitterness which both must drink" (6–7). In an image that interprets imaginary love in a manner uncannily close to how Lacan interprets it, she describes how the lovers' foundational selves grow in roots in the pond "deep below," in comparison to which the actual lovers in their relationship to each other are mere "lilies on the surface" (10–11). These primal imaginary selves that "crav[e] each for each; / [r]esolute and reluctant without speech," (10–11), only momentarily surfacing to form a connection, resemble Lacan's description of imaginary love as a surface bond that hints at repressed depths as love "fill[s] up . . . the primitive gap of the immature subject's libido" (SI, 180). For Christina Rossetti, as for Lacan, the joining of the lovers' faces produces no real unity, only an illusion of it when "a sudden ripple" makes "the faces flow / [o]ne moment joined" (7, 12–13). This contact is instantly cut off, moreover, so that in contrast with Dante Gabriel's emphasis on the preciousness of the imaginary connection, Christina's emphasis is on its brevity and thereby affirms that the subject must look to other, divine forms of love to find a more hospitable place for the heart.

Christina Rossetti most decisively critiques the unreliability of imaginary passion in "A Triad" (1856/1862), which suggests that women are bound to be degraded by it no matter what form of it they undertake. Of the three women characterized in her sonnet,

> One shamed herself in love; one temperately
> Grew gross in soulless love, a sluggish wife;
> One famished died for love.
>
> (9–11)

All of these women erroneously "take death for love" and thus sicken unto death (12). The shameful woman dies of a plaguelike fever "with lips / [c]rimson, with cheeks and bosom in a glow, / [f]lushed to the yellow hair and finger tips"; while the unrequited woman freezes, "blue with famine after love" (1–3, 6). Even human love that has been put on the "symbolic plane," submitted to a cultural framework such as marriage (SI, 141), is spiritually degrading, engendering in the married woman a paralyzing complacency so that she does nothing but "dron[e] in sweetness like a fattened bee" (13). According to Lacan, marriage can produce a symbolic framework for love by binding lovers in relation to a higher principle than their specular attraction and thereby stabilizing the tempestuous character of imaginary passion into a "viable temperate relation" (Four, 276). However, while Lacan finds some form of symbolic structure to be necessary for stabilizing the imaginary self and its bonds, he also points out that symbolic orders can be alienating of the subject in many of their formations; a subject who finds a given symbolic arrangement anathematic must "realign [her]self" within a different one that will allow her to "perfect[ ] her desire" (SI, 197, 14). For Christina Rossetti, whose "A Triad" describes the symbolic stabilization of desire through marriage as not only "temperate[ ]" but also "soulless" (9–10), a realignment toward more-vitalizing forms of sublimation is found to be necessary.

Increasingly over the years, a Christian context to Christina Rossetti's critique of love came to the foreground. "Amor Mundi" (1865/1875), for example, performs a similar exposure of the corruptive force of imaginary passion as "A Triad" while making overt use of iconic biblical and traditional Christian discourses. Reviving the allegorical geography of John Bunyan's *Pilgrim's Progress*, the ballad tells a story about a young woman with "love-locks flowing" who invites a young man to take "the downhill path" into a valley that breathes "honey," signifying the pressures of sensuality (1–2, 6). The two lovers are first described in ways that suggest not corruption but youthful sensuality, particularly in the case of the girl, whose "swift feet seem[ ] to float on / [t]he air like soft twin pigeons too sportive to alight" (7–8). The earthbound quality of her feet acts as an omen, however; and after two pleasant stanzas, ominous signs pass across the bucolic scene: "blackest clouds" that hang, a "scaled and hooded worm" whose "scent comes rich and sickly," and, finally, a shadow of the "thin dead body which waits the eternal term" (9–14, 17). "Amor Mundi" thus roots Rossetti's critique of love in the genre of spiritual warning poems, showing her growing commitment to a specifically Christian philosophy of asceticism.[14] Insofar as "Amor Mundi" shows how the descent into sensual love can lead to spiritual death, its title expresses a double significance, warning both that loving the world is a sin and that erotic love is irredeemably worldly.

Devotional Strategies of Sublimation

Christina Rossetti's ascetic philosophy in her earlier works thus recommended not a renunciation of erotic desire as such but a renunciation of human objects. Discourses of love were not disfavored within her poetic vocabulary but were revised into the ambiguous genre exemplified in "Confluents" that shuttles between amatory referents. Using tropes that are both suggestively erotic and determinedly spiritual, "Confluents" performs semiotic actions that Kristeva has also found in the biblical *Song of Solomon*, which she describes as drawing on biblically coded figures to associate desire with privileged Judeo-Christian contexts, thereby inscribing "the spoken word of law . . . in desire" (*Tales*, 96). Another of Rossetti's erotic poems that resembles *The Song of Solomon* is "A Birthday" (1857/1862), in which lushly aesthetic details, such as the "dais" she would decorate with "vair and purple dyes" and carvings of "doves and pomegranates," invoke sensual jouissance while alluding to biblical discourses of divine royalty and blessed plenitude (9–11). The future tenses of "A Birthday" heighten both erotic anticipation and teleological yearning as the waiting reader comes to anticipate an ideal object. In the midst of this array of symbolic patterning in "A Birthday," there is a compelling image of "peacocks with a hundred eyes" (9); when looked at closely, these are not actual eyes but camouflage eyes of the sort Lacan finds to act in art as a lure to attract the gaze of the symbolic Other (*Four*, 102). The elaborate similes with which Rossetti characterizes her heart—"like a rainbow shell / [t]hat paddles in a halcyon sea" (5–6)—likewise partake of the linguistic fluidity that Kristeva discovers in highly idealistic and potentially sacramental love poetry that produces a confusing sense of the reference and so dissolves the speaker's heart into an evanescent object oriented toward the oceanic experience of "unbeing" (*Tales*, 273). In "A Better Resurrection" (1857/1862), Rossetti's speaker similarly disintegrates herself, finally asking for Jesus to melt her into a "royal cup" so that she can become the vessel of divine rather than mere earthly love (22–23). Through all of these gestures, Rossetti's speaker dramatizes the first stage of sublimation of libido through the dissolving of libido into a more ductile element capable of directing itself toward an ideal object.

But the orientation of desire away from concrete objects and toward ideal ones can only be a preliminary moment in a process of sublimation. As Freud insists, "sublimation is a process that concerns object libido and consists in the instinct's directing itself toward an aim other than, and remote from, that of sexual satisfaction; in this process the accent falls upon deflection from sexuality" ("Narcissism," 94). While Christina Rossetti's poems that combine sexual feeling with religious aspiration are literarily complex and spiritually inspiring, they are also cautionary, proposing that there may be hazards in trying to turn God into a lover. "Weary in Well-Doing" (1864/1866) depicts the speaker's relationship with God as an exhausted plod that sets the speaker up for agonies of amorous frustration and disappointment similar to that experienced by the widow in "Death's Chill Between." The speaker thus protests,

> I go, Lord, where Thou sendest me;
> Day after day I plod and moil:
> But Christ my God, when will it be
> That I may let alone my toil
> And rest with Thee?
> (11–15)

Insofar as this poem nakedly characterizes devotion as a plea without an answer, it suggests that unrequited love for God can be as famishing as unrequited love for a person. The devout's heart breaks and her "soul is wrung" with oscillations of doubts in God as much as any lover's heart and soul are taxed with doubts in the faith of their lover (8–10). Poems such as "Weary in Well-Doing" thus reveal that if one seeks escape from the perils of interhuman amorous desire purely through the refocusing of desire onto an ideal object, one may produce an anthropomorphic religion that replicates the frustration of imaginary loss.

Kristeva and Lacan have accordingly represented the danger of a devotional project that aims to satisfy the personal, imaginary claims of the subject, given that the "transcendental tendency" is, properly, a quest for the symbolic end of language rather than for companionship or erotic fulfillment. In this vein, Kristeva wonders whether Guyon's quest for contact with a perfectly loving God loses its essentially religious qualities, undergoing "slippage" from a symbolic quest for emptiness of the self toward a quest for a perfect unity with another that is essentially narcissistic (*Tales*, 310). Lacan also warns that if a subject's desire for religious sublimation is a quest for a personal response from the Other, one will inevitably suffer disappointment, because "the Other does not respond"; it is "only a metaphor, only the [ultimate] signifier" that one approaches for the sake of total comprehension and meaning (*Four*, 188). A subject's sense that there is a personal God who cares about one may thus be the ultimate imaginary mirage. In general, therefore, Lacanian theory leads us to believe that if there is progress to be had in Christina Rossetti's religious vocation, it is likely to arrive through a route other than purely amorous yearning and will necessarily require incorporating the strategies of the symbolic order through which one may "open out" the self, exchanging personal desire in all of its forms for the impersonal apprehension of a divine totality that Freud characterizes as the end of sublimation.

In "The Lowest Place" (1863/1866), Christina Rossetti exemplifies how the means of the symbolic order can allow one to overcome the disappointments of imaginary yearning with its roots in the egoistic constitution of the subject. "The Lowest Place" is a clever variation on the Christian ethic that "he that humbleth himself shall be exalted" (Luke 14:11), which enacts how the abasement of the ego can lead to the enhancement of another, less egoistic, part of the self. This Christian process (which deems that through refusing limited worldly goods, one can open oneself up to the availability of greater symbolic goods) is consistent with

Lacan's view that in accepting the castration of one's drives, one finds ultimate jouissance "on the inverted ladder of the Law of desire."[15] Rossetti's speaker is at first nervous over her presumption when she asks a favor from God: "Give me the lowest place: not that I dare / Ask for that lowest place" (1–2). But although in the next stanza the speaker asks for further abasement, she has gained the confidence to make a personal demand: "Give me the lowest place: or if for me / The lowest place too high, make one more low" (5–6)—a "daring request," as Dolores Rosenblum points out, given the Christian doctrine that "the last shall be first" ("Religious," 144). Finally, the speaker's request for lowness is revealed to be a demand for the best seat in the house, "where I might sit and see / [m]y God and love Thee so" (5–8). Readers of "The Lowest Place" thus need not be concerned, as some critics have been, that an ostensibly female speaker is enacting her social role of being "subordinate" and "dependent,"[16] because a poem that appears to be about humility is simultaneously saturated with spiritual assuredness. By enacting how acceptance of debasement leads to elevation, Rossetti dramatizes how the humility that "glorifies the annihilation of self in the love of God" can spring from "a vitality and a confidence," in Kristeva's words (*Tales*, 298).

The form of "The Lowest Room" suggests, meanwhile, that this annihilation of the self occurs not instantaneously but through a gradual process of sublimation described by Freud as the "execution" of a discipline ("Narcissism," 407), as it formally dramatizes a discipline of constrained, prayerful repetition. Christina Rossetti's poetry has accordingly been tied to the poetry of the ritual-seeking Oxford movement, and George B. Tennyson particularly notes a link between Rossetti's repetitive style and that of Tractarian poets such as John Keble and Isaac Williams, whose poetry foregrounded its connection to High Anglican liturgy and prayer.[17] In this context, the repetitious nature of Tractarian verse can be understood as having a spiritual function of restoring "precision and pattern to those who felt lost," to borrow the terms of Raymond Chapman.[18] Such a technique of verbal support is evident in "The Lowest Place," in which a repetitive form gives the despairing mind a pattern to follow. Lacan's theory of the symbolic function of language further helps to explain how Christina Rossetti used language as a trenchant device through which to imagine and pursue a condition of symbolic transcendence. As Richard Boothby explains, for Lacan the repetition compulsion and its correlative, the death drive, do not constitute merely a fixation on unpleasurable experiences that Freud described in *Beyond the Pleasure Principle*.[19] Instead, Lacan employs the repetition compulsion as a more general concept descriptive of the function of language, which works through repetition to imprint in the subject a foundational speech that roots the subject in a symbolic system, encompassing "the whole structure of community . . . as being" (SII, 20). According to this logic, the kind of formal repetition enacted in "The Lowest Place" subdues the ego in its relentless pursuit of individualistic attractions and allows the symbolic order to achieve its stability. Lacan's version of the repetition compulsion, which emphasizes the essential normality of the subject's quest for symbolic stability through repetition, can accordingly supervene previous interpretations of the trope of repetition in Christina Rossetti that are based in the original Freudian concept that theorized it as an obsessive involuntary pattern born of trauma.[20] In response to these critical concerns, we may accordingly respond with a Lacanian perspective on the repetition in her verse as a symbolic strategy with transcendental aims. In this regard, it is helpful to observe that Rossetti's repetitions are never static and directionless but evince a gradual progress; Harrison accordingly observes subtle "hierarchical and evolutionary" developments within the stanzas of her devotional verse (Context, 35). These developments in her verse (which belie the implication of paralysis conveyed with Freud's version of the repetition compulsion) can be seen in "The Lowest Place," in which each stanza takes the speaker a step closer to securing a place beside God.

Another spiritually strategic poetic mode practiced by Christina Rossetti is what Harrison calls her "poetics of conciseness," in which syntactic details and references are eschewed (Context, 42). Whereas Harrison portrays the diverse aesthetic and expressive effects of conciseness, such language can be understood as also having sublimatory effects, as by eliminating details, Rossetti engenders the kinds of ambiguity that permits the direction of desire to symbolic ends. The amenability of a poetics of conciseness to transcendental aims is explained by Lacan's comment that "the subject is separated from the Others, the true ones, by the wall of language"; Rossetti's keen desire to overcome all barriers to transcendental truth and contact would have led her to make this wall of language as low as possible (SII, 244). We can see how Rossetti's minimal language supports the anticipation of oceanic dissolution at the end of each stanza of "Confluents," where personal longings are abstracted into linguistic structures so elemental that they assume the status of pure sound:

> As running rivers moan
> On their course alone,

> So I moan
> Left alone.
>   (5–8)

In this fragment, the repetition of words and sounds suggests that the speaker is at the margins of language. Language is further minimized in the final lines of the fourth stanzas:

> Shall I, lone sorrow past,
> Find thee at the last?
> Sorrow past,
> Thee at last?
>   (5–8, 29–32)

Here, the repetition of a few words underscores the poem's sense that the speaker is coming to the end of language and is thus plausibly closer to the Other, who is beyond it.

In an earlier poem, "If I Had Words" (1864/1896), Christina Rossetti even more explicitly portrays language as a route beyond the confines of the self. Her speaker begins by seeking words with which to "to vent [her] misery," a linguistic function that remains on the level of the personal (1). However, she quickly moves on to imagine a function for words that is more overtly sublimatory. The right words, she claims, could help her reach a land "of love / [w]here fountains run which run not dry" (19–20), suggesting with this image Lacan's oceanic state of desire freed from the ego's libidinal attachments. The speaker goes on to claim that if she could find the right "words" they would be like "wings" that would lift her over herself so that she "would not sift the what and why," thus explicitly equating words with the transcendental power to exceed the self's egoistic concerns (24–25). The form of "If I Had Words," meanwhile, mimics the condition of transcendence of self. At the end of each stanza, the speaker uses a few words repetitively, diminishing her language in a way that mirrors the diminishment of ego that would occur through such transcendence:

> I would make haste to love, my rest;
>   To love, my truth that doth not lie:
> Then if I lived it might be best,
>   Or if I died I could but die.
>   (29–32)

The purging of extra words in this passage reflects the purging of self that Christina Rossetti's speaker seems to be trying to achieve through her quest for sublimation. As her voice dissolves into a chainlike repetition of simple terms, the speaker seems to be approaching a condition of ego death, though one that is not a calcification, as it is for the married women in "A Triad," but a liberation into an infinite extension.

In these lines of "If I Had Words," it is evident that the concept of death is linked closely with Christina Rossetti's general hopes for self-transcendence through language, a prospect illuminated by Lacan's suggestion that death is a concept used by the subject to indicate the limits of "the symbolic order in so far . . . as it hasn't been realised" (SII, 326). Explained through this Lacanian lens, Rossetti's invocations of death need not all be taken as neurotically morbid but alternatively as aspirational, in the sense that they aspire to what is beyond what can be encompassed by the ego's categories.[21] For Lacan, paradoxically, only through a relation to the death drive can one "engage in the register of life" (SII, 90). We can find similar testimony of this paradox in works such as Christina Rossetti's "Song" (1848/1862), in which the speaker anticipates entering into an oceanic condition where the cycles of earthly organic being will be unbound and she will "[d]ream[ ] through the twilight / [t]hat doth not rise nor set" (13–14). Continuing in this eschatological vein, the speaker discourages her lover from memorializing her with roses and cypresses that represent love and loss; instead, she requests that her grave display "green grass," thus alluding to the prophecy in Revelation 8:7 that "all green grass [will be] burnt up" after the Apocalypse.[22] With its exaggeratedly impersonal tone, "Song" has the effect of insisting on the supremacy of the permanent symbolic order of heaven over the imaginary order of human love. Incidentally, the year in which "Song" was written suggests that it was intended as a response to "The Blessed Damozel" (1847/1850), Dante Gabriel's poem of the previous year in which a woman remains emotionally bound to her beloved despite the fact that she has died and been symbolically elevated to a Christian heaven. For Christina, one would presume, maintaining a lingering attachment in the face of such cosmic bliss could not have seemed more absurd.

In Christina Rossetti's later "Somewhere or Other" (1863/1866), the speaker continues to invoke death as a symbol of her yearning to move beyond her ego-oriented feelings and cravings that limit the self (SII, 70). This poem dramatizes a complex dialectic of transcendence, in which the speaker at first depicts a search to exceed the specific constraints of her life in imaginary terms, as a search for an unknown face:

> Somewhere or other there must surely be
> The face not seen, the voice not heard
> The heart that not yet—never yet—ah me!
> Made answer to my word.
> (1–4)

In the next two stanzas, however, the speaker ranges beyond these imaginary symbols of the ineffable, looking "clean out of sight" (6). She goes on to wonder whether the entity she seeks lies beyond "wall" and "hedge," invoking images of boundaries to be crossed over within the self (10). The speaker's quest to exceed boundaries ultimately leads her to propose that the meaning she is searching for may be found in "the last leaves of the dying year," thus evoking the death drive as a means to characterize a limitless beyond (11–12).

The glorification of death in such poems is rooted in a Christian understanding of the subject as divided between body and spirit, which sees the possibility of seeking the death of one part of the self from the position of the other part and holds that all elements of the self that are susceptible to death ought to be discarded as soon as possible to liberate the eternal soul. This eschatological framing of the subject is not far from the psychoanalytical framing, which similarly gives credit to the symbolic aspirations of the subject to transcend unstable identifications and yearnings based in the imaginary order. As Lacan holds, "the core of our being does not coincide with the ego," which, though we experience it as an "I," is merely an object with a certain preliminary libidinal function (SII, 43–44). Although there is a definite cost and strain involved in wielding a campaign against this libidinal "I," Freud's theory of sublimation would indicate that such a campaign is not necessarily unviable or productive of neurosis, so long as it ultimately opposes the libidinal drives of the ego not through repression but through a determined will toward self-understanding. Joan Copjec accordingly agrees that the thrust of what she calls the ultimate "will" in the subject is to resist "surrender[ing her] internal conflict, [her] division" against her drives, and that it is through such resistance that the subject aims at her "ultimate freedom" (92).

A similarly intricate structure of self-division is characterized in Christina Rossetti's "Who Shall Deliver Me" (1864/1875), in which the speaker portrays her Christian commitment as one side of her being through which she can whittle down another side (55). After defining the part turned toward God as "me" (in opposition to "myself," who generates the cravings that distract her from that focus), she turns to the "One," who can "deliver" her by helping her to "curb [her]self" (22–24), pleading,

> God harden me against myself
> This coward with pathetic voice
> Who craves for ease, and rest, and joys.
>
> (1–3)

In her representation, the speaker considers her ego an alien rather than a central part of her because it distracts her from her highest destiny; she thus insists that "[m]yself" is "[m]y hollowest friend, my deadliest foe" (19–20). The speaker further describes "myself" as "[m]y clog whatever road I go" (21), approximating in this image the Freudian notion of the ego as a limiting aspect of the self that constrains the subject's self-expansion by fixing the desires of the self on discrete objects.[23] Finally, when the speaker requests that God should "break off the yoke and set me free" (24), her language embodies the thrust of the symbolic order, which seeks incessantly to push beyond the ego and go "beyond the limits of life" (SII, 326). Tonally, the final sounding of the word *free* may strike an alarmingly suicidal note, given the account of frustration that has preceded it; structurally, however, it indicates the momentum of her verse's journey into the reaches of the symbolic order that have not yet been realized, toward a vision whose place the concept of death is merely holding in the meantime.

Experiments in Transcendence: The Sonnet Sequences

In Christina Rossetti's two major sonnet sequences composed in the late 1870s and early 1880s, she provides the fullest picture of the ways in which a subject may use poetry to pursue symbolic transcendence, offering what seem to be a bad and a good example. In her preface to *Monna Innominata* (1880), Christina pledges to emulate Dante Alighieri and Petrarch in their perfection of the courtly love sequences, the genre that Lacan analyzes in *Seminar VII* as a key form of literary sublimation in Western literary history. Ultimately, however, *Monna Innominata* seems designed to prove that a Victorian woman cannot enact her sublimation in such a fashion, and the sonnet sequence fails both as a story of love and as a story of spirit. The love affair is palpably moribund by Sonnet 9, where the Lady complains at the defaulting of "all / [t]hat might have been and now can never be" (1–2). Even more tragically, the Lady's amatory experience, both when it is active and after it has lapsed, does not seem to offer support for any kind of spiritual program. Instead, it supplies a distraction for a religious practice that is autonomous from it, as she indicates as early as Sonnet 6 when she asserts that "I love, as you would have me, God the most; / [w]ould lose not Him, but you, must one be lost" (2–3). This moment when the Lady signals the presence of a competition within herself between two objects may be taken as the pivot point at which the she indicates the failure of the sublimatory process in her handling of it. The sonneteer should not have to subordinate the beloved in any regard, lest the idealizing process that opens up the subject's desire to symbolic potential be short-circuited. Kristeva characterizes the courtly mode as attaching an "excess of meaning" to the love experience to indicate an "Other at the limits of faith," who will only be found through the love experience if an exaggerated and unconditional splendor is attributed to the beloved (*Tales*, 288, 291). In turn, the exercise as a whole comes to naught, because even though the competition for the Lady's trust is inevitably won by God, as the Lady reveals in Sonnet 12 when she wonders, "If I could trust mine own self with your fate, / Shall I not rather trust it in God's hand?" (1–2), the fruits of this conversion come too late. The Lady has wasted too much time in loving and consequently has no sacramental goals to focus on in the final sonnet, where she is instead displayed as mourning for earthly joys: "youth and beauty [that] made a summer morn" and "love that cannot sing again" (14.13–14).

Multiple reasons may be found for why the Lady in Monna Innominata is inhibited from success. In the first place, having the Lady's efforts turn out poorly makes the sequence generally consistent with Christina Rossetti's ideology that human love is bound to be distracting rather than glorifying. Additionally, Rossetti may have been determined to show how the courtly mode of sublimation was bound to be unavailing for a woman. In this regard, her sequence confirms what we may derive from psychoanalytic treatments of courtly sublimation, which is that it is an exclusively male prerogative. The success of a courtly practice of sublimation depends on the sonneteer's willingness to exaggerate the charms of a real human other, a habit that can be linked to the construction of male symbolic desire, whereby men seek substitutes for the phallus that as castrated subjects they by definition lack.[24] As Lacan suggests, a woman of sufficient stature can be made to "signify this phallus" through idealization and the evacuation of her real qualities ("Phallus," 289–90). There is, however, little cultural precedent for women's discursively elevating men in such an extravagant fashion, perhaps because men are viewed (according to the same heterosexual economy) as having the phallus and thus being at a symbolic advantage over women already ("Phallus," 289). As Lacan contends, the woman "finds the signifier of her own desire in the body of him to whom she addresses her desire for love" ("Phallus," 290). For a woman to idealize her real male lover would accordingly not be taken as a charming artifice but instead as a dangerous further subjugation of her own desire. Christina's lady accordingly spends little time praising her beloved and refuses to glamorize his effect on her, as when she fails to recall her and her lover's first "touch hand in hand" (2.14). She also expresses nervousness about a competition with her beloved in Sonnet 4 when the intensity of her beloved's desire is in danger of overwhelming her own:

> I lov'd you first: but afterwards your love
>   Outsoaring mine, sang such a loftier song
> As drown'd the friendly cooings of my dove.
>   Which owes the other most? my love was long,
> And yours one moment seem'd to wax more strong;
> I lov'd and guess'd at you, you construed me—
> And lov'd me for what might or might not be
>   Nay, weights and measures do us both a wrong.
>   (1–8)

As we can see from the example of Christina Rossetti herself, only by taking a sublime object without a body can a woman overcome this problem, for such an object allows the woman to signify her own desire independently of her beloved's. The Lady accordingly expresses no such nervousness about making hyperbolic claims about her God, as she indicates as she waxes lyrical in the second-to-last sonnet about his infinite power and compassion—though, again, apparently too meagerly and too late.

In contrast, Christina demonstrates in *Later Life* how the Victorian female subject who hopes to fully sublimate her imaginary desire must deconstruct her imaginary libido and diffuse herself into a field of symbolic discourse, as Christina's speaker began to do in shorter formats. The sequence thus affirms Freud's argument that a subject who wishes to find "a way out" of desire through sublimation must not only replace the object of the libidinal instinct but also transform the instinct itself, through a process that generates both self-knowledge and intellectual curiosity ("Narcissism," 407–8). Before aiming at this integration, however, the sonnet sequence lays out a system of devotional practice through which the speaker may confess the full scope of her sublime hopes. She signals her intention of launching a pilgrimage in the opening sonnet: "Let us today while it is called today, / Set out" (1.9–10). But she quickly divests herself of this homiletic tone, modulating toward one of confession as she announces that such a seeker feels "[b]lind eyed, deaf-eared, and choked with failing breath" (1.12–14). In general, Christina's speaker revises descriptions of Christian rituals to conform more closely with interior experiences, as, for instance, when she conveys that one should "[r]end hearts and rend not garments for our sins" and "[g]ird sackcloth not on body but on soul" (2.1–2). The speaker's candor in these passages may seem desperate, but it achieves a spiritual function within her verse of enacting what Raymond Chapman has called Tractarian "self-revelation"—a process that, in form at least, draws close to the talking cure of psychoanalysis (154).

To reveal more layers in herself, the speaker deconstructs the nature of her desire in a way that closely resembles the analytics of Lacanian theory:

> We lack, yet cannot fix upon the lack
> Not this, nor that; yet somewhat, certainly
> We see the thing we do not yearn to see
> Around us: and what see we glancing back?
> Lost hopes that leave our hearts upon the rack
> Hopes that were never ours yet seemed to be.
> (6.1–6)

The speaker's account of the elusive content of her lack is surprisingly similar to Lacan's explanations that "desire" has no fixed content but is a negative essence, "a relation of being to lack" (SI, 223). Likewise, Christina Rossetti's statement that "hopes . . . were never ours yet seemed to be" is similar to Lacan's premise that our ego's objects are essentially secondhand, mirrored in those of others. In Lacan's interpretation, this gap between ourselves and our desire means that "desire is essentially a negativity" that seeks to be filled but cannot; Christina observes that desire is sustained despite any attempts to fulfill it, being "not this, nor that; yet somewhat" (6.2).

The speaker's rigorous analyses of the empty nature of her desire may appear to lead toward nihilism. But unlike the Lady in *Monna Innominata*, the *Later Life* sonneteer is not destroyed by her disillusionment; rather, she finds disillusionment an incitement to hardiness. As the speaker consequently observes,

> If thus to look behind is all in vain
> And all in vain to look to left or right,
> Why face we not our future once again,
> Launching with hardier hearts across the main.
> (6.9–12)

By understanding that one's cravings have no genuine personal meaning but are internalizations of others' desire, she is able to see them as all the more dispensable. She thus does not pity herself for lovelessness but instead values her "[s]oul dazed by love and sorrow" as "more blest . . . than mortal tongue can tell" because of how that condition may lead to a deep conversion (7.5–6). Terrifying processes such as that exhibited in this sonnet, through which the speaker both probes the depth of her desire and renegotiates its meaning, play a necessary role in her process of transcendence, as they permit her to interrupt her fixed attachments and seek a more abstract, hence symbolic, goal.

The *Later Life* speaker further distinguishes herself from the Lady of *Monna Innominata* insofar as she does not merely supplement and later replace her lover with God but focuses her desire entirely on God from the outset. Like Christina Rossetti's earlier mystical speakers in "A Better Resurrection" and "Twice," the sonneteer insists that Jesus, who "hath the heart of God sufficed," can equally "satisfy all hearts" (7.13–14). Also like these earlier speakers, the voice of *Later Life* proposes that a love focused on God can even gratify the imaginary level of the subject, which remains ungratified in the *Monna Innominata* sequence. At this point of the sonnet sequence, the speaker extensively elaborates her imaginary desire for God. She claims that our deepest selves can similarly be nourished "if once we turn to Thee," who is "only Life of hearts and Light of eyes / [o]ur life, our light" (8.5–6). We have the means to achieve this transformative vision, the sonneteer proposes, because "thou hast given us souls and wills and breath / [a]nd hearts to Love thee, and to see Thee eyes" (8.13–14). The sonneteer of *Later Life* thus fully engages her scopic desire at this point of the sequence, as she describes the attraction of "glories half unveiled," which, if meditated upon, may "uplift" her both "to longing and to Love" (11.8–10).

Nonetheless, as we have seen, such a diversion of imaginary desire is not symbolic sublimation and thus does not in itself provide the serene "way out" of desire that Freud outlines. Lacan cautions against hoping for such a direct response from the Other, warning that we may thereby engage "the gaze": a perspective we hope that the Other will assume upon the self but that is not guaranteed to be comfortable or affirming. If we "look[ ] at what cannot be seen" and hope that in return "that which is light [will] look at me," we are likely to experience not a sense of being embraced by love but an overwhelming sense of shame (Four, 182, 76). The *Later Life* speaker does not explicitly link her desire for the gaze to an onset of shame, but a discussion of the experience of severe shame follows her expression of scopic desire for the Other. In similar terms with which Lacan describes the shameful subject as a defiling "screen" that blocks the gaze, casting a shadow upon that which it illuminates (97), Christina Rossetti's speaker describes shame as "a shadow cast by sin" that simultaneously produces the effect on her of a burning light (13.5). Rossetti's other descriptions of shame, as "a flame so fierce that we must die[,] / [a]n actual cautery thrust into the heart[,]" further evoke the quality of painfully brilliant light that Lacan associates with the appearance of the Other as it "surprises" the subject in a "function of desire . . . disturbing [her], overwhelming [her], and reducing [her]" (Four, 84). Both Lacan and Christina Rossetti nonetheless indicate that this castration by the gaze is what the subject cannot help but seek, lest she inhabit a terminal meaningless void; moreover, this castration serves the subject's ultimate elevation. In Rossetti's words, "shame gives back" the subject to herself and "sets [her] up on high" (13.13–14).

Chastened by shame in the face of the gaze, Christina Rossetti's speaker moves out of the cauldron of desire and into the more arid sphere of symbolic discourse. She suggests that if one feels "[b]efogged and witless" through excesses of private thought, one should return to discourse: to a "wordy maze," where she claims that a "groping stroll perhaps may do us good; / [i]f cloyed we are with much we have understood" (16.9–12). What this "wordy maze" may be is unclear, though the phrase suggests some sort of puzzling or cryptic language that requires the active interpretation of the reader—biblical or theological discourse, perhaps, given the immediate prior interests of the sonneteer in how to interpret the story of the first couple's departure from Eden. Thus, Rossetti's speaker exits the realm of pure emotional instinct and reenters a discursive community, reenacting a dialectic that she describes explicitly in the following sonnet, where she contrasts the wisdom we derive from "[o]ur teachers" with that wisdom we gain from love, or emotional intuition. As she concludes, if "[o]ur teachers teach that one and one make two," and "[l]ove rules that one and one make one," then we should shun neither kind of knowledge "[b]ut skilfully to each should yield its due" (16.1–4). This sentiment of integration suggests that Rossetti's speaker has come to an eclectic theology that relies on the symbolic functions of knowledge and rationality to complement the imaginary immediacy of love. Throughout the next phase of the sequence, the speaker accordingly envelops herself in discourse, increasingly describing her spiritual path in conventional allegorical frameworks of the seasons (Sonnets 18–21) and of pilgrimage (Sonnets 22–23).

Having regained her composure through a return to discourse, Christina Rossetti's speaker at the end of her sequence is able to bear gracefully a realistic vision of her mortality as a physical experience of "eyes that glaze . . . heart pulse running down" and including the possibility that she "may miss the goal at last" (27.12–14). But she is also able to sustain cautious hope that she will be restored to an enlightened community in the afterlife—a hope of which the Lady in Monna Innominata despaired, in her conviction of a terminal solitude. This speaker thus proposes,

> The unforgotten dearest dead may be
>   Watching us with slumbering eyes and heart
> Brimful of words which cannot yet be said,
>   Brimful of knowledge they may not impart
>
> (28.10–13)

In this way, the speaker confirms the importance of a discursive community to the experience of sublimation in the same way that Lacan does, as he finds that "the operations of sublimation are always ethically, culturally, and socially valorized" (SVII, 144). On the whole, moreover, the sonneteer's final vision of waking eyes and unimaginable words expresses a subtly integrated and infinitely deferred idea of fulfillment on both symbolic and imaginary levels. Her final vision also reflects how her vision has gone beyond the concerns of her ego through this process, as in the last sonnet she anticipates a collective transformation of love for herself and her friends. All in all, Later Life seems to describe a conditionally successful journey of sublimation of desire into a religious quest, conducted through the innovation of linguistic strategies as well as immersion in available discourses. This involvement of symbolic discourse in the pursuit of transcendence is essential, as Kristeva holds, explaining that the mystic, while pursuing "that which is nonrepresentable" (*Tales*, 319), nonetheless must use writing as a symbolic discipline through which "to 'hold fast to renunciation,' in the words of Jeanne Guyon (*Tales*, 308). As Lacan explains, language is the only means by which we can indicate those presences that lie beyond it, as it is the "network" we cast "over the totality of the real" where our "gods" abide (*SI*, 162; *Four*, 45). Moreover, because Rossetti's linguistic structures are formally and aesthetically designed to indicate this beyond, we may find that her devotional practice seems hopeful even when her tone is yearning and desperate. Her candor about the limits of language is what maintains the integrity of her quest, since (as Lacan proposes) the most ethical use of language involves refusing to project the presences we seek, using it instead to "play on this ambiguity" about the limits of representation (*SII*, 244). In this regard, Rossetti's devotional poetry is eminently ethical, as her speakers at the same time confess their failures to absolutely secure a vision of the Other and craft their confessions as illustrations of how their resources for searching are being strengthened.

Putting Faith in Discourse

As we have seen throughout this chapter, there is a way to read Christina Rossetti's dedication to a Christian path of sublimation as indicating an extreme self-assurance and certainty regarding the best way to expend her time on earth, rather than evidencing a masochistic and morbid nature. This self-assurance can be extended even to her reflections on gender, in the consideration that her faith seems to have given her a foundation from which to dismiss potential anxieties relating to her position as a woman. Kristeva has described how the mystic's "confidence" in her spiritual path can lead her to feel indifferent to political conditions, and Christina Rossetti accordingly expressed diffidence toward worldly feminist campaigns, supporting neither suffrage nor the ordination of women (*Tales*, 298; Marsh, *CR*, 464). While this choice to abstain from campaigns to remedy the worldly afflictions of women may seem perverse to modern readers, the acceptance of given conditions appears to have been an essential part of the process of symbolic sublimation for Rossetti, insofar as this process was aided by conditions that affronted the imaginary ego. Rossetti made one exception to her dismissal of feminist causes, which is that in her devotional tract *Seek and Find* (1879), she "voice[d] the female right to speak and be heard in religious discourse," as Marsh notes (*CR*, 464). This stand was, however, consistent with her overall determination to make use of these discourses for sublimatory ends, as she could not benefit from them if she was not permitted to investigate them and elaborate them in her searching ways.

Such a conviction of the necessity for submitting herself to potentially humiliating discursive expressions can be seen in Sonnet 14 of *Later Life*, where Christina Rossetti's speaker attempts to interpret the incident of Adam and Eve's exile from paradise in Genesis chapter 3. She first considers through the romantic claims of her heart, asking hopefully whether "[w]hen Adam and Eve left Paradise / [ ] they lov[ed] on and cl[u]ng together still" (14.1–2). In the next sonnet, however, she cautions that an interpretation must take into account theological discussions of this incident, including those that dwell on Eve's—and, consequently, woman's—error and frailty. In this way, the sonneteer accepts the authority of these symbolic sources even when they oppose her concerns and her intuitions as a woman. What Kristeva calls the mystic's confidence emerges even more fully in Rossetti's framing of the biblical tragedy of the first couple within an apocalyptic context that anticipates the termination of all gender relations; she concludes consolingly, "A morrow cometh which shall sweep away / Thee and thy realm of change" (14.11–12). Rossetti also implies that gender is a temporary source of division in her statement that on Judgment Day, "[l]ove will 'hold[ ] fast / [man's] frailer self'" while "sav[ing] without [woman's] will," implying that divine love will balance out masculinity and femininity by emphasizing male frailty and female will (15.13–14)—thereby collapsing what Lacan describes as the "activity/passivity relation" that differentiates conventional femininity and masculinity (*Four*, 192).

Christina Rossetti makes her most distinctive statements on gender in her last volume of theological writings, *The Face of the Deep* (1892), which forges a vision of humanity in the shadow of an inevitable apocalypse. In this text, Rossetti again expresses her willingness to submit to the conventional dictates of patriarchal Christianity, lecturing to women that "we daughters of Eve" should "be kept humble by that common voice which makes temptation feminine" (357).[25] This comment reveals an attitude of irony toward the cultural tendency to associate women with temptation, which she characterizes as "that common voice" rather than an essential truth. But it also affirms her belief that symbolic discourses—even chauvinistic ones—should be submitted to. Even though the equation of women with temptation exists purely on the level of cultural discourse, Rossetti seems to be saying, women should still heed such popular framings, presumably because they drive women down a path of humility that is always valuable for the Christian seeker. In other words, the merits of a discourse should be evaluated in relation to an apocalyptic context rather than a worldly one: this "common voice" may have the effect of subjugating women in this world, but what is far more important is that it can prospectively liberate them in the one to come.

The most intriguing comment that Christina Rossetti makes about gender in *The Face of the Deep* is the analogy she constructs between gender difference and the difference between right-handedness and left-handedness. In a radical musing, she suggests that although the cultural dominance of right-handedness over left-handedness is a rule, "rules admit of and are proved by exceptions," for "[t]here are left-handed people, and there may arise a left-handed society" (409–10). An extrapolation of her metaphor would dictate that she believed that gender hierarchy, too, was relatively arbitrary and conventional and could prospectively be overturned. Nonetheless, as Colleen Hobbs points out, Rossetti's metaphor does not hold out strong hopes for that happening in her context, given how strong the conventional alignments are (*View*, 422). Rossetti's suggestion that the orientation of power is reversible is therefore to be taken not as a rallying cry but as a consolation with an especial purchase for the apocalyptically focused mind. While the arbitrariness of gender hierarchy does not determine that it is likely to be overturned in her own world, it does provide some assurance that, as a conventional attribute of human society, it will be discarded in the world to come. Rossetti's conviction that gender is an arbitrary and contingent element of human society has a parallel in Lacan's treatment of gender, which likewise envisions it as a construct of the symbolic order. His theory of gender holds that it is a semiotic attribute that is found only within language, not in nature, and is based on the symbolic order's insistence on identifying the gender of the subject based on the absence or presence of the signifier of the phallus, which has a further meaning of signifying desire itself (Lacan, "Phallus," 284). The selection of the signifier of the phallus as a master signifier for desire is, he insists, completely arbitrary, based in a metonymical association to its physiological attributes. By extension, he concludes that all gender characteristics are not essential but conventional: dictates of the symbolic order that is imprinted in the subject as he or she comes to maturity. But in the same way that Christina Rossetti holds out little hope of reversing hierarchy, Lacan does not expect the arbitrary androcentric structure of the symbolic order to change, given how the symbolic order irrevocably reproduces itself (SII, 26).

One significance of this overlap between Christina Rossetti's and Lacan's understanding of gender is how it militates against various readings that have been made of Rossetti's writing that trace the effects within it of what post-Lacanian French feminists Hélène Cixous and Luce Irigaray conceived of as *écriture féminine*. As Grosz explains, the project of these theorists was to describe how elements of women's writing "exceeded or overflowed the oppositional structures and hierarchizing procedures" of the symbolic order, in keeping with the distinct and autonomous nature of feminine sexuality and pleasure (176–79). Proponents of these theories have made numerous discoveries within Christina Rossetti's writing of the actions of an ironic "female self" that speaks against the grain of her writing, sustaining subversive or resistant subtexts to the apparent meanings of her poems, especially insofar as these draw on patriarchal discursive contexts. In the course of these analyses, certain supposedly feminine qualities are observed within Rossetti's writing, such as that it is "freed from law" and "unencumbered by moderation"; "turbulent" and "non-unified"; and "obliqu[e] and indirect[ ]" in its meanings.[26] As a whole, the invocation of *écriture féminine* in interpretations of Rossetti's poetry holds that she does not authentically subject herself to the patriarchal Christian discourses of which she makes such manifest use in her writing but instead occupies a paratextual or subtextual position in relation to these discourses from which she subverts the poem's "ostensible meanings" and "speak[s] beyond patriarchy" (Foster, 76, 67).

This conjecture that we should read against the discursive grain that Christina Rossetti develops in her writing to find their true meanings is highly problematic, in terms of both the Lacanian theory of gender as located in the symbolic order and her view of gender as similarly conventional and contingent in scope. Whereas Rossetti with her Christian perspective on gender seems to have regarded femaleness as a fleeting surface, theories of *écriture féminine* designate a biological location in woman outside the symbolic order whence a more profound order of signification issues.[27] This prospect is logically impossible within Lacanian theory because all of the subject's means of communication are symbolically mediated, as Rose points out. Moreover, the very femininity that is supposed to support this alternative form of communication is nothing more than a set of symbolic conventions because "for Lacan, men and women are only ever in language" (49). Lacanian theory accordingly opposes such essentialist accounts of gender that would directly attribute certain types of signifying styles to men and others to women by founding them in the biological strata of sex. Moreover, the idea that the true meanings of Christina Rossetti's poems originate in a "female" space beyond the work that she is doing in mobilizing and interweaving the Christian discourses is at variance with Rossetti's perspective on her femaleness, which, as we have seen, does not hold it to be deeper than her symbolic commitments. To the contrary, Rossetti possessed an eschatological sense that in the apocalypse her soul will be liberated from gender as we understand it, as well as a theological sense that symbolic discourses avail the subject who is seeking sublime emancipation from the conditions of worldly selfhood. Another problem is that the terms of *écriture féminine* that attribute to Christina Rossetti's writing qualities such as "turbulence" and "freedom from law" seem inapplicable to much of her work, which evinces a highly regulated and precise nature, Rossetti having been a practitioner "of exact meaning," as Marsh describes her (CR, 473).

Christina Rossetti's linguistic virtuosity is if anything better accounted for by Kristeva, who likewise contends that language has multiply gendered facets but does not thereby insist that members of one gender are likely to be more prone to the use of one than the other. Kristeva's theory of language—which elaborates Lacan's theory backwards in time to envision another strata in its founding—describes it as featuring a symbolic level of meaning rooted in the subject's internalization of the paternal order of the law, along with a semiotic order of sound and rhythm that is founded in the subject's earlier relationship with the mother and that challenges the regulative function of the former (*Desire*, 134). While this division that Kristeva describes is rooted in the sexed experiences of development, its effects do not thereby polarize the genders; indeed, Kristeva proposes that women are likely to be virtuosic users of symbolic functions because they are challenged to symbolize their excluded experiences, which leads them to expand the power of the symbolic order "by giving it an object beyond its limits" (146).[28] Thus, instead of seeing Christina Rossetti as a writer who, despite her overt commitments to the symbolic meanings and discourses she drew upon, was actually oriented against them, we may see her as a writer who continually set herself the challenge of expanding the realm of symbolic meaning and the uses of symbolic discourses—maximizing their power to characterize her emotional and libidinal struggles and to pursue the sublime projects of the self.

two

The Superegoic Demon in Christina Rossetti's Gothic and Fantasy Writings

> The super-ego is at one and the same time the law and its destruction. . . . The law is entirely reduced to something, which cannot even be expressed, like the *You must*, which is speech deprived of all its meaning. It is in this sense that the super-ego ends up by being identified with only what is most devastating, most fascinating, in the primitive experiences in the subject. It ends up being identified with what I call the ferocious figure.
>
> <div align="right">Jacques Lacan, <i>Seminar I</i></div>

A CONSISTENT THEME IN Christina Rossetti's writing is the desire to submit the self to a greater will. Although this quest for submission is most often portrayed in Rossetti's writing as an ultimate pursuit of self-realization, other kinds of submission detailed in her oeuvre are not virtuous but guilty, and they result in not redemption but loss. These other, darker poems provide a warning that the subject must carefully discriminate between different opportunities for submission, entrusting one's fate to only the most meritorious authorities. Rossetti's gothic poem "Shut Out" (1856/1862), for example, characterizes an authority figure who demands submission rather than permitting an opportunity for it; consequently, the poem appears to be a description of a damaging enthrallment rather than a parable of a goal that the self may seek. The poem describes the figure of a "shadowless spirit" who is building a tower around the speaker, cutting off a world of color and life. The speaker describes her terrifying fate:

> The door was shut. I looked between
>   Its iron bars; and saw it lie,

> My garden, mine, beneath the sky,
> Pied with all flowers bedewed and green.
>
> (1–4)

This cruel obstruction of sight by the shadowless spirit exemplifies a phenomenon of obstructed scopophilia that Lorraine Janzen Kooistra observes more broadly in Christina Rossetti's writings such as *Goblin Market*, in which women's desire to look is subject to prohibition.[1] The speaker's fate in "Shut Out," however, does not represent a prohibition in the social world but reflects a condition of obstruction within the self, an internal blocking of an allegorical landscape that "had been [hers]" but later "was lost" (8). The interior nature of this obstruction is evident in how the captive heroine not only resists her prohibition, asking for "some buds to cheer [her] outcast state" (12), but also adds to her obstruction by "blind[ing herself] with tears" (22)—a motif that Rossetti also uses to describe self-repression in her accounts of Eve after the fall from grace, in "An Afterthought" (1855/1862) and "Eve" (1865/1866). The speaker also confirms that the "delightful land" being barred to her is not a concrete place but symbolic of some existential condition when she reveals that its loss cannot be compensated for by the "violet bed" and "lark" she still has access to, which are "good" but "not the best"—a status held by her allegorical garden (24–28).

Within this conflict, the shadowless spirit who initiates the heroine's repression in "Shut Out" holds an ambiguous position. On the one hand, he is comparable to the angels in several of Christina Rossetti's poems who exorcise forbidden scenes of color. For example, the "fiery messenger" in "An Afterthought" cuts Eve off from her paradise of "roses redder . . . / [t]han they blossom otherwhere" (2–3). Likewise, after Rossetti's speaker in the apocalyptic reverie "My Dream" (1855/1862) has an alluring vision of a colorful Euphrates—the origin of false, beastly gods in the Book of Revelation—the vision is cut off by an "avenging ghost" (27). In cases such as these, the repressive agencies are understood to be agents of divine justice who strike out visions that are patently forbidden or legitimately lost. On the other hand, there is the more arbitrary character of the shadowless spirit and his remorseless captivity of the speaker behind "iron bars," harkening back to the demon lovers of the gothic poems that Rossetti wrote at approximately the same time as "Shut Out." In 1856, Rossetti composed many explicitly gothic poems in which women are lured to isolated locales where all prospects of human delight are absent. Such poems as "The Hour and the Ghost" (1856/1862) and the fragmentary "A Coast-Nightmare" (1857/1896) feature malevolent demon lovers who, like the shadowless spirit, bear women off to castles that suggest immurement, where the women are forced to hide their eyes and their actions are restricted. These demons reproduce the conventions of vampirism that David F. Morrill observes running through Christina Rossetti's oeuvre, in which agencies of threat loosely based on characters from popular gothic novels such as *The Vampyre*, by her uncle John Polidori, "tear away masks of innocence and drain lives."[2]

These two archetypes of the authority figure—the avenging angel and the restrictive vampire—overlap in Christina Rossetti's writing and suggest a troubling zone in her work in which two types of repression intersect. This zone seems to center on the figure of the shadowless spirit of "Shut Out," one of Rossetti's poems that is most ambiguous about the reasons for and causes of repression in the subject. We may be tempted, given how these two types of divine and demonic authority overlap in Rossetti's work, to collapse them into a single ominous specter of the superego, which Freud has described most generally as a psychic agency that "dominate[s] the ego . . . in the form of conscience or perhaps of an unconscious sense of guilt" (*Ego*, 25). Freud's basic concept of the superego is of a legacy of the father that functions both as the ego-ideal, an elevated ideal with which the subject identifies, and the "general character of harshness and cruelty exhibited by the ideal—its dictatorial 'Thou shalt'" (*Ego*, 44–45). This conceptualization of a singular representative of paternal authority within the self that expresses both idealized and restrictive qualities does not, however, adequately account for Christina Rossetti's poetic intuition that some agencies of restriction may be beneficial to the ethical and spiritual development of the subject while others encapsulate purely mortifying tendencies. Following upon Christ's abjuration in Matthew 12:1 that his disciples should pluck out their eyes if what they see obstructs their spiritual progress, Rossetti's speaker asks in "Who Shall Deliver Me" (1864/1875) for God to "wall / [s]elf from myself," hardening her against distracting "ease, and rest, and joys," so that such obstruction will lead to a "lightened heart" and freedom from her "yoke" (8–9, 18, 14). In "An Afterthought" and "My Dream," the angel Gabriel and the fiery sword similarly represent God's clear authority, as they "[w]ill[ ] with the perfect will" just and deserved restrictions within a Judeo-Christian context ("Afterthought," 33). In contrast, Rossetti's shadowless spirit in "Shut Out" represents no apparent law, inflicts repressions for no perceived reason, promotes no good outcome for the speaker, and thus seems stringently distinguished from the former figures, who, however stern, are nonetheless defined as servants of their speakers' transcendental processes (33–35).

Although Freud did not express this distinction between benign and malignant internal authorities, Lacan did, strengthening the Freudian distinction between the concepts of the ego-ideal and the superego and adding to the former a relation to his concept of the symbolic law that integrates the subject in relation to her culture.[3] The ego-ideal—which can, as in Christina Rossetti's case, be expressed by an image of a God—is a projected personification of a law that is elevating insofar as it orients one's quest for meaning and models how to improve one's ethical character (SI, 142). In contrast, the superego is an internalization of authority within the subject that does not "exalt[ ]" her but instead "constrain[s]" her, perpetuating over her a tyrannous regime born of the drives (SI, 102). The superegoic form of authority, Lacan suggests, is a corrupted form of the symbolic law in the subject: a set of mistakes in interpretation that have induced a "schism . . . in [her] relation" with the symbolic law (196). This senseless and destructive internalization of authority holds extreme and immoral power over the subject that is inseparable from her desires and is pictured by the subject as the "ferocious figure" of her nightmares (102). Lacan's distinction between exalting and constraining forms of authority within the self is thus perceptive about the way in which inner agencies of authority may support true ethics that enhance social cohesion and overall self-realization or, contrarily, may drive the subject to destructive and self-alienating actions.

Lacan's observation that the superego is represented in compelling but fearful figures of false authority helps, moreover, to interpret the recurrent imagery of demons in Christina Rossetti's writings as negative authorities to be contrasted with good ones. In particular, his observation helps to place the significance of the category of Rossetti's fantasy figures that prey on characters to corrupt them; among these demonic authorities, we may include her disturbing panoply of beasts, goblins, and demon lovers. Although Lacan never specifically links the superego to fantasy, his account of the superego as an almost demonic figure within the psyche that is "linked to primitive traumas the child has suffered, whatever these are" suggests that the superego might be a symptom of a disturbed oedipal complex that the subject has been unable to complete (SI, 102). Psychoanalytic theorists Jean Laplanche and Jean-Bertrand Pontalis accordingly describe how fantasies record unique personal traumas and thereby "provide a representation of, and a solution to, major enigmas" of development in a "reverie" that is perpetually "live[d] out."[4] Fantasy is a personal code in which one may locate vestigial representations of whatever momentous experiences preceded or exceeded the infantile subject's power of signification; some frequently imaged fantasies are, for instance, episodes of seduction and castration that can harken back to the subject's first experiences of the drives' outbreak and their prohibition by the symbolic order (Laplanche and Pontalis, 19). While the shadowless spirit in "Shut Out" is not as sexually seductive as some of Christina Rossetti's other demons, his actions seem nonetheless to hint at a primal origin in which boundless desire was incited and then punished.

The meanings of the ongoing fantasy running through Christina Rossetti's oeuvre, centered on figures that are at once agencies of seduction and enactors of sadistic prohibitions or punishments in response to the transgressions they have initiated, may have been personal to Rossetti but also directly participate in various literary and religious discourses of the demon. The fantasy, as articulated in several subgenres in Christina Rossetti's writing (primarily gothic writing, fantasy writing, and narratives about Eve), went through several shifts and adjustments, but these do not undermine its coherence, in keeping with Lacan's observation that an individual's fantasy takes the form of a unique "signifying ensemble" that grows "ever more complex" over the course of the subject's life (Four, 185). The different versions of the fantasy thus sustain many of the features of "Shut Out," including scopic delight in a primal scene that is repressed, an ambiguously compelling authority figure, and experiences of shame, chastening, or blindness. The fantasy also transformed over the course of Christina Rossetti's career, becoming increasingly characterized by its differentiation from her religious quest and by a sense of her recognition of and control over the fantasy as an author. Thus, while the speakers and narrator of early versions of the fantasy (such as "Shut Out") express incomprehension and helplessness in the face of demonic entities, characters in Rossetti's later fantasy writings reveal strategies to distinguish and disarm demons, including resistance from a position of symbolic security and narrative containment within the symbolic order.

A reading of Christina Rossetti's quasi-autobiographical short story *Maude* (1850/1897) reveals this work to be an inchoate yet particularly fatal form of Rossetti's fantasy. Although Maude is an avid writer of religious poetry, the narrative gradually reveals that she is not writing to fulfill a transcendental imperative but is instead in the grip of a sinister, erotic entrapment by an obscure internal demon. Christina Rossetti's oeuvre exhibits more-obvious fantasies of demonic possession during her brief gothic period, when she became fascinated with demons that tempt women toward obscure forms of gratification and then destroy the women. Later, she wrote poems that have been described as fantasy proper, including *Goblin Market* (1859/1862) and the stories in *Speaking Likenesses* (1874). In these writings, Rossetti depicts what Kristeva portrays as apocalyptic conflicts within the subject between primordial desire and symbolic stability, figuring them literally in the terms of the Book of Revelation as conflicts between the beast's reign of sensuality and a subsequent divine reign of purity (Kristeva, *Powers*, 208). These stories reveal a program for how the subject can be empowered to resist her darkest appetites by becoming a writer who is master of her demonology.

Maude's Superego

One of Christina Rossetti's most ambiguous narratives about the dangers of false subservience is her early story, *Maude*, the tale of a precocious poetess with an uncannily self-mortifying impulse.[5] Maude is a fifteen-year-old who is not known by her friends to have suffered any unhappy experiences, yet she writes poems about how hard it is "to bear hated life":

> To strive with hands and knees weary of strife;
> To drag the heavy chain whose every link
> Galls to the bone; to stand upon the brink
> Of the deep grave . . .
> To hold with steady hand the knife
> Nor strike home.
>   (*Maude*, 20)

Maude's circle receives these poems with perplexity, given that Maude at first does not even seem outwardly gloomy, greeting new friends "with the manner of a practised woman of the world" (23). That she is, at least initially, fascinated by a Romantic literary mode of melancholia rather than personally gripped by any root cause of it is affirmed in the narrator's description of how Maude completes the sonnet only to "yawn[ ], lean[ ] back in her chair, and wonder[ ] how she should fill up the time until dinner" (20).[6]

Displaying a strange reversal of the cause and effects of literary expression, however, Maude begins to show signs of a growing tendency toward self-mortification that doubles the content of her poetry. This tendency is first shown when she plays *boutes-rimes* with her friends, a game of sonnet writing that allows her to show off her literary skill. The day afterwards, she is grave and expresses herself "sick of display and poetry and acting" (28). During another visit the following year, her anxiety regarding what is supposedly a sin of pride that she is discovering in herself is induced when new friends "attack[ ] on either hand with questions concerning her verses" (33); this show of attention leads her to avoid further contact with these young women. After this incident, Maude begins a more serious symptomatic deterioration. She suffers from "headache" and shows herself to be "pale, languid, almost in pain"; meanwhile, she writes increasingly punctilious poems that reproach herself for "vanity" and "false heart" (33–34). Most damagingly, she refuses to take communion, considering herself a "hypocrite" for not "avoiding putting [herself] forward and displaying [her] verses" (34).[7] Within the year, Maude begins her approach toward the "deep grave," undergoing a carriage accident that results in vague internal injuries that precipitate her death (20).

Although this accident is not properly in the field of her control, within the structure of the story it provides a fitting and conveniently obscure closure to her morbid narrative. Overall, this tale thus seems to outline the progress of a "death drive" within Maude that readers have analyzed in different ways. Most critics have depicted the poetess's demise as the fulfillment of a conventional norm that in some way stifles creative women, for instance, by legislating that a destiny of death is suitable for the Victorian authoress.[8] In other words, they characterize Maude's will to die as the exponent of a norm that is given to her by her symbolic order, her death being the fulfillment of a law that has been "bred" into its subjects. From a Lacanian point of view, however, this way of accounting for the conflicts that Maude expresses in her life and works is too simplistic a solution. In Copjec's terms, these kinds of analysis fall prey to monistic theorizations of the subject developed by Louis Althusser that conceive of desire "as a realization of the law," and say "simply that the law causes us to *have* a desire" (24). In contrast, Lacanian theory considers the character of the social law as inadequate, in itself, to explain the dynamics of something as obviously perverse and antisocial as Maude's death drive, which orients her in a way quite opposed to how her fellow schoolgirls develop and thus seems to suggest the rootedness in her not of a cultural norm but of a strangely perverted process.

An examination of Rossetti's various images of Maude writing death-driven poems and falling away from the church shows that in doing so, Maude is not in the least obeying the cultural norms of her society. The baffled and distressed responses of Maude's friends to her behavior suggest that such behavior does not properly represent what Lacan describes as the symbolic law of "[one's] parents, [one's] neighbours, [and] the whole structure of [one's] community" (SII, 120). Rather, what seems to kill Maude is a deviant, personal form of that law—a version such as Lacan outlines in his idea of the superego. As Lacan holds, the superego does not encourage the subject along a path of true enhancement but instead induces in the subject "a failure to understand the law" (SI, 102). Kristeva further elaborates the Lacanian description of the superego by describing it as a prospectively deceptive and fraudulent internal authority that "corrupts, uses . . . [and] takes advantage of" symbolic laws, "the better to deny them" (Powers, 15). We can see the difference between proper, lawful behavior and Maude's perverse self-punishment when Maude's friend Agnes begs her not to "deprive [her]self of the appointed means of grace" by refusing to go to communion but to take it and thus find "safety . . . in obedience" (35). Maude, in turn, shows herself in thrall to the punishing part of herself that mercilessly refuses her any scope for salvation when, in a paralyzing fit of self-loathing, she cries, "I cannot go tomorrow; it is of no use" (36). Evidently, Maude is not bound by a determining social law but is in thrall to some other drive that only seems to derive its authority from some morality, being actually the representative of what Lacan calls "anti-legal morality" (SI, 102). The sense of a split within Maude against the symbolic law is further evident when she offers "strange prayers" to God with "a divided heart" that is simultaneously frightened and reproachful (35–36). Her relentless habit of self-reproach indeed places her in the category of what Freud calls a moral masochist, who endlessly exaggerates her own wrongs and thereby "produces criminality" for herself (Ego, 42).[9] Freud's reason for why a girl like Maude would flagellate herself this way is illuminating: the superego, he holds, is conscience "mixed with libido," and the moral masochist persists in relentless accusation to permit "relief" from an obscure sense of guilt by "fasten[ing] this unconscious sense of guilt on to something real and immediate" (Ego, 42). Thus, Freud points to the drives and to a sense of primal guilt felt by the subject over how these drives are directed for the solution of why Maude is both exaggeratedly mortifying herself for small infractions and isolating herself from the community that could help to save her from them.

The tradition that explores the compulsion by perverse drives, which Christina Rossetti seems to be invoking in her presentation of Maude, is the gothic. Effects in *Maude* seem particularly to resemble a motif observed by Fred Botting in Charles Brockden Brown's influential gothic novel

Wieland, of "spirit[s] possessing the body" who produce "strange voices" that resemble "emanations from God."[10] Maude's automatic manner of writing poems that by all appearances exceed her personal experience further suggests a case of gothic possession, a condition also denoted by Maude's generally pallid demeanor and intermittent enervation, which Morrill finds represented in the traditions and literature surrounding vampires (*Twilight*, 6). Maude is "languid" and of fixed "paleness" except when she reads her poetry, at which times her "sleepy eyes . . . light up with wonderful brilliancy" (21). Even after she has become distinctly sickly, reciting produces "inexhaustible" fund of energy in her, while the writing of it is an exhausting compulsion, as Agnes notes when she discovers Maude "pale, languid, almost in pain," surrounded by her manuscripts after a busy day of Christmas preparations (25, 34). Further signs of possession can be seen in Maude's growing isolation and unfitness for normal social activities. Because she refuses to "wear ornament" (23), Maude hangs back from the circuit of girlish enjoyments that are directed toward securing marriages and family lives for the girls—a destiny for which she is portrayed as being poorly adapted, as when a baby given to Maude and responds to her "advances with a howl of intense dismay" (22). Some involuntary obstacle to the normal course of feminine life seems at play in her, given that her fatal injury occurs when she is on her way to a wedding, and later, when she inquires whether the husband is handsome and proposes that she "should love a baby of [Mary's]," her pain breaks out with new violence (40–41).

Kristeva explains how superegoic symptoms can block expressions of normative sexuality by relating the superegoic complex to the introverted function of narcissism. According to Kristeva, a powerful superego will "jealous[ly] . . . block the desire craving an other" so that "desire and its signifiers turn back toward the 'same'" (14–15). Maude's superego's blocking of marriage can thus be seen as similar to her "anti-legal" superegoic obstruction of church attendance, as each of these reactions expresses the superego's demonic drive not to advance but to prevent benign forms of symbolic pursuit through which—as a devotee or a wife—she may "give herself, to a god, to something transcendent," in Lacan's words (SII, 263). In this way, the superegoic drives hold Maude captive to themselves, catching her terminally in narcissistic self-absorption. Maude is shut off by her superego not only from marriage but also from another option for the young ladies in her circle: the convent. She thus responds to a suggestion by the convent-bound Magdalen that Maude may someday also do so by proposing that she is unsuited for that destiny as well, owing to some darkness that inhabits her: "[Magdalen] is so good she never can conceive what I am" (39). As Maude elsewhere confirms, she is not "fit or inclined" for the convent and does not "fancy [she] ever could have talked to the poor people or done the slightest good" (29).

More signs of Maude's superego's jealous inhibition of transcendence emerge, moreover, as she meditates on the reason for her unfitness for the convent by writing a poem called "Three Nuns" that surveys various good and bad reasons for becoming a nun.[11] The best motivation is that of the third nun in the poem, who sought with a pure heart a "[v]oice to guide me . . . till I reach Heaven's strand" (149–51). A misguided reason is advanced by the second nun, who was lovelorn and sought the convent in consolation for her grief; the proper vocation for this woman was marriage. But the worst candidate for the convent is the first nun, who in a death-driven impulse entered the convent to "shut out all the troublesome noise of life" (6–7). Like the desire to escape suffering that Maude expresses in her earliest poetry, this nun's form of death drive thus seems to have been not sublimatory but genuinely suicidal:

> Shadow, shadow on the wall
> > Spread thy shelter over me
> Wrap me with a heavy pall
> > With the dark that none may see
> Fold thyself around me; come.
>
> (1–5)

This nun goes on to compare life in the convent to a "winding sheet" that can allow her to be "buried before [she is] dead" (10–11). This first sort of nun appears to be a version of Maude, who goes so far as to deny and to obstruct the connection, declaring that "no one can suspect [the nun] of being myself . . . [because] my hair is far from yellow" and not curly (*Maude*, 40).

While the morbid nature of the first nun's desire is patent, there is a simultaneously an erotic component to her request for obliteration that points to the rootedness of this request in narcissistic desire. As this nun asks the shadow to "fold thyself around me" and to "lay thy cool upon my breast," she seems to be invoking some sort of a terminal sexual fantasy (5–12). A sense that the first nun's vocation is narcissistic is, moreover, confirmed in her description of the kind of isolation that the cloister of the convent represents to her. Its insulation from the outer world reminds her of a wood to which she had retreated as a child,

whose thick sheltering atmosphere protected her from being "found
[ ]or sought" (59):

> In the thickest of the wood,
>   I remember, long ago,
> How a stately oak-tree stood
>   With a sluggish pool below
> Almost shadowed out of sight.
>
> (50–54)

The nun's memory of being able to live "as in a dream" and to feel as "pure" as the "lilies on the stream" evokes a background of perfection and completeness that suggests the imaginary order casting back to its origins in the subject's primordial sense of wholeness, before the alienating effects of the mirror stage and symbolic subjectification took effect (60–62). The wood itself resembles Kristeva's account of the condition of primary narcissism, where "light touches, scents, sighs, cadences . . . arise, shroud me, carry me away" (*Powers*, 58–61). The presence of the pool is an obvious gesture toward Narcissus, while its "sluggish" quality exemplifies how repressed imaginary desire is "dissolv[ed] in the raptures of a bottomless memory" that tends not to exist in a pristine state within the self (Kristeva, *Powers*, 14). Instead, the locus of narcissistic drives within the self is muddied with what Kristeva terms the abject: the impression of horror and repulsion by which the symbolic order retroactively enforces the forbiddenness of return.

Within this context of revived narcissistic desire, the nun's stately oak tree stands like Kristeva's proto-phallic superego, a foreign object that "settle[s] in place and stead" of the self among the narcissistic drives, both drawing the subject toward himself through layers of repression and punishing the subject who is so venal as to take that journey (10).[12] The psychoanalytical theory of fantasy provides a link between this image of a primordial phallic presence and the nun's account of how she—like Maude—has been compelled to avoid normative forms of sexuality. The nun describes how before she entered the convent "[m]en saw and called [her] fair" (23), but she thwarted opportunities for courtship by hampering alluring aspects of her appearance and generally avoiding display, shearing her curls and becoming "curtained from intruding eyes" (30).[13] While we may feel sympathy for the nun's desire— which is not notably different from that expressed by the winsome speaker of "Winter: My Secret" (1857/1862), who longs for protective garments to protect her privacy in the form of "a shawl, / [a] veil, a cloak, and other wraps" (10–11)—the nun's avoidance of the kinds of self-display that could lead to courtship and marriage patently seem related to her attraction to the more insular form of eroticism that she projects onto the shadow of the nunnery and onto the phallic oak tree that rises up in her childhood memory. The latter, narcissistic form of sexuality might indeed have precluded her participation in the former, symbolically normative kind, in keeping with Susan Isaacs's description of fantasy as a defensive function that protects an initial route of desire to a lost object by blocking other routes.[14] Insofar as the first nun appears to be the narrative self-reflection of Maude, meanwhile, the poem helps to explain the actions of Maude's superego, which similarly punishes vanity within her to an excessive degree that seems more socially obstructive than religiously promotive. *Maude* as a whole, moreover, portrays how the evasion by a young girl of normative feminine sexuality is not necessarily benign and emancipatory.[15] As Copjec points out, the impulse to "conflict with and disrupt . . . social relations" is generally an expression of a prior, narcissistic desire that is excluded by those relations (23), and *Maude* shows how this prior desire can be at least as tyrannical as the entry into the symbolic order that it obstructs. The wish to be "curtained from intruding eyes" takes on a sinister character when the evasion of a symbolically ordered sexual life deprives the female subject of all relationships, isolating her within herself.[16]

At the same time, the prospect held out in *Maude* that religious vocation may be confused with sexual evasion by no means affirms that Christina Rossetti's ultimate spiritual project as a whole was an expression of perverted desire, as has been suggested.[17] For another kind of religious pursuit is undertaken by Maude at the end of the story, when she becomes released from her superegoic compulsion toward immurement into a clearer mode of symbolic transcendence. When Maude lies suffering and dying, she at first continues to indulge her gothic mood, composing a poem in which she solicits a luxurious and deadly shadow who will "[s]hut out the light" and "lull [her], languid as a dream" into death—as the first nun asked the shadow on the nunnery wall to do (*Maude*, 50). However, after Maude has died, two more poems are unearthed that the narrator suggests were "evidently composed at a subsequent period" to the former (50). The first begins to signal a departure from neurotic morbidity toward a more transcendental perspective, as it anticipates how in dying, "we shall come the sooner back to pleasant spring" (51). In the last poem, Maude reveals herself to be even more distinctly illuminated by a sublime vision, as she senses that in the presence of Christ "the powers of darkness . . . [she] needst not fear" (51). The shift from the dark imagery that dominates Maude's earlier poems to the light-filled imagery of these final poems suggest that Maude finally found an escape from narcissistic forms of self-persecution and discovered the third nun's exalting faith. And although Christina Rossetti was not able to accomplish this shift from demonic habit to genuine illumination as spontaneously as Maude did—as we will see, she had to write a great deal of poetry before the darkness cleared from her religious vision—her body of work suggests a growing confidence that through diligent and patient writing, she too could work the gothic compulsions of the superego out of her religious vocation.

Entrapments in Ghostland

Between 1856 and 1857, Christina Rossetti's writing suggests that she peered most distinctly at her inner darkness, "convey[ing] the impression of something seeking expression," according to biographer Jan Marsh, that was "bound in with half-glimpsed fear" (CR, 199). During these years, Rossetti produced the poems that most overtly employ gothic motifs (such as demon lovers and wild landscapes) as other nineteenth-century works use them, to describe the "irruption of fantasies, suppressed wishes and emotional and sexual conflicts" (Botting, 11). Kristeva likewise notes how the nineteenth century developed the language of gothic horror to encode our "most intimate and most serious apocalypses," which she elaborates as being eruptions out of the schisms between the "religious, moral and ideological codes" that try to secure the subject on symbolic ground and the persistent narcissistic impulses that seek jouissance in dangerous and abject formations (Powers, 209, 9). A perfect exemplar of this logic, Rossetti's version of gothic similarly depicts subjects who are torn between tantalizing but destructive zones of libidinal jouissance and normative symbolic orders in which desire never seems adequately fulfilled, thus guaranteeing her heroines' attraction to what these orders exclude.

Christina Rossetti's gothic writing has not been examined very thoroughly, perhaps because it seems highly conventional, founded more on borrowings than on innovations.[18] But Rossetti's version of the gothic is worth studying, especially because of the stark emphasis on the maleficence of its contents—an emphasis that many other Victorian writers of gothic efface. As Anne Williams notes, the demonic lovers characterized by late-Romantic and Victorian writers such as Jane Austen and Charlotte Brontë are only superficially "mysterious," and "otherworldly"; their actual natures are eventually realized when they are found to be capable of symbolically legitimate companionate marriages.[19] By offering readers gothic demons who are redeemable and marriageable, these novels commit a sleight-of-hand, permitting gothic thrills while hiding the literary and psychological truths that demons are alluring precisely because they resist and thwart symbolic containment. Christina Rossetti's gothic, in contrast, uncompromisingly maintains a schism between illicit, abject gratification and symbolic conformity. She thus depicts scenarios in which women are about to enter sensible, conventional marriages with loving but unexceptional men, only to be overwhelmed by alluring but deadly outlaws. These poems are genuine psychomachia, in which, like Spenserian heroes, Rossetti's heroines are forced to make momentous choices among the claims of different parts of themselves, with the gothic complication that Rossetti's heroines have no choice, because they have already been condemned by their susceptibilities to a desire for a jouissance tinged with sin.

"The Hour and the Ghost" is constructed as two overlapping conversations, one between a bride and a bridegroom and one between the same bride and a ghost who attempts to draw her away from her marriage to his rugged place "beyond the hills and pines" (4–6). This demon has knowledge of the bride's desires, as he bids her, "[C]ome with me . . . to our home" and reminds her of a prior time when she "wast not afraid"; he also refers to the bride's "fair frail sin," of having previously submitted to the ghost's wooing, thus making irresistible appeals to both her desire and her guilt (12, 15, 51). Embodying the "corrupt" legality of the superego, the ghost distorts the words of the marriage ceremony to imply that she is already bound to him: "For better and worse, / For life and death . . . / Come, crown our vows" (34–36). As long as she can, the bride resists the call, asking her groom to hold her "one moment longer" (18). Finally, she speaks to her groom as though she were dying, telling him, "Keep thy faith true and bright / Thro' the lone cold winter night / Perhaps I may come to thee" (45–47). The groom fails to comprehend the cause of his bride's drifting and demands, "Who spoke of death or change but aught of ease?" (50). Readers of gothic fiction will recognize that it is not real death that threatens the bride but a far worse living death in the nebulous zone of limbo, which Christina Rossetti once described as "the most horrible of all deaths imaginable" (quoted in Morrill, 9). Generically, such a death is a direct cause of the subject's submission to exorbitant desire, which ushers in an enchantment that Morrill describes as "a doppelgänger process in which [one] confronts [one's] desirous other self" (24). Rossetti conveys such a possession through the ghost's description of the "outcast weather" in which he and the bride will "toss and howl and spin" (62)—an image representing narcissistic stasis in terms similar to those used by Dante Alighieri to describe Paolo and Francesca, the illicit lovers who inhabit Dante's stormy second circle of hell, reserved for the wanton.[20] The ghost who is at once the bride's seducer and her jailer thus seems the paradigm of Lacan's and Kristeva's superego, a character who is both "fascinating" and "devastating" and invokes moral authority for an immoral end, which is to trap the subject in a permanent narcissistic isolation (Lacan, SI, 102). In the same way as Maude's superego obstructs normative sexual expression to lure her toward a pole within herself, this demon deceptively lures the bride away from conventional happiness, not only by offering her a desirable alternative but also by coercing and deceiving her. Having lured her with a promise of support, assuring her that she may "lean on [him]," he guides her to a solitary cell where no love awaits (29–31). Like a vampire, he finally gloats over how she has become a banished wanderer similar to himself, as one who will "visit" the bridegroom "[t]o watch his heart grow cold; / [t]o see one much more fair / [f]ill up the vacant chair" (3–8). In this superegoic fashion, the ghost thus torments the bride with the consequences of the same infraction against symbolic normality that, as a representative of her drives, he impelled in her.

"Love from the North" (1856/1862) is another ballad of a bride torn between normal love and exorbitant narcissistic passion. The bridal drama plays on an opposition briefly hinted at in "The Hour and the Ghost" between southern civility and Nordic vigor and freedom, as the ghost is said to come from "beyond the pines" to disrupt that wedding.[21] Here, the woman is about to marry, in a bounteous church celebration "flushed with sun and flowers," a temperate man who is servile to her needs, having "waited on my lightest breath / [a]nd never dared to say me nay" (10, 3–4). Suddenly the northern man bursts into the marriage ceremony, offering a contrasting picture of rough and austere eroticism as he offers to bear the bride off in "strong white arms ... o'er crag, morass, and hairbreadth pass" (14–16). Although the bride initially resists this bracing alternative to conventional marriage offered by the northern man, she eventually succumbs to his persuasion, though in a moment when it is not quite distinguishable from coercion. Her fantasy of submission accords with Kristeva's representation of a kind of subject that Kristeva calls a "stray," who does not entirely desire (but nonetheless enjoys) the "jouissance" of the "abominable" drives, becoming a "fascinated victim[ ], if not [a] submissive and willing one[ ]" (*Powers*, 9). Kristeva's distinction between desire and enjoyment thus helps to explain why the bride is overcome by a seduction that she does not seek but nonetheless cannot resist—a "clutch" from which "she cannot withhold" herself, in Rossetti's terms (20, 23). Here we can see how Rossetti's emphasis on the degrading and destructive effects of demonic temptations presents a counterexample to certain nineteenth-century demon lovers who act as vehicles of female empowerment and creativity for Victorian women. The demon lovers that Anne Williams itemizes, for instance, end up helping gothic heroines by "expressing disruptions in the law of the father" that produce "spaces . . . for women to enter" (72–73).[22] But Rossetti's demon lovers grant her heroines a permanent and unhappy exile from symbolic normality. Rossetti's demon lovers thereby feature a degree of psychological realism and consistency that is missing from the ones Williams tends to emphasize, who are readily convertable into intriguing husbands. Rossetti's demon lovers never are, because they mirror the narcissistic core within the heroines that resists such symbolic restraints—a reflection that is at the heart of their attraction.

Kristeva further helps to explain the origin of the northern man's irresistible attraction for the bride through her conceptualization of "strays": subjects in whom the seal of secondary repression, which blocks off the memory of the condition of narcissistic wholeness in which the self existed before symbolic subjection, is not fully secure. For such subjects, "the unconscious contents remain excluded but in a strange fashion: not radically enough to allow for a secure differentiation between subject and object, and yet clearly enough for a defensive position to be established . . . between Inside and Outside" (*Powers*, 7). Such subjects are particularly susceptible to revivals of primary narcissism, which is not as fully blocked from their memory as it is from more soundly subjectified individuals. In the course of such relapses, these subjects can lose their symbolic ability to distinguish themselves from other objects, falling prey to a fragile infantile logic through which the mother teaches her child to resist the encroaching world, demarcating a "universe with fluid confines" (*Powers*, 8). The bride accordingly describes how she is overcome by the force coming from all directions, which pummels her like a "blast" she "cannot stem" ("Love," 3). In response, the bridegroom attempts to get her to focus on the objects that surround them: "Only ourselves, earth and skies, / Are present here: be wise" (28–29). But the bride is unable to "be wise" in this way, as she cannot distinguish rational facts such as the difference between her dialogue with the groom and her interior dialogue with the ghost (9).

Kristeva's explanation that such an object-annihilating logic has a basis in the primordial relationship between a child and its mother further helps to explain why the demonic ghost ultimately seems to offer the bride not precisely sexual thrills but security: the prospect that the bride may "lean on" him and receive a more satisfying "house and bed" than the groom can offer ("Love," 29, 32).[23] Such narcissistic promises of a return to maternal security do not, however, yield what they seem to promise. Christina Rossetti's man from the north turns out to embody neither virility nor narcissistic security but rather sterility and cruelty. He seduces the bride by making himself out to be an alternative lover, proposing a time of happiness for the two of them equivalent to what the bride expects with her bridegroom, "in which I will not say thee nay" (24)—a lie, since the man from the north never again asks the bride "yea or nay" (28). Seduction turns into compelled confinement that is both outer and inner, as the demon makes "her fast with book and bell" and binds her with "links of love" that eliminate any signs of her earlier will, so that the bride finally has "neither heart nor power / [n]or will nor wish to say him nay" (29–32). In exchange for a prospectively happy but bland marriage ratified by the symbolic order, the bride thus obtains only enslavement to a wasted and colonized version of her maternal legacy, not the revival of maternal wholeness in the hopes of which one regresses to narcissism (Kristeva, Powers, 6).

A maternal context to horror is even more explicitly denoted in "A Chilly Night" (1856/1896) and "A Coast-Nightmare," two poems by Christina Rossetti that contain ghost lands that distinctly resemble the landscape of the womb. In "A Chilly Night," a speaker rises to "look for my Mother's ghost, / [w]here the ghostly moonlight shone" (2–3)—thereby, in Kristeva's terms, breaking through the wall of repression that drapes our primordial relation to the mother and to the condition of original narcissism that we experienced at that time (Powers, 13–14). In this realm of the drives to which the speaker returns, there are unearthly ghosts that speak "without [ ] voice[s]," indicating their externality to symbolic ordering ("Chilly Night," 13). The speaker further shows herself bereft within the ordinary, symbolic world, as she "sobs" and entreats "O my mother kind," asking her mother to "make a lonely bed for [her] / [a]nd shelter it from the wind" (15–18). That the speaker's voyage is a narcissistic attempt to recover a lost connection to the maternal era seems explicit, as she seeks this retreat with her lost mother as an escape, begging her lost mother, "Tell the others not to come / to see me" (19–20). But the landscape does not contain the security that the speaker yearns for, and she must conclude that the "dead had failed" her (49), confirming Kristeva's proposition that any seeming opportunity of narcissistic return to the maternal era provides "no solace" (*Powers*, 63).

In "A Coast-Nightmare," a speaker is lured to a similar wasteland of the drives by a lover who has become a vampiric citizen of "ghostland" (1). The landscape of this world is as deathly as that of "A Chilly Night": here, her lover hovers "thro the darkness black as ink" and drinks "death's tideless waters" (32, 28). A maternal background of this ghostland is implied in womblike images of "blood-red seaweeds drip[ping] along that coastland" (3). As in "A Chilly Night," however, this maternal zone is sterile rather than fertile, characterized by an "unripe harvest" and an "unripe vineyard in . . . unprofitable space" ("Coast," 9–12). The landscape is also associated specifically with sexual sin, signified by the lover's return from ghostland to show her "a blasting sight" that is "a secret [she] must keep" and to tell her "the worldless secrets of the death's deep" (40, 34). Once she has learned these secrets, her guilty knowledge gives him power over her: "If I sleep he like a trump compels me / To stalk forth in my sleep: / If I wake, he rides me like a nightmare" (34, 36–38). "A Coast-Nightmare" thus fully imagines the guilty aftermath of a visit to the primal repressed, portraying it as a landscape saturated with sin, with its biblical "unripe harvest" that signals God's disapproval and its *Inferno*-like "troops, yea swarms, of dead men's souls" (19). As Kristeva explains, the symbolic order must retroactively impose a framework of "defilement, taboo, or sin" on the primal repressed, transforming the desired into "the banished" and "fascination into shame" to ward off further returns to this zone, where its own regime does not hold (*Powers*, 15, 8).

The speaker's conviction that the "blasted sight" she has seen in a ghostland must remain a "secret," meanwhile, indicates a new concern in Christina Rossetti's fantasy about the suitability of representing primal visions. As Kristeva points out, returns to the primal repressed are forbidden by the symbolic order because the drives, once released, threaten to annihilate the symbolically forged identity and projects of the subject (*Powers*, 14). "A Coast-Nightmare" is one of Rossetti's last gothic poems, affirming that she may have begun to judge such presymbolic visions unsuitable for poetry. Rossetti, who (as discussed in chapter 1) identified to an increasing degree with her symbolic goals, seems to have finally retreated from such a threat to symbolic bearings. Even before the writing of "A Coast-Nightmare," Rossetti's gothic poems begin to feature hints of a punishment for viewing the untoward secrets of the presymbolic experience, enacting further repressions to block their memory. In "A Chilly Night," for instance, the "subtle ghosts" that the daughter had traveled to see in the maternal sublime ultimately fade from sight, so that "from midnight to the cockcrow / [she] watched till all were gone" (45–46). Such an image affirms that one aim of secondary repression is to cut the subject off from the memory of a unitarily powerful mother (Grosz, 156).

Christina Rossetti's poems about the fall of Eve—one of which, "An Afterthought" (1855/1862), she wrote around the same time as her gothic poetry—are another context in her writing in which a transgressive return to an ostensibly maternal realm is punished with blinding. In "An Afterthought," Eve's lost garden is characterized as the place where the "first mother" was "lulled to rest" and as a place that was saturated with a "first love of all" that was "[w]armer, deeper, better worth / [t]han has warmed poor hearts of earth" (15–17, 9–10). In Genesis, paradise is the realm in which obedience to God's paternal order was total; however, by overlaying the biblical version with imagery of a sleeping mother and maternal love, Rossetti recasts that perfect place as the subject's maternal era. Accordingly, as Eve looks back at paradise, her vision fades as though through a secondary form of repression, so that she cannot ascertain the validity of her intuition of that perfection: whether "the roses [were] redder there, / [t]han they blossom otherwhere?" (24–26, 1–2).[24] This Eve, like the heroines of "Eve" and of "Shut Out," abrades her eyes in punishment for sin, streaming "tears that would not cease" and "weep[ing] sore" (1–2, 3). These images of women blinding themselves reveal an intersection between Rossetti's biblically themed poems and her gothic poems, in which the angels who enforce Eve's secondary repression assume a role parallel to that held by superegoic demons, and Rossetti consequently comes close to effacing the distinction between legitimate and illegitimate authorities that she elsewhere sustains.

In each of her demonic poems, Christina Rossetti thus describes perilous presymbolic conditions that tempt the subject but wield punishments for those who accede to them, reiterating the claims of her devotional poetry that temptations by imaginary libido should be resisted. Arseneau has proposed that Rossetti's poems about demonic enchantment are consistent with her devotional poems, perpetuating a central Christian myth in which "the sexualized imaginative world is infinitely attractive but sterile and destructive, and those who commit themselves to longing for it waste away in gloom and frustration, cut off from natural human life" ("Incarnation," 91). In psychoanalytical terms as well, Rossetti's devotional and gothic modes are consistent, because while her gothic poems dramatize fantasies that the devotional modes abjure, they also tend to recommend solidly against these fantasies, illustrating how subjects must learn to recognize, forgo, and—if necessary—recover from the diverse attractions and compulsions of narcissistic regression to claim the benefits of symbolic transcendence. At the same time, the gothic poems, like the story Maude, shed light on how narcissistic compulsions could corrupt a religious vocation by causing the subject to be confused about proper objects of submission and proportionate procedures of mortification. In this regard, it may be that Rossetti's gothic period of 1855–56 constituted for her a confessional moment in which she was able to give form to, and thereby purge, her most confusing and contaminating impulses.

Fantasy of the Beast

Appropriately, Christina Rossetti's works that most distinctly elaborate a developing fantasy are her so-called fantasy writings, which include the poems "So I Grew Half Delirious and Quite Sick" (1849/1904), "My Dream" (1855/1862), and Goblin Market (1859/1862), as well as a collection of tales, Speaking Likenesses (1874). These works fall into the category of Victorian fantasy writing identified by Steven Prickett that features loose structures, surreal imagery, and themes of primitive desire, which he observes to have developed out of eighteenth-century and Romantic forms of associative writing that expressed the quality of a dream or daydream.[25] This romantic context of dream-writing is particularly significant to Rossetti's fantasy writing, which tends to express a basis in dreams and even to explicitly foreground such a basis in the cases of "So I Grew Half Delirious and Quite Sick" and "My Dream." Marsh additionally postulates that real dreams may lie behind some of Rossetti's fantasy writings, as "all her life Christina was apt to remember dreams, and often made poems from them" (CR, 105). Rossetti's fantasy poems frequently seem to contain the suppressed erotic subtexts that Freud observed in dreams.[26] For Prickett, Rossetti's fantasy writings sustain underlying themes of forbidden sexuality and thereby "hold a mirror to the darker and more mysterious sides" of human life that were otherwise not represented in Victorian literature (xv–xvi). Morrill specifically reads Rossetti's most famous fantasy poem, Goblin Market, as concerned with the "sensual possibilities of an evil, seductive brotherhood" of vampire literature, based on how her goblins offer exotic pleasures to young women, with pernicious consequences (1). Rossetti's fantasy writings have thus struck critics as coded accounts of unconscious eroticism that are perhaps more fully camouflaged but no less libidinally charged than her gothic writings.

But while Christina Rossetti's fantasy writings contain traces of literary and psychological eroticism, they also hint at the moralistic discourses of religion insofar as they prominently feature familiar demonic creatures from Revelation and other religious texts, such as Dante Alighieri's *Commedia*. Northrop Frye has defined apocalyptic visions as forms of literature that retell the biblical story of how "heathen kingdoms are cast into darkness,"[27] and Christina Rossetti's fantasy writings belong to this category with their parables of beastlike creatures associated with sin that have great authority at the outset but are ultimately subdued by a higher power (Revelation 13:2). Given this biblical intertext to Rossetti's fantasy writings, many of these works can been seen to function as Christian allegories as well as dreams. Psychoanalytically, however, there is no necessary inconsistency between allegorical and erotic interpretations of her fantasy writings, because apocalypses occur on the personal level of the subject as much as they do on the religious level of a community, as Kristeva indicates (*Powers*, 208). Likewise, the narratives of seduction that are invoked by subjects to explain the origins of their individual sexualities, according to Laplanche and Pontalis (19), are congruent with Judeo-Christian explanations of the collective fall from grace owing to temptation and the defiance of prohibitions. These overlaps between psychoanalytical and biblical discourse suggest that Rossetti's dreams of Leviathan-like monsters can refer both to a biblical battleground of lush indulgence and austere but beneficent discipline and to a psychoanalytic fantasy of the same.

Christina Rossetti wrote the first of her fantasy poems, "So I Grew Half Delirious and Quite Sick," as an exercise in *boutes-rimes*, the sonnet-writing game practiced by the characters in *Maude*. The exercise evoked poetry that seems both personally and universally prophetic. In the poem, the speaker describes a dream of an abject landscape of desire, where a monster "put[s] forth a fin" and "lick[s] my hand" (2–6). The dreamer then passes through a crisis, experiencing a "quick pulsation of my heart . . . the fight / [o]f life and death within me" and losing track of the monster (8–10). When she wakes up, she weeps for the loss of the "creature" who "had love for me," his dark and moist world having been replaced by an apparently lonelier and brighter world where the "sun [was] at its height" (14, 12). While the narrative of "So I Grew Half Delirious and Quite Sick" is an oddly surreal product of spontaneous writing, Rossetti's speaker hints at its broader significance in her ambiguous comment toward the end of the sonnet that "this thing is true" (11). There are numerous possible interpretations to be made of her speaker's insistence on the truth of her dream. One can focus on the religious truth embedded in the poem's language, making reference to Kristeva's description of horror as depicting an intimate apocalypse (*Power*, 208) and to Frye's assertion that apocalyptic discourse is not merely prophetic but portrays "the inner meaning . . . of everything that is happening now," acting as a kind of revelation (146). Marsh accordingly observes that Christina suffered a breakdown at age fifteen in the course of which she simultaneously wrote apocalyptically toned poetry "to exercise the evil lurking within like a horned and abominable beast" (53). Given Christina's background, it is not surprising that the speaker's description of an encounter with dreamlike desire in "So I Grew Half Delirious and Quite Sick" draws imagery from the Book of Revelation, with her account of how "thro' the darkness . . . strange faces grin / of monsters at me" (2–3) resembling the biblical speaker's account of how he "saw a beast rise out of the sea" (Revelation 13:1). The landscape of Christina's poem is very similar to Dante's description of Malbowges, the abyssal eighth circle of hell, in which, as Dante narrates, Virgil throws his girdle into the "thick murky air" (16:131).[28] When the speaker describes monstrous grinning faces and fins extending through the darkness (2–3), there seems a reference to the image of Geryon, a version of the apocalyptic beast who is the "unclean image of Fraud," as he "comes swimming up [in] a shape most marvellously / [s]trange for even a steadfast heart to bear"—offering a parable for how sin can be so tempting (*Inferno*, 16:131–32).

But while "So I Grew Half Delirious and Quite Sick" is redolent with theological meaning, the speaker's description of how "strange faces" frightened her and a monster "touched [her] clammily" (4–9) also seems psychoanalytically laden, tinted with shades of the fluidity, "clamminess," "repulsion," and "fear" that according to Kristeva accompany a narcissistic crisis, characterized as a descent into the primal drives, according to Kristeva (*Powers*, 6, 14). The speaker's strange encounter with the fleshy sea creature can thus also be read as recording a psychoanalytically true account of "the origin and upsurge of sexuality," in the terms of Laplanche and Pontalis's account of the language of fantasies (19). The abrupt manner in which the encounter with the beast who offers "love" is cut off in "So I Grew Half Delirious and Quite Sick" similarly suggests the onset of a symbolic prohibition (11–12). The image of the sun that the speaker describes as rising over the newly purified scene of her dream has accordingly been classified by Kristeva as a typical poetic symbol of the "limiting structure [of] paternal law" that binds and contains libido (*Desire*, 28–29).[29] Fantasies may, in turn, draw on literary reference points available to the speaker, and the moment in Christina's dream when she grieves the loss of her beast, "knowing that one new / [c]reature had love for me" (12–13), accords with Dante's contention that one may be easily fooled by Geryon into overvaluing his charms, which hide the fact that he "pollutes the whole wide world" (*Inferno*, 16:1, 16:7). Read in this way, the poem is a fantasy that may encode a moment in the speaker's history when her lingering attraction to her condition of primary narcissism caused her to resist the symbolic subjection that nonetheless contained the seeds of her salvation.

A final way in which the poem may have been true is as literally so. Marsh interprets the poem in this way, proposing that its narrative of "delirium, sickness [and] fainting" literally recollects Christina's breakdown of 1845 and, moreover, that the account of an ambiguous and confusing incident in which the drives of a "monstrous 'bad self'" overwhelm the dreamer may hint at an incestuous event that lay behind this breakdown (CR, 259–60, 167). Kristeva's reflections about the abject suggest that an incident of incest in Christina's background might be captured in fantasy as an encounter with an abject superegoic authority figure. Superegoic figures, Kristeva finds, are particularly animated among those who have simultaneously suffered "too much strictness on the part of the Other" as well as "the lapse of the Other"—both potentially suggestive of improper encounters with filial figures who loom large in childhood (*Powers*, 15). Nonetheless, the psychoanalytical theory of fantasy suggests that we cannot tie Christina's demonic and beastly imagery with assurance to a concrete incident in her background, given how fantasy contents are more generally pieced together by subjects out of a collective "metapsychological structure" to help explain whatever "major enigmas" haunt the subject (Lapanche and Pontalis, 19). A seduction fantasy that uses an abstract myth to explain a traumatic and ambivalent onset of sexuality could presumably be keyed to a wide range of actual incidents.

Chrstina Rossetti's poem "My Dream," written five years later, also envisions a beast-usurper who resembles the Leviathan from Revelation and Geryon from Dante's *Inferno*. The poem begins in a prophetic key, with the speaker announcing, "Hear now a curious dream I dreamed last night, / Each word where of is weighed and sifted truth" (1–2). She goes on to mimic the biblical passage that describes the emergence of the Leviathan with "seven heads and ten crown" (Revelation 13:1), narrating a birth of crocodiles who put on armor of "massive gold / and polished stones," among whom one wears "kinglier girdle and a kingly crown / [w]hilst crowns and orbs and sceptres starred his breast" (13–16). In his showy glamour, the crocodile also recollects Dante's Geryon, who wore "coloured stuff . . . rainbow trammed" (*Inferno*, 17.7). Like these figures, the crocodile of "My Dream" is described as powerfully and even perversely sexual, a phallic object "broad as a rafter, potent as a flail" (22). A presymbolic context of the crocodile is further indicated through imagery of a "swell[ing] river" that "waxe[s] and colour[s] sensibly to sight," which resembles the source of presymbolic identity that Kristeva calls the "chora," in which "drives hold sway and constitute a strange space" (*Desire*, 14).

The "white vessel" that arrives on the scene to terminate the reign of the crocodile offers a distinct contrast to the colorful river (38). Kristeva proposes in her analysis of medieval iconic art that white stands for the "transcendental dominion of One meaning" (*Desire*, 234); the function of this white vessel is evidently to impose paternal order upon this heterogeneity scene. The vessel vanquishes the crocodile, along with the entire river from which he emerged, revealing him as a fraud who hypocritically "shed[s] appropriate tears and wr[ings] his hands" (22, 48). Like "So I Grew Half Delirious and Quite Sick," however, Rossetti's vision seems to resist overt moralism despite its borrowing of morally freighted Dantesque and biblical imagery. Whereas the Leviathan in his moments reveals his vile and damned nature, vomiting up "three unclean spirits like frogs" and being "cast alive into a lake of fire" (Revelation 16:13, 16:19), Rossetti's crocodile seems merely comically reduced. Rossetti's speaker seems, moreover, far more impartial than the speaker of Revelation, who champions the "new heaven and a new earth" obtained through the destruction of the usurper (Revelation 21:1), as she regards with awe—but not joy—the violence of the "avenging ghost," who "level[s] strong Euphrates in its course . . . [t]ill not a murmur swelled or billow beat" (31–32, 40–45). "My Dream" thus continues to present a subject who, like Rossetti's Eve in "An Afterthought," recalls an oedipal event with ambivalence and thus seems to remain partly in thrall to the charms of the presymbolic era that her fantasies cast back to and to the demonic figures that superintend them.

By the time Christina Rossetti wrote *Goblin Market* (1859/1862), however, her fantasy had become far less morally equivocal and her characters assumed a more prudent resistance toward the primal repressed. "We must not look at Goblin Men," Lizzie warns her sister, Laura (42), revealing a determined morality that contrasts with the susceptibility of the speakers of "My Dream" and "So I Grew Half Delirious and Quite Sick," who look at monstrous creatures without qualms. Lizzie's concern in *Goblin Market* about forbidden visions thus extends the anxiety that had begun to emerge at the end of Rossetti's gothic period. At the same time, Lizzie's caution reveals a maturation in Rossetti's fantasy insofar as her characters are developing the means to avoid scenes of primal desire so that they are not destroyed by their desires. Nonetheless, *Goblin Market* fits decidedly into the larger pattern of Rossetti's fantasy poetry, with goblins this time assuming the place of the grotesque and fraudulent superegoic beast. Like Rossetti's gothic demons, the goblins are purveyors of fraud, promising delight but "offering only empty promises and death" (85–86). The goblins promise Lizzie hospitality, reaching out to her "to be welcome guest" (381), but are in fact out for themselves, turning on her when she rejects their fruit and "no longer wagging, purring" as "[t]heir tones wax[ ] loud, / [t]heir looks [are] evil" (391–97). Like Rossetti's gothic demons, moreover, the goblins combine persuasion with coercion: when Lizzie does not give up her money voluntarily, they seek violent ways to compel her, "[s]cratch[ing] her, pinch[ing] her black as ink" (427). As Morrill elaborates, "the goblins in Rossetti's poem are hardly the sprightly, mischievous elves of folklore who skim the cream off milk. . . . [T]hey are darker, more mysterious, more powerful, more terrifying, and more human. Above all, their actions are vampiric: they dole out strange, exotic fruits to young women who become drained, languid, bloodless" (2). The motif of vampirism particularly emerges in how the goblins destroy a third girl, Jeanie, who "should have been a bride; / [b]ut who for joys brides hope to have / [f]ell sick and died" (278–79). Laura's incipient decay from the goblin fruit as she "dwindle[s] as the fair moon doth turn to swift decay and burn[s], / [h]er fire away" (480–81) similarly resembles the states of possession in "A Coast-Nightmare" and *Maude* that draw women beyond the reach of normal life and relationships.

It may seem counterintuitive to link the pleasure-offering goblins with the superego. But upon examination, the goblins, like Christina Rossetti's other ferocious tyrants, are frauds who "mislead, corrupt, use" and "take advantage" of societal laws and rules to trap their victims in confusion and double binds (Kristeva, *Powers*, 15). The goblins thus apply what Copjec finds to be a primary source of superegoic pressure within utilitarian society, which is its "violen[t] and obscen[e]" way of inciting one to indulge in a "boundless and aggressive enjoyment" (92). Despite the goblins' nefarious intentions, their social pressure is hard to resist. They operate from the base of the capitalist market, by which they derive a sense of legitimacy as well as the power to pressure Lizzie, given that in the marketplace, exchange is accepted as a form of civility, as Terence Holt points out.[30] As a result, when Lizzie returns to the goblins on Laura's behalf, the goblins shame her for not buying their fruit, calling her "proud, cross-grained, uncivil" (394–95). Interpreting the male goblins as a form of the superego that contests the regime of a genuine symbolic Other by extending false claims can help to explain the difficulty that Lizzie and Laura have in avoiding such dangers, which requires not only that they resist pleasure but also that they discriminate between conflicting imperatives. Arseneau has read *Goblin Market* as a poem about making proper distinctions in the Christian sense: she finds that Laura is drawn to the superficially tempting fruit because she lacks the "symbolic sense" described within Tractarian philosophy, which lets humans observe divine values beyond attractive appearances and thereby make difficult moral distinctions in a physical world (81). This symbolic sense, Arseneau argues, is what allows Lizzie to see the demonic character underlying the pleasing appearance of the "unnatural, illusory and deceptive" goblin fruit ("Incarnation," 85).

Arseneau's explanation of the Christian ethic of resistance that the sisters in *Goblin Market* must learn to apply is, meanwhile, similar to Copjec's account of the psychoanalytic ethic of resistance to the superego that always urges the subject toward demonic excesses. To resist the demonic appeals of the superego, Copjec asserts, one needs to deepen one's awareness of the symbolic relation that creates distance between "evidence of a thing" and the "real" of the thing (98, 103). Modern subjects, she finds, have lost this suspicion of appearances because of the "fantasy of the maximization of pleasure" that has been created through the utilitarian—essentially capitalist—definition of the subject as a "pure positive drive towards realisation" (103). But psychoanalytic theory revives the Christian suspicion of pleasure, defining the subject as not only alienated by the symbolic law that looks askance at excessive pleasure and attempts to regulate it, but also as saved by this law, given that the subject is occupied by a superego fueled by the id that would pressure her to indulge her drives to the fatal limit.

In the face of the superego's imperative of boundless enjoyment, there are several possible means of resistance. For Copjec, one resists the superego's pressures through intellectual separation of oneself from one's own desires as one erects a barrier "against [one's] aggression or [one's] enjoyment," even at the expense of "prolonging conflict with the self" (92). We may accordingly see Lizzie crudely resisting the goblin's calls—and the calls of her own senses—when she "thrust[s] a dimpled finger / [i]n each ear," shuts her eyes, and runs (68). But Lizzie's separation of herself from her enjoyment is not enough to protect her when she has to more closely approach the goblin market on Laura's behalf. Kristeva thus additionally proposes that some means to "deal[ ] with narcissism" as well as "sin and fiendish characters" are embedded in "theologies and literatures" (*Tales*, 7), which, as she elsewhere explains, provide the subject with fundamental strategies of separation and purification that are rooted in the symbolic law (*Powers*, 94). Lizzie accordingly emulates a distinctively theological attitude of purity when she braves the scene of the goblins the second time, standing "[w]hite and [g]olden" (408) and thereby embodying the stance of the angels in Revelation who are "clothed in pure and white linens" and "golden girdles" (Revelation 15:6).

Finally, Kristeva notes another, more radical way of dealing with sin within Christianity, which is to convert it into "jouissance and beauty" through "familiarity with abjection" and "subtle transgression" (*Powers*, 123, 31). Kristeva accordingly cites Christ's seeking out of lepers to strengthen his spiritual purity as the paradigm of how "sin, turned upside down into love, attains . . . beauty" (*Powers*, 128). Kristeva's account of the paradox of Christian purity-within-abjection provides an answer to one of the major paradoxes of *Goblin Market*, which is why the goblin's fruit is at one point poison for Laura and at another point her cure. Kristeva likewise indicates that while contact with the abject is dangerous, the representation of the abject in art "provide[s] sinners with the opportunity to live" by setting "the joy of their dissipation . . . into signs, painting, music, words" (*Powers*, 131). Interestingly, Laura seems to respond to Lizzie's costume of fruit as to an extreme kind of art, leaping and singing as she licks up the signs of sin (495). Kristeva's description of how such art produces jouissance (*Powers*, 123) also may explain why Laura's response to eating the fruit off Lizzie resembles a "biblical frenzy," as Dorothy Mermin finds.[31] Encounters with the abject for the sake of holiness are rare, Kristeva proposes, being typically permitted only in esoteric mystical sects (*Powers*, 131). But where the deliberate familiarization with the abject occurs, it is an even stronger tool against sin than is resistance or separation, providing a means to include within symbolic discourses what these discourses exclude so that individuals who have fallen away from the symbolic law can potentially be reintegrated. In a similar way, Christina Rossetti believed that it was necessary to imagine desire in order to help those whose knowledge of desire has been damning, such as the women in St. Magdalene's asylum, claiming that "'the poet's mind' should be . . . able to construct [an illegitimate woman] from her own inner consciousness" (Marsh, CR, 229). Rossetti's philosophy of writing thus appears to have accorded with Kristeva's, which holds that familiarity with the abject extremes of desire can allow them to be "subsumed into a speech that gathers and restrains" and sin can be thereby "toppled . . . into the Other" (Powers, 131, 130).

A particular form of writing that helps in this process of enlarging the means of the symbolic order to redeem the fallen is the confessional kind, and Rossetti accordingly has Laura infinitely rehearse her frightening story before her and her sister's children, reliving her horror at the experience with the fruit merchants and her gratitude for "how her sister stood, / [i]n deadly peril to do her good" (554–58). In making Laura a storyteller, Rossetti indicates that a key way to conquer demons is to turn the lessons learned from them to the public good. This final image of *Goblin Market*, of Laura producing stories out of sin, is extended in Rossetti's later *Speaking Likenesses* (1874), three salutary stories about goblins that are told by an aunt to her nieces. These stories, cast in the form of cautionary juvenile fairy tales, contain imagery that is in some regards as uncanny and disturbing as that of Rossetti's earlier fantasy works, prompting a contemporaneous reviewer to register "an uncomfortable feeling that a great deal more is meant than appears on the surface, and that every part of it ought to mean something if we only knew what it was."[32] Nonetheless, the stories told by the aunt are more morally determined than Christina Rossetti's other fantasies: indeed, the collection is called "anti-fantasy" by its modern editors David A. Kent and P. G. Stanwood, presumably because the moralizing tone of the work contrasts with the daring spontaneity of Rossetti's earlier fantasy works. In this regard, the stories culminate the trend we have seen in Rossetti's fantasy writing as a whole, which has been moving in the direction of moral certainty and determinacy. The modes of narcissism that concern this aunt are far less brazen than they were in the case of Rossetti's earlier speakers, with the elderly aunt concerned with deterring not exorbitant sexual sin but garden-variety forms of egotism—a direction that detracts from the horror and suspense of Rossetti's fantasy writings but augments her ability to make salutary examples out of her characters. Accordingly, the diminution of Rossetti's fantasy in *Speaking Likenesses* may reveal that, by 1874, Rossetti's own demons had dwindled into quotidian spiritual problems, her truly ferocious figures having been largely vanquished in the remote past.

One character who must pursue a course of moral improvement is an irritable birthday girl named Flora presented in the aunt's first tale. Flora discovers a parallel party amid a "multitude of mirrors" with children who double the egotistical qualities of herself and her invitees (125). Flora is matched with a bossy queen, girls "exude[ ] a sticky fluid," and boys are "hung round with hooks" and "pricky quills," conveying in unpleasantly sexualized ways the destructive nature of children's egoistic drives (129). The self-centered qualities of the mirrored children are also reflected in the aggressive games they play, including a game called "Self Help," where the boys attack the girls with their hooks and quills, representing the perverse selfishness one finds amid the egoistic drives.[33] Finally, the children build houses of colored glass bricks that threaten to cage Flora in with the unpleasant queen, producing a parodic reenactment of the narcissistic captivity inflicted on the heroine in "Shut Out" (133). By experiencing these demon-children's bad behavior, Flora learns not to listen to her inner "queen," a greedy superegoic authority that would, if unfettered, force her to seek her own satisfaction at the expense of every other value.

The other tales in *Speaking Likenesses* also portray pleasure-seeking impulses within children as tyrannical demons. In the second tale, a young girl named Edith wants to boil water without help from her family. She subsequently finds herself beneath a "cluster of . . . purple grapes . . . hanging high above her head" and by a "pool," revealing through this image that Edith's self-assertion is a narcissistically tempting but fraudulent good, like the fruit in *Goblin Market* (139). In the third tale, a girl named Maggie is sent on an important journey through the woods. After she becomes diverted by a piece of chocolate on the ground, she is accosted by a horrifying boy with "only one feature . . . a wide mouth," who represents the insufficiently tempered appetite that leads Maggie away from her pilgrimage (147). Maggie is frightened enough to run away from the boy as well as the chocolate, thus learning to ignore the demands of her gluttonous appetite. The point of the story is clearly not that Maggie should perversely deprive herself—an imperative that would resurrect one of Christina's own vanquished demons—since back at home she is permitted to enjoy a healthy snack of "buttered toast" (150). Rather, the point is that she should be able to make ethical distinctions, forgoing excess of appetite for the sake of carrying out her social duty.

As we can see, a common feature of these stories is that the demons in them are no longer private apparitions in nightmares but instead are social demons that break out at birthday parties and in family contexts.[34] Within Christina Rossetti's trajectory of fantasy, her gradual relocating of demons outside of private nightmares and social scenes seems to be yet another way that she gradually subsumes abjection into the symbolic order of the Other. Kristeva implies a similar development in the artist, who, upon mastering the materials of the abject, moves beyond confession and becomes a source of social authority. At this juncture, "power no longer belongs to the judge-God" but rather belongs to "the act of judgment expressed in speech and . . . in all the signs (poetry, painting, music, sculpture) that are contingent upon it" (Powers, 132). This social facet of *Speaking Likenesses* thus helps to explain why it is so important that Laura tell her stories to her children at the end of *Goblin Market*. By doing so, Laura moves beyond paralysis and also beyond confession to become an artist who recovers her experience of the abject through signs and who can thus school others in making subtle moral distinctions. Laura thus improves on Lizzie's general warning not to "look at goblin men" as she describes to her children the precise attraction of the "wicked, quaint fruit-merchant men" and "their fruits like honey to the throat / [b]ut poison to the blood" (552–54). In turn, *Speaking Likenesses* represents a final shift in Christina Rossetti's demonic art, toward stories in which a speaker wields an active moral stance, deploying the imagery of demons not nervously but assuredly, in strategic contexts where they can induce discursive renewal.

As we have seen, Christina Rossetti's fantasy first presented itself as a dissociated trauma of abjection over which the speaker exercises no understanding, in "My Dream." It subsequently emerged in horror stories through which Rossetti could represent the danger that these fantasies held and then was enclosed in the fable of *Goblin Market*, which both expresses the fantasy's power in a mythical form and uses that myth to contain its power. *Speaking Likenesses* is another moment in this development that foregrounds the act of narrative as the means by which salutary morals can be derived from encounters with demons, though they may continue to present themselves in baffling new forms. We can see here a pattern that is similar to that expressed in a psychoanalytical treatment, whereby even though the author does not banish demons by writing about them, she attains a means of reckoning with them. Analysis does not preempt pathological reactions, Freud claims. Rather, by making the subject aware of her drives, it "give[s] the patient's ego *freedom to decide*" whether to obey the pathological imperatives of the superego (*Ego*, 40n). Similarly, the author who tells stories about a malevolent and greedy superegoic demon may never vanquish it, though she may minimize its power over her. In *Speaking Likenesses,* the superegoic demons that haunted Christina Rossetti's young heroines have been knocked from their perches, their basis in bad conscience reintegrated into discourses of wisdom. Demons no longer loom up in vicious dreams but provide their lessons and are, for the moment, banished with a snack of buttered toast. And if the pathology of superegoic demons continues to haunt Christina Rossetti's characters, these characters at least have, in Freud's words, the "freedom to decide" whether to heed their demons.

three

Imaginary Oscillation in Dante Gabriel Rossetti's Illustrations of Dante

> It is the nature of desire to be radically torn.... If the object perceived from without has its own identity, the latter places the man who sees it in a state of tension, because he perceives himself as desire, and as unsatisfied desire. Inversely, when he grasps his unity, on the contrary it is the world which for him becomes decomposed, loses its meaning, and takes on an alienated and discordant aspect. It is this imaginary oscillation which gives to all human perception the dramatic subjacency experienced by the subject, in so far as his interest is truly aroused.
>
> —Jacques Lacan, *Seminar II*

WILLIAM GAUNT HAS OBSERVED that "the Rossettis carried Dante with them like a totem."[1] Gabriele Rossetti, the father, was a scholar of Dante Alighieri who made himself notorious through his stringently political interpretation of Dante's books, and to some degree, each of his artistic offspring likewise defined their own artistic visions, as well as spiritual and philosophical frameworks, upon Dante's examples.[2] We have seen allusions in Christina Rossetti's oeuvre to the path of sublimation dramatized by Dante, through which he forgoes human desire to attain ultimate spiritual knowledge and transcendence. Dante Gabriel Rossetti was also riveted by this process, although Dante remained an ambiguous as well as an admired icon for the brother, who gradually showed himself to be patently unsuited for the path of spiritual purification outlined in the *Commedia*.[3] Consequently, Dante Gabriel Rossetti saw Dante not as a model but as a basis for productive innovation, through which Rossetti could produce the kinds of "errors of recreation" that would distinguish him from his ideal precursor, in the terms of Harold Bloom.[4] While remaining consistently focused on the details of Dante's vision, Rossetti swerved away from Dante's sacramental metaphysics toward a worldview that emphasized earthly and aesthetic rewards, as Rossetti reformulated for himself where the deepest human satisfactions lie.

The evidently autobiographical sonnet "Dantis Tenebrae" (1861/1870) provides an overview of the different ways in which Dante Gabriel Rossetti and Dante treat both spirituality and sexuality. In the title, which can be translated as "Dante of the darkness" or "Dante of the lower world," Rossetti summarizes what aspects of Dante's legacy he has, and has not, inherited with the great writer's name. As he declares in an implicit address to his late father, he finds himself in a "vale" (6) that resembles Dante's "valley's wandering maze" at the opening of canto 1 of the *Inferno*, which symbolizes the condition of sin (1.14). Rossetti adds that he has, like Dante, been taken up by a patronizing Beatrice who "declin[es] her eyes" upon him ("Dantis," 4). However, for the remainder of the poem, Rossetti indicates that he has a different trajectory from that of Dante, who was sent by Beatrice on an epic journey that led him to imaginatively scale the heights of heaven. Rossetti accordingly describes how his "foot-track" extends "to the hills" but implicitly not up them ("Dantis," 5–7). Another difference between Dante Gabriel Rossetti's journey in "Dantis Tenebrae" and that of his namesake is that Rossetti departs at sunset rather than at sunrise, which is when Dante begins his travels ("Dantis," 9), suggesting that Rossetti knew he lacked Dante's scope to achieve spiritual redemption within his lifetime. This imagery of dusk, which captures the widespread Victorian sensation of spiritual decline,[5] adds to the sense that Rossetti regarded Dante's heights as an ideal to admire rather than an achievement to follow. That Rossetti was primarily interested in Dante as a source of aesthetic inspiration (in keeping with Rossetti's identification of himself as an "Art Catholic" rather than a bona fide spiritual pilgrim) is confirmed in his description of how at the same time as his path aims downward into the vale, his face is lifted and gazes at heights that cannot possibly be mounted, being only clouds ("Dantis," 10–12).

The sharpest distinctions between Dante Gabriel Rossetti and Dante, however, are evident in the two artists' respective ideas about sin and about woman. For Rossetti, the valley he finds himself in is not a source of dread, as it is for Dante. Rather, it is a repository of Romantic enchantments, where "wisdom's living fountain to his chaunt / [t]rembles in music" ("Dantis," 8–9). Jerome McGann has appropriately argued that Rossetti's trajectory as an artist reverses Dante's, in "descending from various illusory heavens ... to the nightmares and hells" of his later works, especially *The House of Life*.⁶ In "Dantis Tenebrae," Rossetti captures a sense of this downward fate—although his depths are depicted as a fascinating goal rather than a condition of nightmarish disenchantment. Rossetti's sense of hell is not as horrifying as McGann implies, however, because it is not only an intellectual condition but also a libidinal condition, as is signaled by the presence of the woman who resides there: a sorceress who has "accept[ed] [him] to be of those that haunt" those depths ("Dantis," 5–6). Rossetti's indication that he is bound to indulge in and explore certain mysterious and dark depths hints at his attraction to what Lacan calls the "imaginary domain," where the subject's libidinal investments are dominant (SI, 225). It accordingly anticipates the thrust of Freud's epigraph to *The Interpretation of Dreams*, "Flectere si nequeo superos, Acheronta Movebo"—"If I cannot influence the heavens, I will move Hell"—in which Juno's reference to the depths of hell in the *Aeneid* is used to figure the depths of the psyche where the structures of desire reside. Translator Dorothy L. Sayers has described how Dante's journey in the *Commedia* through hellish views to blessed vistas establishes a sublime triumph over "disordered desires";⁷ in this sense, Rossetti's "Dantis Tenebrae" can be taken as a declaration of the later poet's insistence on lingering amid the precise disorder from which Dante emerges.

Nonetheless, the perspective of the climbing clouds piling up before Rossetti suggests that he idealized Dante for achieving sublimation even as he resisted Dante's example—a combination of attitudes that, according to Freud, is likely to produce a subject who harbors some degree of neuroticism. In "On Narcissism," Freud defines the ego-ideal as the subject's projection of his lost childhood perfection on another, who becomes "the substitute for the lost narcissism of his childhood in which he was his own ideal" (94). Taking such an ideal exerts a pressure on the subject to elevate and purify his own being to match up with, and thus be worthy of, the ego-ideal he has taken. A person who holds a high ego-ideal without the genuine capacity to transform his desire through a process of sublimation will fall prey to repression and consequently to neurosis (95). Freud further proposes that it is particularly among subjects with a significant amount of displaced narcissism that the attraction to an ego ideal is strong (94). The record of Dante Gabriel Rossetti suggests that he is a candidate for this sort of diagnosis, his writing and biography being permeated both by the narcissistic idealization and by syndromes of neurotic anxiety and depression (Marsh, DGR, 488). In contrast, while Dante could be said to neurotically idealize Beatrice at the beginning of *La Vita Nuova* when he describes how "the natural functions of his body began to be vexed and impeded" under her influence (82), he gradually de-emphasizes the ideal of Beatrice and eventually converts his libidinal instinct into a pursuit of intellectual and spiritual knowledge, in keeping with Freud's definition of sublimation.[8] As Kristeva argues, by the time of the *Commedia*, Dante's desire for Beatrice has been sublimated into a desire for the meaning symbolized by the crystal rose at the terminus of *Paradiso*, and the narrative of secondary narcissism according to which Dante perseveres in his quest of Beatrice through all levels of the cosmos is "no more than a fiction" (*Tales*, 293–94).

The term *narcissism* is frequently used in relation to Dante Gabriel Rossetti, but the kind of narcissism implicated in Rossetti's literary oeuvre and biography is not the same as the self-loving narcissism that destroyed Narcissus. Narcissus's was a "primary" narcissism characterized by eroticized self-love, whereby one seeks oneself "as a love-object" (Freud, "Narcissism," 88). Freud contrasts primary narcissism with what he calls the "secondary narcissism" of a subject who mirrors lost perfections of the self upon others and consequently feels love, devotion, and dependence upon them (94).[9] Kristeva likewise explains that a lover's narcissism is not the kind in which the ego "projects and glorifies itself" but instead is where the ego "shatters into pieces and is engulfed, when it admires itself in the mirror of an idealized [o]ther—sublime, incomparable, as worthy (of me?) as I can be unworthy of him, and yet made for our indissoluble union" (*Tales*, 6–7). Lacan similarly describes the state of secondary narcissism as one of "imaginary oscillation," in which the subject alternately "recognises his unity in an object" and "feels himself to be in disarray in relation to the [object]" (*SII*, 166). The neurotic consequences of narcissistic idealization are partly rooted in this effect of shattering and merging, the result of which is that the subject never feels entirely distinct from the other, or entirely whole, and so fixes onto the other as an organizing ideal that ends up intimidating and diminishing him. In *The House of Life*, when Rossetti's speaker tells his lover that he cannot tell "thee from myself," he portrays being haunted by the same kind of disorienting secondary narcissism—a jouissance he never renounces ("Heart's Hope," 8).

If a persistent career of narcissistic idealization likely made Rossetti neurotic, however, his compulsions also lend his oeuvre its own peculiar grandeur, his art emphasizing throughout the particular glories of the interpersonal relationship and seeking untiringly for some form of redemption that can be attained through the libidinal drives of the subject rather than in exchange for them. This possibility—that an ongoing commitment to imaginary order compulsions underlies a modern ethic that emphasizes individuality and relationships—has recently been proposed by a number of Lacanian theorists. Ellie Ragland Sullivan has derived from Lacanian theory that secondary narcissism adds a personal and human element to interpersonal relations, individualizing and innovating upon otherwise-rigid social mores.[10] Marshall Alcorn has similarly theorized that the narcissistic subject will develop new kinds of representation and discourse to depict his "fundamental response to an image of otherness," thus potentially remaking the symbolic order to more closely satisfy his needs.[11] Some readers of Rossetti have likewise observed that, in deviating from Dante, Rossetti mapped out some key functions for the "modern" artist, marking out a path of symbolic development for those who are forced or inclined to "substitute human love for the lost comfort of divine love."[12] In other words, by accepting his nature as "Dantis Tenebrae," Rossetti seized the opportunity to replace Dante's holy metaphysics with a damned one that nonetheless contains ethical potential in our post-Romantic era.

Dante Gabriel Rossetti's illustrations of Dante's writings thus serve as a case study of how Rossetti carved out an identity in relation to, and in conflict with, the Dantean myth that occupied a central place in his artistic and poetic pantheon. In particular, Rossetti emphasized, glamorized, and heightened whatever indications of narcissistic passion he found in Dante's aspirational writing in accordance with his role as a "Dante of the darkness," driven to reformulate his predecessor's imagery according to his own fallen value structure. For example, Rossetti signals an underlying narcissistic basis to Dante and Beatrice's relationship by representing them in ways that thwart normative hierarchies and gender distinctions, in keeping with Copjec's observation that a subject's narcissistic impulses will cause him to "conflict with and disrupt . . . social relations," a tendency that can be a recipe for persistent immaturity in a subject but can also make him a vehicle of social evolution (23).[13] Another way in which Rossetti's narcissistic impulses led him to challenge established mores was by representing male passion, thereby participating in a general Pre-Raphaelite attack on the Victorian ideal of masculinity as emotionally stoical.[14] Rossetti's earlier illustrations of Dante show him throwing special attention on Dante's account of love as a trauma that induces what Lacan refers to as disarray in the male subject. Nevertheless, Rossetti eventually succumbed in his painting to Victorian canons of aesthetic decorum for representing male desire, in part by increasing the presence of symbolic hierarchy and sanctification in his paintings of Dante and in part by heightening the presence of fetishistic imagery in them, which Slavoj Žižek characterizes as a "step towards universalization" (104).

Revisioning Dante's Erotics

The most sustained account that Dante Gabriel Rossetti gives of desire, apart from that captured in *The House of Life* sonnet sequence, is his series of illustrations of the major love stories in Dante's writings: those of Dante and Beatrice and of Paolo and Francesca da Rimini. While these two themes within Rossetti's painting complement each other, their visual depictions required very different strategies. Rossetti was presumably interested in Paolo and Francesca because they are literature's preeminent narcissistic lovers: a sister-in-law and brother-in-law damned to hell for their illicit affair. In Dante's telling of the story through Francesca, the imaginary character of her mutual attachment to Paolo snared the two in a relentless and fatal passion:

> Love, that to no loved heart remits love's score,
>   Took me with such great joy of him, that see!
>   It holds me yet and never shall leave me more.
> Love to a single death brought him and me[.]
>   (*Inferno*, 5.103–6)

As Dante commentator Charles Williams has pointed out, while the formal sin of these lovers is adultery, their poetic sin is "shrinking from the adult love demanded of them" and refusing "the opportunity of glory"—in other words, resisting the regulations of the symbolic order that would remake their desire according to its sacramental norms.[15]

What is striking about Rossetti's *Paolo and Francesca da Rimini* (1855) is how it challenges the need of such glory, emphasizing the permanent quality of these lovers' strong passion over and above the painful condition of their damnation (fig. 1). In the left-hand panel, Rossetti focuses his artistic efforts on memorializing the excitement of the moment in which passion gripped them. In Dante's *Inferno*, Francesca describes how, through exchanged glances, she and Paolo fell prey to an intense imaginary attraction that is signaled in their mutually reflected gazes:

> As we read on, our eyes met now and then,
>   And to our cheeks the changing colour started,

> But just one moment overcame us—when
> We read of the smile, desired of lips long-thwarted
> ...We read no more that day[.]
>
> (5.130–38)

Lacan describes this sort of instantaneous overwhelming by another's glance as the experience of a "specular mirage" in which "the subject recognises his unity in an object" (Four, 168). A lack of separation between the lovers in Francesca's speech, which uses no individuating pronouns but only the unifying we, dramatizes how the couple is becoming bound within one joint identity (SI, 276). This moment of merging is what Rossetti eternalizes in the left-hand panel of *Paolo and Francesca da Rimini*, where the couple is wrapped in the embrace Francesca describes. Rossetti's symmetrical positioning of these two lovers with their hands knotted and their lips kissing renders them as mirrored reflections of narcissistic unity. The two lovers are mirrored again in the opposed panels of the triptych, as the right-hand panel registers them in an identical embrace in hell, at odds with Dante's description of the lovers, "hand in hand on the dark wind drifting" (Inferno, 5.75).

Where Rossetti most seriously deviates from Dante, meanwhile, is that while Dante describes the couple as having arrived at a "dolorous pass," such that Paolo "wail[s] on [Dante] with a sound ... lamentable" (5.140–41), Rossetti's illustration registers none of this misery—an omission noted by his colleague Ford Madox Brown, who observed that "it is

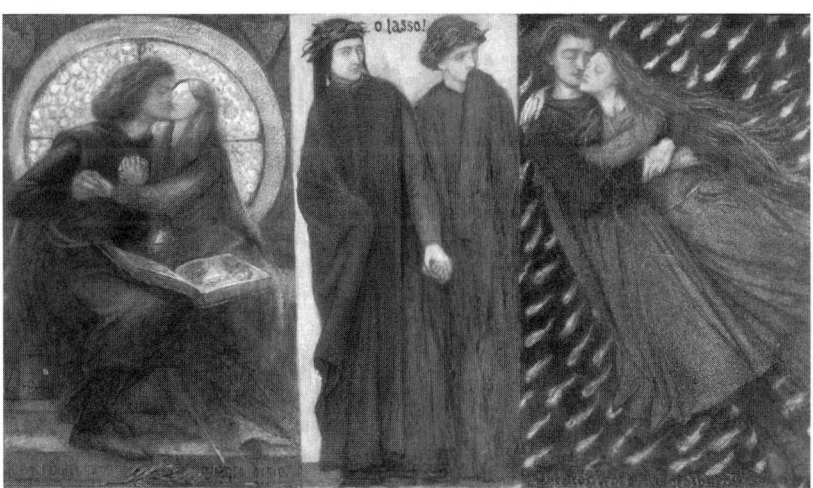

FIGURE 1. D. G. Rossetti, *Paolo and Francesca da Rimini* (1855). Watercolor on paper, 25.4 × 44.9 cm. Tate Gallery, London. Photo credit: Tate, London/Art Resource, NY.

impossible to suppose that when DGR painted it he . . . thought that the two lovers were really suffering."[16] The only indication in the right-hand panel of Rossetti's painting that the couple has been relocated to the Inferno is a background of blustery raindrops signifying the winds of the Circle of Lust, a "blast of hell that never rests from whirling" (*Inferno*, 5.31). In the graphic context of the painting, however, the storming rain around the lovers seems not to bother them but instead heightens the attraction of their embrace by conveying the stormy thrill of imaginary disarray—how "lovers drift[ ] into self-indulgence and [are] carried away by their passions," according to the translator.[17] Rossetti thus elides in his portrayal the bleaker suggestion of Dante's anecdote that Sayers points to, of how love without symbolic ordering is a hell of "howling darkness of helpless discomfort"—a quality of experience affirmed by Lacan when he describes imaginary passion as "always unsatisfying" (*Four*, 102). The only suggestion of symbolic transgression in Rossetti's triptych is provided by the figures of Virgil and Dante in the center panel; as they look upon the scene, Virgil seems to represent the regulating gaze of the symbolic Other that Paolo and Francesca defied and that—at least in Rossetti's illustration—they continue to resist (5.72). This painting thus dramatically envisions how amatory bliss might be prolonged in defiance of a symbolic order that would compel one to relinquish it through measures of intimidation that include the concept of hell.

In contrast with the affair of Paolo and Francesca, which with its visual content and scopic reference points seems to have been relatively easy for Rossetti to pictorially compose, Dante's asymmetrical, abstract, and increasingly sublime love for Beatrice appears to have presented more of a challenge.[18] Some of the difficulty that Rossetti had in conveying the magnificent drama of desire that is *La Vita Nuova* surely arose from the natural mismatch between Dante's highly poetic love for Beatrice and the visual medium into which Rossetti was trying to translate Dante's stories. Courtly love inspires great poetry because sonneteers can saturate their language with their own desire, transmitting it metonymically along the circuit of signifiers, in the terminology of Lacan (*Four*, 154). However, the delicate and unconsummated nature of a courtly affair, conducted with all of the formality that such affairs tend to feature, is such that it is likely to lack visual content. To make this highly inward form of love pictorially dramatic, Rossetti was consequently forced to introduce some creative interpolations.

One strategy he developed for maximizing the excitement of Dante and Beatrice's uneventful meetings in the streets of Florence was to heighten the suggestion of mutual imaginary attraction to a degree far beyond what was presumed by Dante. This tactic is most evident in Rossetti's painting *Beatrice Meeting Dante at a Marriage Feast, Denies Him Her Salutation* (1851; fig. 2), which captures the infatuated Dante trying to engage Beatrice's attention but failing because others had "misfame[d] [him] of vice."[19] This incident, in which Beatrice "denie[s][him] her most sweet salutation, in the which alone was [his] blessedness," is anticlimactic in Dante's report (*Vita Nuova*, 87). Rossetti obtains some visual drama for his illustration by heightening the effect of Beatrice's aloofness toward Dante: emphasizing her inaccessibility by surrounding her with a bastion of bridesmaids and emphasizing her coolness by coloring the women's dresses green to contrast with Dante's fiery red cloak. Rossetti thereby captures the signature qualities of courtly love according to Lacan, which is that the lady is "surrounded and isolated by a barrier" and is "terrifying" in her cruelty—two effects that encourage the love directed toward her to be delibidinized along a route of sublimation (*SVII*, 149–50). But Rossetti's *Beatrice Meeting Dante* strains against not only Dante's account of the incident but also the premise of Beatrice's indifference that Lacan considers foundational, by hinting at a thwarted imaginary attraction between the two Florentines. In the first place, Rossetti depicts them in an exclusive exchange of glances despite Beatrice's refusal to formally greet Dante, the effect of which is to suggest a secret thrill. He further underlines this imaginary frisson by juxtaposing a parallel encounter on the other side of the canvas, in which a young man reaches to pluck a grape from a basket being carried by a young peasant woman. In contrast to Beatrice, this woman glances sweetly up at her young pursuer—therein hinting that perhaps Beatrice would likewise return Dante's desire if she were not restrained by her compulsory courtly hauteur. In adding this other pair of lovers, in other words, Rossetti allows us to glimpse a hint of imaginary naturalness beneath the symbolic freight of transcendental courtly love.

Another depiction of an encounter between Dante and Beatrice employs further measures to suggest that there might be a mutual imaginary attraction between them. *The Salutation of Beatrice* (1859/1864) is a two-paneled work that juxtaposes Dante's and Beatrice's first meeting in the Florence street with the meeting that Dante later envisions them having in paradise (fig. 3). In the left-hand panel, Rossetti appears to have painted the very moment of the inception of Dante's love, when Beatrice "turn[s] her eyes thither . . . [and] salute[s] [him] with so virtuous a bearing that [he] seemed then and there to behold the very limits of blessedness" (*Vita Nuova*, 80). Rossetti appears to have required several drafts and versions

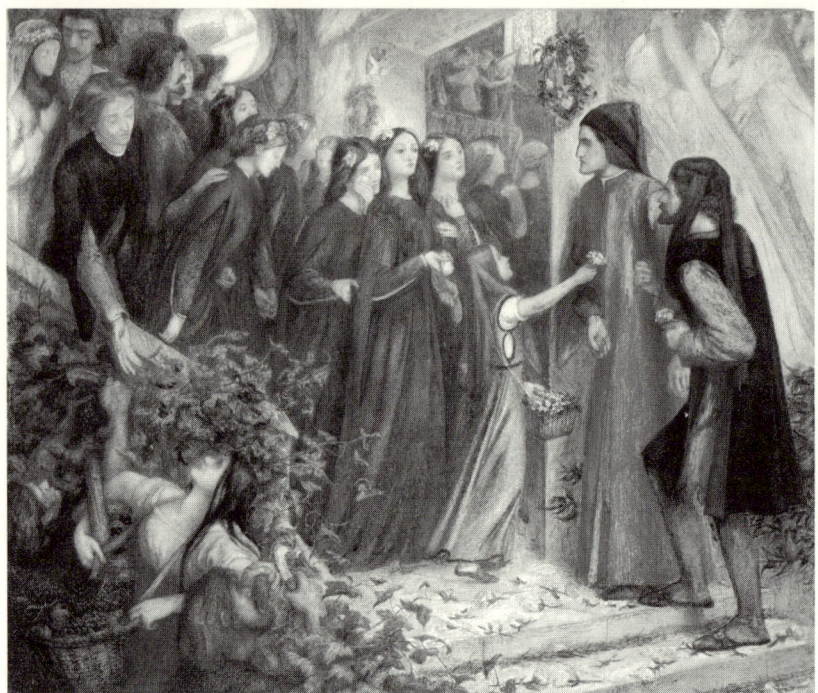

FIGURE 2. D. G. Rossetti, *Beatrice Meeting Dante at a Marriage Feast, Denies Him Her Salutation*. Watercolor on paper. *Courtesy of Ashmolean Museum of Art and Archaeology, University of Oxford*.

to determine how to maximize the imaginary suggestiveness of the incidents described by Dante—in particular, how to overcome the onesidedness of the attraction as Dante narrates it. In early sketches of the meeting on the Florence street, Rossetti portrays Dante with fidelity to the canons of courtly respect, standing at a remote distance from Beatrice as she greets him with "virtuous . . . bearing" (*Vita Nuova*, 80). But in the left-hand panel of the version of 1864, Rossetti transgresses Dante's norm of courtly distance to graphically dramatize the internal excitement that punctures the surface reserve. In this rendition, Dante and Beatrice pause and look at each other on the same step of an incline in the street while Beatrice's attendants stand on different steps. The juxtaposition of Beatrice's descent and Dante's ascent in the left-hand panel anticipates the conditions of their later meeting in the *Commedia*. However, the conceit also racily isolates the two figures in a private meeting, thus defying the courtly motif of the barrier observed by Lacan. It also produces an effect of mirroring between the man and the woman, who are symmetrically opposed in the composition in a similar way to Paolo

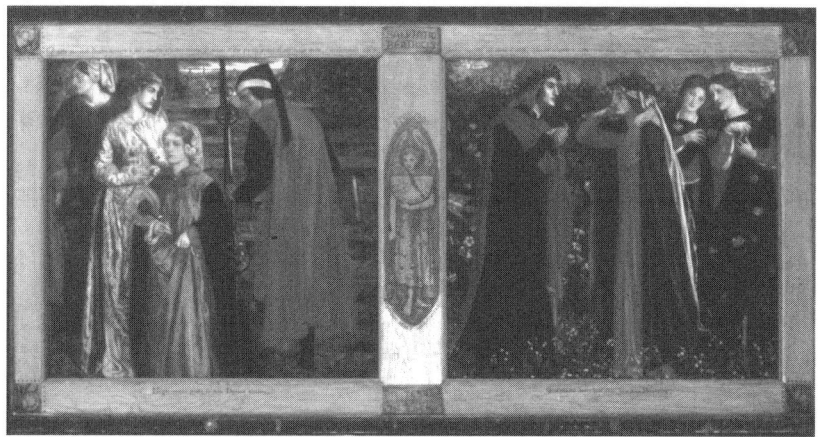

FIGURE 3. D. G. Rossetti, *The Salutation of Beatrice* (1859). Oil on two panels, each 74.9 x 80 cm. Courtesy of National Gallery of Canada.

and Francesca. The suggestion of imaginary intimacy is underlined by Rossetti through his inscription of a radically decontextualized line from the *Vita Nuova*'s sonnet of the same name at the base of the panel: "My lady carries love within her eyes" (*Vita Nuova*, 100). In its proper context in a sonnet in section 13 of *La Vita Nuova*, about halfway through the narrative, the line means that Beatrice's eyes radiate *agape* to the world, not exclusive *eros* for Dante. In his relocation of the line, Rossetti thus produces what Bloom calls a swerve, whereby a poet misinterprets his precursor to layer his own poetic vision onto a preexistent text (30).

Imaginary symmetry between Dante and Beatrice is further heightened insofar as Rossetti depicts Dante stooping, thus ensuring that his gaze meets Beatrice's on a level plane. Rossetti thus reprises the effects of imaginary symmetry from *Paolo and Francesca da Rimini* and cancels out some of the obstructive effects of the courtly distance that divide Dante and Beatrice in Dante's narrative. By cementing the exchange of glances between these counterparts through the equalization of their heights, Rossetti suggests in his pictorial treatment that a narcissistic exchange can overcome the hierarchies and divisions that might otherwise formalize symbolic relationships. Another socially subversive effect of Rossetti's having Dante stoop is that the painter thereby defies the Victorian aesthetic canons of "minor beauty" and "major beauty" that insisted that women be portrayed as delicate and small and that men be portrayed as contrastingly grand and powerful. Rossetti's strategy here is in keeping with a pattern that Susan P. Casteras observes broadly within Pre-Raphaelite art, which radically favored representations of tall, large-boned women as well as sensitive and diminutive men.[20] Within psychoanalytic theory, this capacity to defy symbolically normative systems such as aesthetic canons is rooted specifically in narcissistic impulses of desire, which have an individual basis in the subject's panoply of interior images, as Alcorn suggests.[21] These gender-dissolving forces of narcissism in Rossetti's works have not been generally noted; instead, Rossetti's narcissism has typically been seen as an impulse that enforces male identity. For J. Hillis Miller, Rossetti's representations of male narcissistic responses to women ultimately reassure men of women's inferiority, as the woman reflects "the perpetual too little or too much" so that the male subject who "look[s] in the mirror and see[s] a sister image" discovers that the sister image "does not fit him" (344). Essentially, Miller finds that Rossetti's narcissism amounts to another form of fetishism, reprising in another form the problem of feminine lack: "If she has [no phallus] then I do, or do I?" (344). But Copjec has specifically warned against this kind of conflation of narcissistic and masculinist effects, recalling that one of the fundamental tenets of psychoanalysis is its dualism—in this case, the opposition it sustains between "the unbinding force of narcissism and the binding force of social relations" (23). While examples of these binding and unbinding impulses are likely to be found in any given work of art, that does not mean that one reduces to the other. In the case of Rossetti, I would argue, the animating tension of his visual as well as poetic work emerges insofar as it is torn between the individualizing effects of narcissism and the normalizing effects of symbolization and fetishism.

The ongoing conflict between narcissistic resistance and symbolic ordering in Dante Gabriel Rossetti's art is evinced through a comparative reading of the first panel of the *Salutation* with the second panel. Here Rossetti appears to have illustrated the highly formal moment in *Purgatorio* when Beatrice pushes back a veil from her eyes and Dante is permitted to glimpse her face far above him, in her holy "chariot" (30.15). The *Salutation* is thus conceived in a similar way to *Paolo and Francesca da Rimini*, as another diptych that mirrors earthly and eternal versions of what Lacan calls the "specular moment" of desire (SI, 177). But in portraying the second episode, Rossetti is far more careful to reflect the sacramental and formal context of the *Commedia*, according to which all human activity is organized within the ladderlike structure of the cosmos. What is unexpected, however, is that Rossetti has reimagined the dominant symbolic order in very different terms from those used by Dante in Dante's account of the meeting at the base of paradise. For Dante, the process of sublimating his desires has elevated Beatrice so that she has become more "regal of aspect" and "formidable" (30.70). In contrast, Rossetti gives the incident the appearance of a wedding, so that Dante and Beatrice again face each other, but as a bride and a groom might—tenderly, with a somewhat shortened Beatrice turning back her veil. In a sense, a wedding is a plausible symbolic replacement for the meeting envisioned by Dante, as marriage is another way besides sublimation of submitting imaginary desire to a transcendental symbolic principle (SII, 263). But Rossetti's expression of the symbolic hierarchy of man and woman ultimately has the effect of inverting Dante's, in keeping with what Lacan observes to be the androcentric structure of marriage (SII, 261). This radical adjustment of Dante's texts suggests that in the Victorian period, the idealization of woman can only ever be a private narcissistic response, since the available systems of symbolic ordering tend to enforce female subordination.

When Beatrice dies halfway through La Vita Nuova and Dante's love grows even more abstract and mournful, Rossetti's challenge in illustrating the story is altered—he must find his material in Dante's dreams and visions of Beatrice insofar as these are filtered through Dante's derangement by grief. Fortunately, these visions are rife with visually interesting indications of narcissistic disarray. Rossetti's first painting on the theme of the grieving Dante, *The First Anniversary of the Death of Beatrice* (1849; fig. 4), thus interprets a quotation from La Vita Nuova in which Dante explains, "I betook myself to draw the resemblance of an Angel upon certain tablets. And while I did thus, chancing to turn my head, I perceived that some were standing beside me to whom I should have given courteous welcome, and that they were observing what I did: also I learned afterwards that they had been there a while before I perceived them. Perceiving whom, I arose for salutation, and said: 'Another was with me'" (340). The "another" whom Dante imagines to have been embodied in the image of the angel is presumably the angel Love, the recurrent personification of the concept that Dante insists on portraying in La Vita Nuova as "not only a spiritual essence, but a bodily substance also" (332). In this scene, therefore, Dante is in a sense comparable to an artist captivated by a visual image that seems more alive to him than to others, and *First Anniversary* is one of the few paintings in Rossetti's oeuvre that deals directly with the allurements and dangers of the image as such.

Rossetti appears to agree with Lacan that desire is triggered in response to an image (SI, 188), a theory that holds the possibility that desire can be

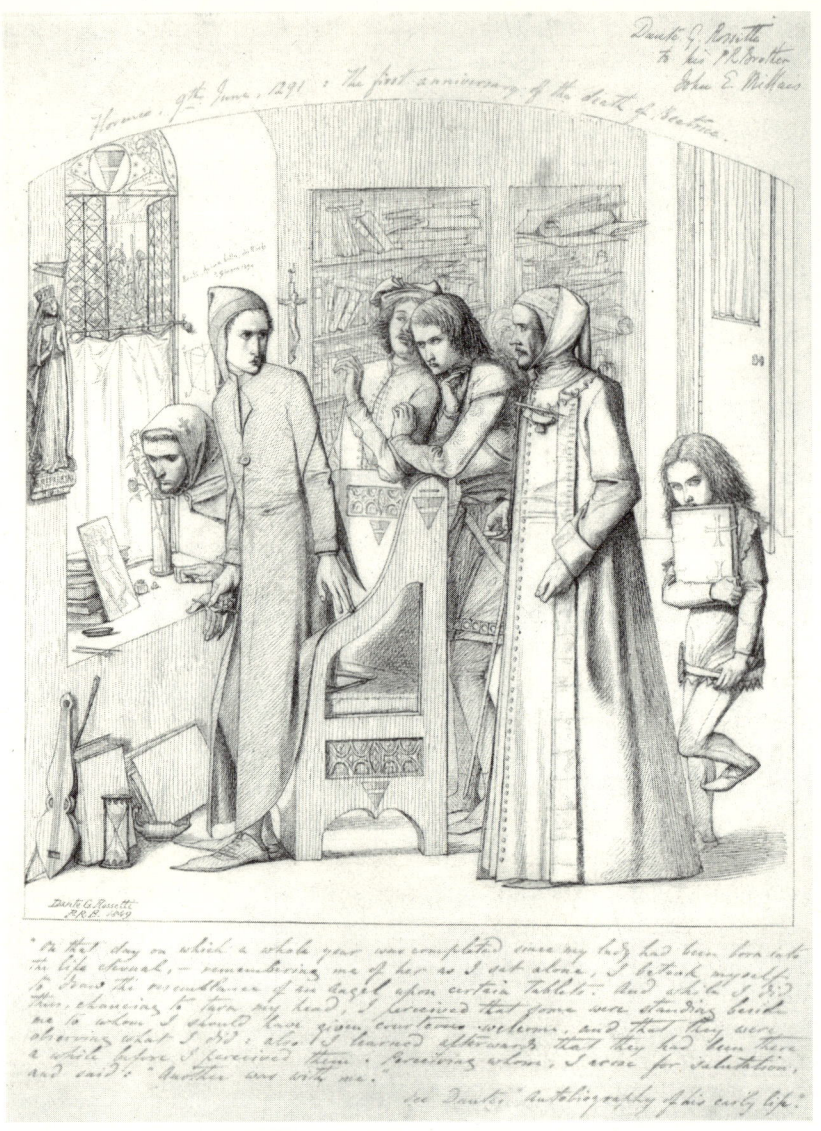

FIGURE 4. D. G. Rossetti, *The First Anniversary of the Death of Beatrice* (1849). Courtesy Birmingham Museums and Art Gallery.

aroused by a simulacrum of the other as well as the original. He explores the potential danger of this susceptibility in poems such as "The Portrait" (1847/1870), where the speaker stands compelled before a painting of his dead beloved, "gaz[ing] until she seems to stir" (5)—a situation of gothic possession that intensifies the hazards of abyssal absorption hinted at in this Dantesque episode. In his early sketch of *First Anniversary*, however, Rossetti does not seem to be as concerned about this danger as he shows himself to be in his final rendition of it. In the first version, Dante stands up in conspicuous irritation at the intruders, anticipating the moment when they will leave and he can "set [him]self again . . . to the drawing figures of angels," as in *La Vita Nuova* he subsequently does (120). These visitors are thereby depicted by Rossetti as an unattractive group of intruders who offer nothing to compete with Dante's narcissistic unity with his image.

In the second version of *First Anniversary* (1853; fig. 5), however, Rossetti goes much further in emphasizing the perilous nature of the imaginary order that he elides in the first version. Correcting his previous account of blissful tranquility, he makes Dante's drawing surface the cover of a disorderly cabinet of objects, thus indicating how disarray accompanies Dante's imaginary fixation on the image. Rossetti also conveys the danger of Dante's dangerous fixation on his image by ornamenting the paneling across Dante's studio with a repeated female face. As Lawrence J. Starzyk has previously noted, instances of endless and nonproductive recursiveness in Rossetti's paintings and writings generally indicate a snare of desire and disillusionment.[22] Freud likewise indicates in his essay "The Uncanny" that "the constant recurrence of the same thing" in art tends to

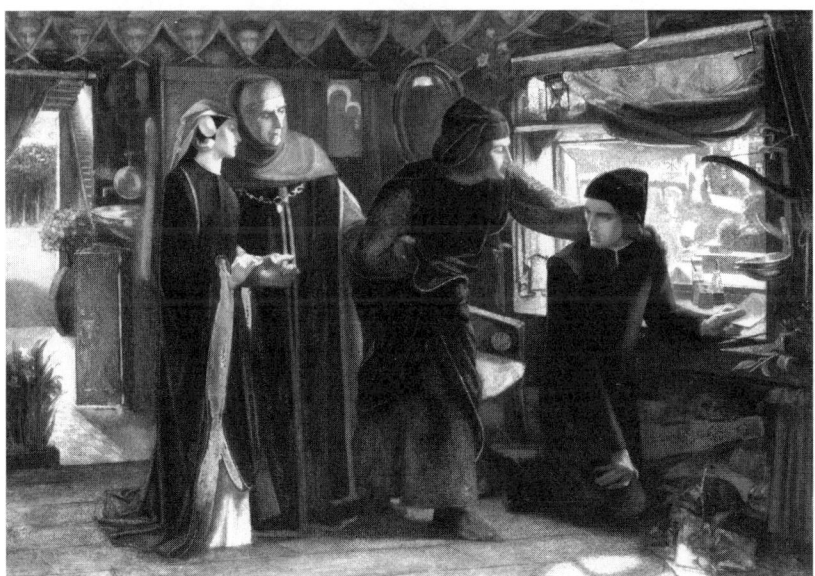

FIGURE 5. D. G. Rossetti, *The First Anniversary of the Death of Beatrice* (1853). Watercolor on paper. Courtesy of Ashmolean Museum of Art and Archaeology, University of Oxford.

indicate the return of repressed narcissism and can be an "uncanny harbinger of death" (356–57). In *First Anniversary*, the repeated images of a woman that line Dante's walls indicate that Dante's equilibrium is being disturbed by his narcissistic relation to the recollected image of Beatrice, which produces a vertigo of incessant mirroring doubled in his repetitious habit of drawing angels. In comparison with these signs of imaginary disturbance, moreover, Dante's guests in the later version of *First Anniversary* are comparatively respectable and serene, as Rossetti's cataloguer Virginia Surtees has observed, noting how "the confusion of the objects in the room contrasts sharply with the three visitors who stand quietly watching Dante at his work, the calmness of their concentration being particularly marked" (22). Rossetti further has Dante reflect on the disturbing quality of narcissistic desire by having Dante kneel before these noble visitors with a dazed appearance, as though he knows he has been weakened by his desire and requires their intervention between himself and the libidinally invested image. Dante's guests thus function as a chastening contrast to narcissistic desire in the same way that Virgil does in *Paolo and Francesca da Rimini*, representing the relations that provide a subject with a fluid position within a language and a culture that unfixes him from the rigid attachments of the imaginary ego (Lacan, SII, 263; SI, 174).

The Fetish as Cover

In the illustrations of Dante and Beatrice so far discussed, Rossetti heightens the appearances of narcissistic desire to hint at an exciting, and possibly mutual, passion lying behind their constrained relationship. Over the course of painting *Dante's Dream at the Time of the Death of Beatrice* (1856/1871), an illustration of another Dantesque incident, Rossetti moved away from his typically celebratory representation of imaginary passion. *Dante's Dream* dramatizes a moment from *La Vita Nuova* after Dante learns of Beatrice's passing, as he dreams that he "be[held] his lady in death" (104): the composition is of Beatrice unconscious on a bier, with her attendants lowering a veil over her and Dante in the foreground gazing upon her. Harrison has observed that Pre-Raphaelite art is often intensely focused on dreams and dream-visions,[23] and in the 1856 watercolor (fig. 6), the theme of dreaming seems to have stimulated Rossetti to include various details that suggest a proto-psychoanalytical interest in Dante's unconscious libidinal investments. The dream becomes a vehicle for Rossetti to explore repressed imaginary structures in Dante's work, in keeping with Lacan's proposition that dream thoughts disclose "the diversified images of

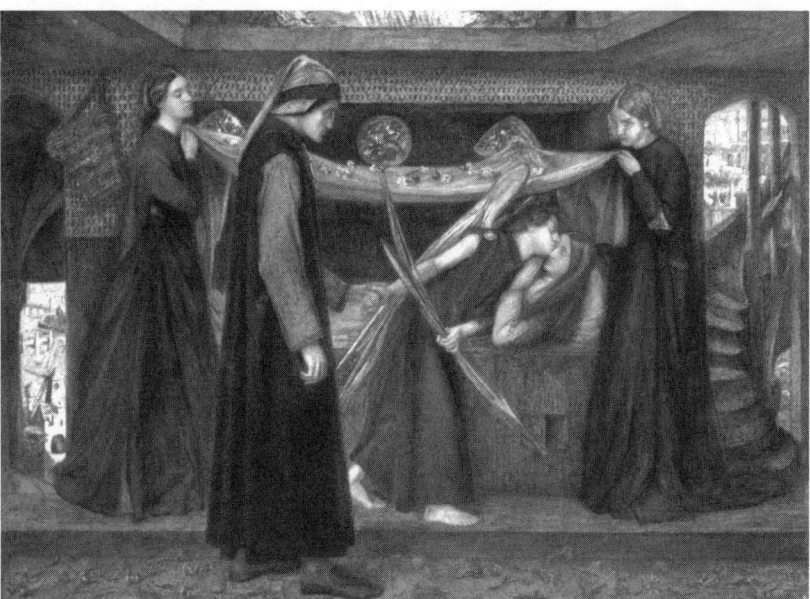

FIGURE 6. D. G. Rossetti, *Dante's Dream at the Time of the Death of Beatrice* (1856). Tate Gallery, London. Photo credit: Tate, London / Art Resource, NY.

[the subject's] ego" around which imaginary relations are forged (SII, 167).[24] There are thus strange bags and apertures around Beatrice's bed-cabinet that suggest inaccessible unconscious mysteries in the dreamer and that Freud more specifically interprets as sexual symbols of female genitalia (*Interpretation*, 390, 419). Rossetti further anticipates the psychoanalytic treatments of dreams by surrealist artists through his distorted depictions of objects, such as strangely twisting staircases that presumably lead up and down to heaven and hell but in their style suggest routes into the unconscious. Rossetti's use of imagery in this illustration is also more than usually chaotic, suggesting the jumbled quality of dream imagery: for example, a small cabinet in Beatrice's bier seems to have no functional purpose other than to contribute another peculiar orifice to the presentation.

In the 1871 version of *Dante's Dream*, Rossetti removes or stabilizes many of the most indeterminate images from the first version (fig. 7). Twisting staircases are normalized and apertures and windows that suggested unconscious conduits in the first version are removed or clarified. A bag marked with an obscure ecclesiastical symbol that hangs beside the bier in the watercolor is replaced with a legible scroll reading "Quomodo sedet solo civitas" ("Every city shall be forsaken"), which is Jeremiah's

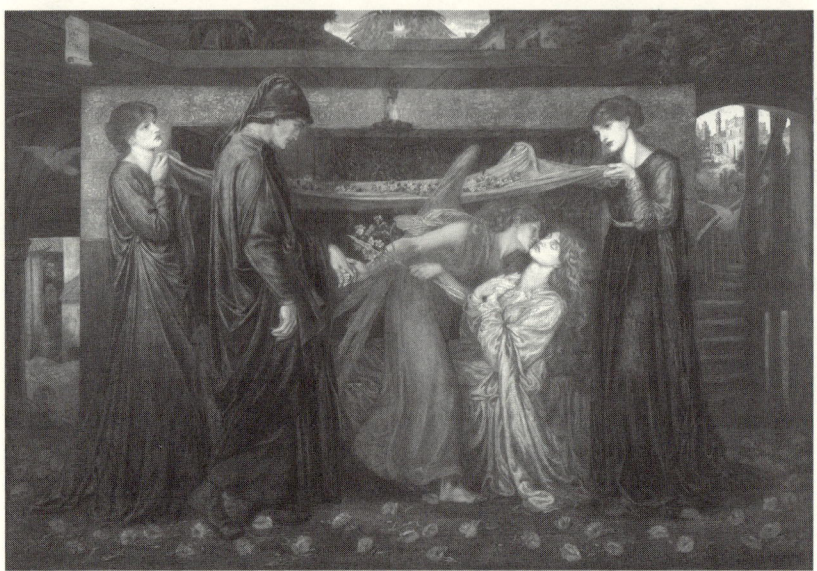

FIGURE 7. D. G. Rossetti, *Dante's Dream at the Time of the Death of Beatrice* (1871). Oil on canvas, 210.8 x 317.5 cm. Walker Art Gallery, National Museums Liverpool. © Board of Trustees of the National Museums and Galleries on Merseyside.

lamentation of the Second Coming, thus exchanging an obscure cipher for a symbolically determinate message. Rossetti also augments the Christian tone of the painting, adding traditional images such as crimson angels to carry off the soul of Beatrice, a lamp to suggest Christian piety, and a dove to represent the presence of the Holy Ghost.[25] The general effect of these revisions is to transform the illustration of Dante's dream from a view into the individual unconscious into a sacramental vision. Lothar Honnighausen has broadly described how Pre-Raphaelitism spiritualized art through the insertion of familiar symbols that linked their desire-laden images with shared codes, thus giving an effect of the ordering, and ultimately the sublimation, of libido.[26] In a similar sense, Lacan proposes that playing with symbols permits the subject to submit his desire to "a human field which universalizes significations" and thereby to locate his subjective experience within a transcendental myth (*SI*, 190). Kristeva likewise contends that the codification of symbols in art and literature as well as specifically sacred rituals and discourse allows subjects to submit narcissism to the patriarchal law, thereby "elevat[ing], spiritualiz[ing], and sublimat[ing] physical desire" (*Powers*, 120). Rossetti's changes from the first version of *Dante's Dream* to the second accordingly seem to be a strategy to represent Dante as no longer the overwrought lover of *La Vita Nuova* but as a man fit to be the sublime prophet of the *Commedia*.

Other measures to subdue narcissism are also in place in the second version of *Dante's Dream*, such as the imposition of greater symbolic decorum. For instance, Rossetti seems to have gone to some trouble to differentiate the heights of the men and women in the frame, as he indicates in a letter he wrote to Ford Madox Brown during its composition: "My soul is vexed with the following point:—The women in my picture being 62 inches high, will it do for the man to be 65 inches, or should he be taller? I've got him traced on the canvas, and fancy he looks all right, but am rather nervous about beginning to paint him lest he should possibly need heightening."[27] This anecdote evinces that in revising *Dante's Dream*, Rossetti struggled against a spontaneous impulse to portray female figures as tall as male ones—having finally succumbed, it would seem, to the canonical regulations about major and minor beauty.

A final change that Rossetti made in the second version of *Dante's Dream* is an increase in the density of fetishistic elements. Several critics have observed a general tendency to fetishism in Rossetti's later images and textures of femininity, which feature ornamentation by profuse flowers, flowing silk clothes, and crinkly hair.[28] Fetishism is markedly less prominent in Rossetti's works of the 1850s, such as in the first version of *Dante's Dream*, in which the Beatrice's is straight and her garments are plain and restrained. In the 1871 version, by contrast, Rossetti's fetish for profuse hair and cloth is fully expressed; there are signs, moreover, that this fetishism performs a function in the painting that is not merely aesthetic but libidinal. Beatrice's originally straight nightgown has been turned into a mass of extravagant silk drapery that ripples like a curtain over the precise place where, in the first version, the small, enigmatic cabinet had opened into the bier. Given the sexual suggestiveness of that cabinet, Beatrice's lavish nightgown seems fetishistic in exactly the way that Freud means when he described the fetish as a "substitution for the sexual object."[29] According to Freud, a fetish tends to substitute either for some part of the body (such as the foot or hair) that is in general inappropriate for sexual purposes or for some inanimate object that bears an assignable relation to the person whom it replaces. In *Dante's Dream*, the silk cloth substitutes for what in the previous version of the painting is a plausible symbol of genital desire. The fetish thus indicates a retreat from the erotic intensity of the imaginary order, in keeping with Žižek's account of the fetish as a "desperate attempt" by the subject to separate himself from an imaginary object (104).[30]

While previous critics of Dante Gabriel Rossetti's art have cited Freud's interpretation of the fetish as a substitute for direct genital desire in the case of Rossetti, I find that they tend to overstate the absolute character of his fetishistic response to women. As Freud suggests, "in the majority of instances the pathological character in a perversion is found to lie not in the *content* of the new sexual aim, but . . . *alongside* the normal sexual aim and object" ("Fetishism," 161: emphasis in original). Lynda Pearce, for instance, observes that fetishism in Rossetti's works is an "expression of extreme psychosexual trauma" (55), while Griselda Pollock sees Rossetti's fetishism as a fortress of isolation by which he protects his self from objects (47). But the manner in which fetishistic details in the second version of *Dante's Dream* are placed to mask the transparency of sexual desire in the first version—thereby introducing a measure of pictorial restraint and decorum—suggests that Rossetti's fetishism does not so much defend the subject *against* the object as defend him against his already exorbitant desire *for* the object. Rossetti's fetish is thus a crude version of symbolization, in keeping with Žižek's explanation that the fetish's fixation on a particular aspect of the other is a first, transitional step of the subject beyond imaginary attachment and toward "the dimension of universality" that culminates in symbolic order subjectification (104). Pollock meanwhile seems to mistake the effect of fetishism in Rossetti's work for that of an empowering gaze in her observation that fetishism empowers the male viewer by reducing women to "screen[s] across which masculine fantasies of knowledge, power and possession can be enjoyed in a ceaseless play" (123). Pollock bases her understanding of the fetish on Laura Mulvey's idea of fetishistic images of women in mass culture, which Mulvey claims emerge from the male unconscious so that woman becomes the narcissistic projection of the man.[31] But Žižek insists that the fetish is not a narcissistic projection whereby the subject remakes the other according to his authentic, imaginary desire. Rather, the fetish is an anticipation of what distorted form the relationship to the other will assume in the symbolic order: it is not a "'lower stage' of development . . . but a symptom of the inherent contradiction within the 'higher stage'" (Žižek, 124n16). In other words, the fantasies produced through fetishism reflect the subject's insecurities because of the divisive formations of the symbolic order, which splits humanity subjects from their desires. The subject thus does not obtain power through the use of a fetish but offers it up to the symbolic Other in a "staging of castration" (Žižek, 104).

In the case of *Dante's Dream*, the fact that Beatrice has become a more sublime as well as more stylized object in the second version of *Dante's*

Dream thus does not suggest that either Dante or Rossetti is assuming more power over Beatrice but rather that a symbolic regime reigns more fully over this scene at the cost of the spontaneous imaginary libido of Dante—as well, implicitly, at a cost to that of the artist and the viewer. Given this psychoanalytical explanation of the fetish as a protection from more-overwhelming forms of libido, one can trace how Rossetti's fetishism may have arisen on a personal as well as artistic level. Freud claims that forms of perversion such as the fetish normally arise when "circumstances unfavorable to [the normal sexual aim and object] and favorable to [the fetish] arise" ("Fetishism," 161). Between 1856, when Rossetti composed his first *Dante's Dream*, and the full eruption of Rossetti's hair fetish in the late 1850s, such a combination of unfavorable and favorable circumstances apparently emerged in Rossetti's life. Around this period, Elizabeth Siddal was in Italy and France for six months, and a schism opened between the two lovers that would never close, although they would marry in 1860 (Marsh, DGR, 157). Rossetti wrote in a letter "come back dear Liz," but he also widened his interest to encompass other women who aesthetically attracted him (DGR, 157). He was drawn first to Ruth Herbert, whom he made his model, claiming in a letter that "[s]he has the most varied and highest expression . . . besides abundant beauty, golden hair, etc." (DGR, 157). Thus, at the same time as Rossetti suffered an unfavorable loss of ordinary, happy sexual passion, he entered into circumstances favorable to the fetish, as his sexual life became aestheticized into the admiration and painting of women whose features could be substituted for the genital goal, in the same way that Beatrice's drapery in Rossetti's 1871 version of *Dante's Dream* is substituted for the earlier cabinet.[32]

Another anecdote that provides insight into Rossetti's shift toward more-fetishistic styles of representation in the late 1850s is contained in a note in the catalogue raisonné that Virginia Surtees made of his visual works, in which she remarks that "with the declining health of Elizabeth Siddal [in 1859] the small angular figures with their medieval accessories familiar from earlier water-colors gradually disappear, and in her place appears a new type of woman already observed earlier in the pencil portrait of Ruth Herbert, in which the sweep of the neck, the curved lips, the indolent pose of the head and the emphasis given to the fall of the hair foreshadow his prolific output of studies of women" (Surtees, 68–69). Apart from itemizing many of Rossetti's renowned painterly fetishes in his later work, which refract desire into a generic array of effects, Surtees emphasizes how the appearance of Rossetti's later female subjects tended to project the quality of sexual unavailability. Such women were "sensual and voluptuous, mystical and inscrutable but always humorless, gazing into the distance with hair outspread and hands resting on a parapet, often with some heavily scented flower completing the design. As the face of the model changed with the years, so the eyes became more wistful, the feeling of distance more remote, until in 1879 the apogee was reached with Mrs. William Morris as the *Donna Della Finestra*" (68–69). Surtees points to the particular importance within Rossetti's fetishistic structure of Jane Morris (formerly Jane Burden), who married William Morris in 1858 and increasingly came to epitomize Rossetti's ideal, which essentially revived for him the courtly motif of the inaccessible lady. We may thus gather that, in part because Rossetti lacked Dante's facility for the symbolic sublimation of desire in the face of an inaccessible object, he was forced in the case of Jane Morris, as in the case of Ruth Herbert, to rely on strategies of fetishism to displace his desire from the pursuit of a "genital goal" that would have been inopportune for him in each case.[33] At the same time, the sentiments expressed in *The House of Life* (discussed in the next chapter) prove without a doubt that Rossetti's adoration of Morris would ultimately go far beyond an attraction to her hair and thus confirm Freud's position that fetishism can very readily coexist "*alongside* the normal sexual aim and object" if more favorable opportunities for the latter open up ("Fetishism," 161). As Lacan equally holds, a subject's sexual drive is always a montage of disparate components (*Four*, 169). This multiplicity of libidinal effects seems conspicuously true of Rossetti, even when he is engaged in representing women most fetishistically and symbolically.

We can see through this overview of Rossetti's illustrations of Dante and Beatrice that whereas in earlier cases his revisionary process was directed toward maximizing the suggestion of imaginary intensity, in later cases his revisions tended to subtract that same kind of intensity to favor suggestions of symbolic decorum and control. In this regard, Rossetti indicates a maturing vision that for Lacan tends to favor more-stable relationships. As narcissism is banished and desire of the other "enters into the mediation of language [and] . . . into the order of a law," love grows closer to being a genuinely intersubjective relationship: a "symbolic relation of I and you" in which there can be "relation[s] of mutual recognition and transcendence" (*SI*, 177). At the same time, however, some measure of spontaneity tends to be lost in a love relationship as imaginary passion is traded for symbolic stability, and we can see a parallel, aesthetic version of that loss in which Rossetti's revisions overwrite his original eccentric details with ones that are more decorous, canonical, and fetishistic. It is as such that Lacan describes the ideal trajectory of love as a dialectic between the two orders, in which love that is first inscribed in the narcissistic framework subsequently transcends that and settles into an "intermediate, ambiguous zone, between the symbolic and the imaginary," with access to the resources of both (SI, 217). We may similarly derive that Rossetti's artistic practice likewise is at its most fertile when signs of imaginary and symbolic ordering are animated in a dynamic tension—as in the *Salutation of Beatrice*, which was painted in 1859 at the essential turning point between Rossetti's earlier and later periods, for its two-panel formula produces an engaging narrative of how the spontaneity of human love and the sacramental character of cosmic love coexist eternally in Dante's work.

For Lacan, the ultimate medium for containing such a dynamic tension is, however, that of language, which he describes as a "mill-wheel" that allows the subject to fully thresh out his desire, allowing the symbolic order to "determine the greater or lesser degree of perfection, of completeness, of approximation, of the imaginary" (SI, 141, 179). Kristeva has suggested that painting since the Renaissance is a relatively conservative medium insofar as it tends to seek an aesthetic goal of "integrat[ing] its transgressions," with artists typically deploying their experiments with color and form in ways that express and serve the ideologies of the time (*Desire*, 215, 232). This may explain why, after Rossetti's painting declined into wholesale fetishism in the 1860s, he never recovered his earlier power to represent the spontaneous, life-giving charge of interpersonal desire, instead becoming absorbed within the symbolic process of anticipating and reflecting his own age's symbolic needs and fetishes. As we will see in chapter 5, in producing what Dianne Sachko MacLeod calls his "Venetian" portraiture,[34] he got caught up in a repetition compulsion whereby he represented the same allegories of desire and castration over and over again. Rossetti expressed his awareness of this problem in an 1868 letter to Thomas Gordon Hake, in which he admitted that the conditions of commercialization had "led to a good deal of my painting being pot-boiling and no more"—in other words, that he had succumbed to producing offerings that would appeal to the base symbolic requirements of the masses (*Letters*, 2:849–50). Rossetti likewise hints in this letter at the deadening effects of repetition on his painting, suggesting that he had succumbed to the production of "re-created forms." He therefore decided to redefine himself as "a poet (within the limits of [his] powers)," hoping that he could thereby revive his powers of expression, as his poetry, "being unprofitable, has remained unprostituted." Rossetti's visual project of making an impression in the art world thus gave way to the verbal project of compiling and refining the *House of Life* sequence, which would engage him for thirteen years and revive in him the ability to plumb the human passions in increasingly innovative and intensive ways.

four

The Symbolic Perfection of the Imaginary in Dante Gabriel Rossetti's *The House of Life*

> It is speech, the symbolic relation, which determines the greater or lesser degree of perfection, of completeness, of approximation, of the imaginary.
>
> —Jacques Lacan, *Seminar I*

DURING THE 1840S, while the Renaissance tradition of the amatory sonnet was being revived by Victorian poets who had fallen under the inspiration of Keats,[1] Dante Gabriel Rossetti was developing a fascination with the sonnet under a more personal and more distinctly Italianate impetus. At age nineteen, he chanced to read his father's mystical analysis of medieval Italian love poetry, *Il mistero dell' amor platonico del medio evo* (1840), as well as several anthologies in the Rossetti library containing works by Cavalcanti, Guinicelli, and others. He was particularly ravished by Dante Alighieri, his brother William Michael wrote, noting that Dante Gabriel was "glowing from the flame breath" of the Florentine as he undertook to produce the volume of translation he entitled *Early Italian Poets from Ciullo d'Alcamo to Dante Alighieri*.[2] Subsequently, Dante Gabriel made his important and widely praised translation of Dante's *Vita Nuova*, which reintroduced the work to English literary culture in the nineteenth century when it appeared in 1862.[3]

Dante Gabriel Rossetti absorbed the spirit of Dante in his work not only as a translator but also as a poet. During the 1840s, Dante Gabriel and William Michael would spend the evenings giving each other rhymes to improvise their own *boutes-rimes*; one can see in some of the spontaneous sonnets produced in this exercise the early stimulation of Dante's *La Vita Nuova*, with its motif of the elevating impact of the beloved lady. In "An

Altar-Flame" (1848), for instance, the speaker writes that his beloved's effect is that of "a most awful strain / [o]f music, heard in some cathedral fanned / [w]ith the deep breath of prayer" (5–7).[4] Similar musings had already found outlet in "The Blessed Damozel" (1847/1850), with its wry modernization of the Dantean logic of the angelic other who has no power to guide her beloved to heaven but can only sensuously await him. Here, in the spontaneous sonnet, the treatment of the beloved is even more in the manner of Dante and the other passionate *Stilnovisti* sonneteers. Like Beatrice, who in the early chapters of *La Vita Nuova* excites Dante to the point of derangement but later inspires him up into the cool reaches of the heavenly heights, this beloved begins by "weigh[ing]" with her presence on his brain but ultimately "perfect[s] a noble calmness in him" through her sublime beauty (5, 9–10). Thus, we can see Rossetti at this young age holding up Dante's *La Vita Nuova* as a kind of hopeful ideal for himself, according to which love and beauty might similarly send "[t]hrough [his] weak heart to [his] strong mind / a rule of life" to orient his impetuous being (11–12).

But this rule of life would not adhere; as we have seen in the previous chapter, Rossetti would chart a wayward course that would allow him to save some of the imaginary passion that he never fully disdained, while incorporating his idiosyncratic cooling measures, such as aestheticism and fetishism. At the beginning of his career, however, he had no other model but Dante, and indeed the example of *La Vita Nuova* would persevere in him as a literary if not a spiritual model. Of all of the Italian sonneteers, Dante was the one who best provided "proof that the theme [of love] redeemed the singer," in the terms of David Larg, who in *Trial by Virgins* imagines the platonic spell that Rossetti must have fallen under in his encounter with Dante after already having been seduced by the Christianized medievalism of Sir Walter Scott.[5] The theme of love as a vehicle for enlarging the soul and achieving divine grace was elaborated maximally by Dante and his influential saint, the eleventh-century Bernard of Clairvaux, the final spiritual guide of the *Paradiso*, who, Kristeva proposes, "imposed upon Europe the idea of man as an amatory subject" (*Tales*, 152). In Bernard's treatment, and Dante's, courtly desire for the lady is a means to an ennobled end, preparing the religious novice for elevation by enlarging his capacity for desiring God. As Kristeva explains, the Christian telos gave all of the proverbial suffering of courtly love a point: "lack" is introduced by such writers "into the very heart of love's violence for the purpose of overcoming it" (*Tales*, 153). One could imagine no more pleasing model for a teenaged man who was both amorous and high-minded than that exemplified in the pattern of *La Vita Nuova*, whereby Dante works his way out of an unsettling, humiliating attraction to a lady by using it as material to forge for himself a new life as a spiritual pilgrim who worships that same lady in "high heaven" (*Vita Nuova*, 116). And even if Rossetti did not repeat that pilgrimage of sublimation as such—having ultimately become aware that his life's journey would not conform to the pattern laid out by Dante—he still held the basic narrative before him of love redeeming the singer as a template.

What has been insufficiently recognized is how Rossetti, in *The House of Life*, gently echoes the redemptive narrative of the sonnet sequences laid out by Dante as well as Petrarch, while at the same time he forges a new and distinctive process for the symbolic transformation of desire. Like *La Vita Nuova* and Christina Rossetti's *Monna Innominata*, *The House of Life* marks out a distinct set of moments in the evolution of the self, portraying how a robust symbolic identity may be created out of the same amatory materials that initially produce confusion and grief.[6] Like Dante, who describes how in meeting Beatrice he experienced compelling intuitions both that his "beatitude hath now been made manifest to [him]" and that he would "often . . . be disturbed from this time forth" (*Vita Nuova*, 79n5), the Rossettian speaker begins by rehearsing the joys and problems of imaginary desire. Also like Dante, who gradually learns to find his happiness not in the greeting of his lady but "in those words that do praise my lady" (*Vita Nuova*, 96), the Rossettian speaker learns how to use language to "perfect[ ] . . . the imaginary" and thereby give his self stability in the symbolic order (SI, 171). To be sure, this is not the stability of Christian devotion ultimately sought by Dante and by the sonneteers of CR's sequences *Monna Innominata* and *Later Life*. Instead, it is a stability in which the other bears a symbolic value for the self and is simultaneously the counterpart in a symbolic exchange, which presents a compensating advantage of allowing the speaker to preserve a personal and living relationship with his adored other.

A redemptive perspective on *The House of Life* is particularly evident through an assessment of the chronological sequence of its writing. Presumably to lend his sequence the narrative coherence of a work such as Petrarch's *Canzoniere*—whose 366 sonnets record his meditations on a love affair over a year and a day—Rossetti organized diverse sonnets written at different times and under starkly different circumstances into a broadly themed two-part structure that essentially mirrors Petrarch's. The first two-thirds of Petrarch's *Canzoniere* is entitled *To Laura in Life*, while the latter third is entitled *To Laura in Death*, with the writer assuming an attitude of praise in the first section and one of grief, leavened by the quest for some compensatory perspective, in the second. Rossetti likewise formed the 1881 version of *The House of Life* into a two-part structure, with roughly the first two-thirds charting the vicissitudes of love and the last third tracing various responses to the problem of love lost. The resulting effect is decidedly downbeat, with the result that most of its critics regard the sequence as a whole as a gloomy affair in which the speaker falls prey to the consequences of his earlier indulgences.[7] Reading the sonnets chronologically, however, foregrounds the sonneteer's increasing sophistication, as Rossetti moved from a relatively puerile attachment to Elizabeth Siddal in the 1840s and 1850s toward the far more philosophically reflective passion for Jane Morris of the 1860s and 1870s. Juxtaposed in this manner, the sonnets written by Rossetti in the 1850s portray love as a disturbing imaginary intoxication that renders the young man as discombobulated as Dante is at the beginning of *La Vita Nuova*, while the sonnets of the late 1860s and 1870s virtuosically synthesize multiple facets of love, from its narcissistic imaginary aspects to the symbolic enjoyments that promise greater scope for genuine intersubjectivity. The narrative of transcendence that the sequence reveals is thus a secular and modern quest for the limits of the grace achievable through love, which for Freud "reopen[s] the door . . . to perfection."[8]

That Rossetti sought not merely artistic expression but also personal transformation in the production of his sonnet sequence is patent in the narrative of its assembly in the late 1860s and 1870s. The idea that the sonnet sequence could be a vehicle for working out new interior possibilities seems to have come upon Rossetti as a solution to stasis in other areas in his life. As discussed in the previous chapter, Rossetti had recognized in 1868 that his painting craft had degenerated into a repetitive production of projects to meet the demand for the Pre-Raphaelite fetishes that he had engendered. At this juncture, he reached toward new expressive power in poetry, as he expressed in a letter to George Hake, anticipating that he "should wish to deal in poetry chiefly with personified emotions" and thereby "put in action a complete dramatis personae of the soul" (*Letters*, 849–50). Poetry thus seemed to offer Rossetti the prospect of excavating a more authentic interior landscape. To begin this new approach of unconscious excavation, however, he had to undertake a notorious literal excavation, asking his friend Charles A. Howell to dig up poems buried in his wife Elizabeth Siddal's grave, so that he could use them as the beginnings of a new opus and a new career.[9]

If we can forgive the brutality of the plundering, we can see that this resurrection of the poetry of his youth as a starting point for a new literary career was emotionally worthwhile; as biographer Jan Marsh observes, "the resumption of poetry . . . signaled the opening of [Dante Gabriel Rossetti's] emotional shutter, the reawakening of his heart and need to speak" (DGR, 357–58). Lacan's account of the experience of clinical psychoanalysis helps to explain Rossetti's feeling that poetry held a special potential for expressing the dynamics of desire that had become alienated from his painting. Of all the forms of symbolization, Lacan argues, verbal language is the medium that can be most "full" in its power to deftly mediate the unconscious (SI, 50–52). Language "aims at . . . the truth," allowing one to move beyond the static and conventional use of symbols to "change[ ] the nature of the . . . beings present" (SI, 107–9). In a similar manner, Rossetti apparently saw poetry as an exponent of truth as well as change, as he conveys in the titles he gave the two sections of *The House of Life*, "Youth and Change" and "Change and Fate," as well as in the names he gave some of the later sonnets, such as "Love's Testament" (1870), "Through Death to Love" (1871), and "Transfigured Life" (1871). Even the introductory manifesto of *The House of Life*, which characterizes the sonnet as a "monument," sees this monument as an animated one that can transport "memorials from the Soul's eternity / [t]o one dead deathless hour" (2–3)—a relocation of truth from the inward places of the self to the stability of the text that recollects Lacan's account of how language allows one to "determine[ ] the greater or lesser degree of perfection, of completeness, of approximation, of the imaginary" (SI, 141).

Three moments in Rossetti's chronological development of the *House of Life* sequence outline a metamorphosis in the Rossetti speaker that is decidedly redemptive, if not sacramental. The first consists of the speaker in a desperate and torn condition owing to the ravages of his imaginary desire, which makes it difficult for him to steel himself to the symbolic goals that importune him. Next, the poet turns his attention to the problem of imaginary desire fifteen years later and in this more mature condition develops a far more nimble and sophisticated account of the imaginary condition. Finally, Rossetti develops an alternative signifying practice that hinges on the relationship to the other, including a process of meditation on unique aspects of her being that anticipates Lacan's concept of the *objet petit a*, wherein the subject uses language to devise an ever-shifting response to his fundamental lack.

Amatory Confusion in the Sonnets of the 1850s

The journey in *The House of Life* through and beyond imaginary desire begins in the earliest poems about love that Rossetti included in the sequence: "The Birth Bond" (1853), "Broken Music" (1852), and "Known in Vain"

(1853). These sonnets, whose writing was presumably triggered by Rossetti's meeting Elizabeth Siddal in 1852,[10] express the narcissistic themes that David Riede finds frequently reflected in Rossetti's writing, of "the union of lover and beloved in images of perfect reciprocity" and the "blurring of the boundaries between self and other" (122). Some of these sonnets, moreover, do not merely convey the quality of what Lacan would call the imaginary experience but anatomize it in a way that is reminiscent of Lacan's accounting for the phenomenon throughout his writings. As Lacan proposes, the subject as an infant receives his primordial form by reflecting his self upon an other, or "imago," at which point he internalizes within himself a "homeomorphic identification" that is both formative and erogenic ("Mirror," 4, 3). The subject's libidinal being is subsequently stimulated when he encounters another person who seems to revive the original source of the reflection, activating an illusion that leads to his tendency to become fascinated by and to overestimate the virtues of that person (SI, 126). Rossetti's "The Birth Bond," likewise, roots the experience of love in an experience of primordial intimacy as it metaphorically compares the beloved other to the sister one might share with a lost mother from a superceded marriage, "nursed on the forgotten breast and knee" (4), thus portraying her as someone who displays an uncannily strong kinship with the self. Amid the tumult of family life, such close siblings would have "silent speech, / [a]nd in a word complete community," similar to that which the speaker feels with the beloved (6–7). The speaker proposes that the special sibling to whom the lover is compared could even be a twin, a "soul's birth-partner": "one nearer kindred than life hinted at / born with me somewhere that men forget," thus producing an intrauterine mirroring that would account for the sense of primordial closeness inherent in the intensity of love's imaginary illusion (14, 11). This imagery of a uterine basis for the narcissistic closeness between lovers further anticipates theories that found the imaginary experience in the "continuous relation with the mother" before the subject has the means to signify himself as a separate being (Kristeva, *Desire*, 134).

While "The Birth Bond," is wholly celebratory of the radically narcissistic basis upon which love rests, "Broken Music" raises the disconcerting prospect reflected in paintings such as *The First Anniversary of the Death of Beatrice*, that absorption in imaginary desire can distract one from symbolic ambitions. In particular, the speaker of "Broken Music" worries that his love affair has the power to divert him from his goal of writing poetry. The primordial basis of imaginary desire in the maternal relationship is suggested in this sonnet as well, as the sonnet figures the speaker's soul as that of a newborn bird's, which "at length [finds] tongue" for the "sweet music" that will turn its mother's head toward it (7–8). This progression from the subject's relationship to the mother to the beginnings of his use of speech resembles that which is captured in Kristeva's concept of the semiotic order, an "instinctual and maternal" precursor to signification that subsists in language's rhythmic and musical functions, which she proposes takes root in the subject directly before the mirror stage (*Desire*, 134). This capacity in the subject for musical speech becomes paralyzed in the sestet: in the last lines, the speaker's soul, which has been feminized as the mother, now fails to catch any of the "breath of song" that normally issues from the self, becoming as paralyzed as a "speech-bound sea-shell" that can utter only a "low importunate strain"; it thereupon suffers the "pang of unpermitted prayer" (11, 14). The reason for the paralysis of symbolic forms of speech such as prayer is the state of love in which the narrator has fallen, such that all that can be heard is "thy voice"—that of the beloved (12).[11] The imaginary condition of exchanged and intermingling selves is thus portrayed here as an incursion as well as a regression, and the hapless speaker consequently refers to the other as his "bitterly beloved" (14).

The critique of imaginary love in "Broken Music" suggests that, as early as 1852, Rossetti began to attain a different perspective on narcissistic absorption that he more generally glamorized. Rossetti's father died in 1853, and this year seems to have generally been one in which Rossetti began to cast about for how he might attain a more mature and symbolically stabilized identity. We can see such a quest being worked out in "Known in Vain" (1853) and "The Landmark" (1854). Each of these sonnets is implicitly critical of imaginary indulgence, insofar as it presents what Copjec calls an "impediment" to the subject's "founding" in the symbolic order (21). In the first of these sonnets, "Known in Vain," Rossetti's speaker worries that "Work and Will" may "awake too late" (4), describing this shortfall of will through the metaphor of a love affair that distracts lovers from their duty toward God. These metaphoric lovers fall prey to a love that seems "first foolish," though its scope "widen[s] . . . to music high and soft / [t]he Holy and holies" (2–3). But this sacramental experience of love does not redeem the lovers, as it merely reminds them of the spiritual paths they have forfeited; they can subsequently only sit together passively apprehending their "hopeless sight of hope" (8). Rossetti's speaker thus portrays imaginary love as a false holiness and an intoxicating but decadent distraction from higher aims. On this note, he indicates his distance from the conviction, which he would arrive at decades later, that the indulgence in love provides its own means to such aims.

In another poem of this transitional period, "The Landmark," a speaker reflects on how he has missed his "path," having been distracted by a well into which he has "flung the pebbles from its brink / [i]n sport to send its imaged skies pell-mell, / (And mine own image, had I noted well!)" (3–5). The well that contains his image is clearly the pool of Narcissus, while the speaker's absorption in the "pell-mell" break-up of his reflection appears to be a fascination with something resembling the imaginary "disarray" of subjectivity described by Lacan (SI, 166). The speaker then revises the meaning of the well and drinks from that pool to obtain nourishment to seek his proper "goal" (8–14), thereby drawing on Christian symbolism of the pilgrimage. In Dante Gabriel's characterization of a young man's laggard disposition, he anticipates Christina's "Prince's Progress" (1863), whose prince similarly idles in languid pleasure and puts off pilgrimage (83). Although Christina regards her tardy prince—often regarded as a figure of Dante Gabriel—pessimistically and has him arrive too late to marry his allegorical princess, "The Landmark" displays the speaker growing increasingly aware of the hazardous quality of his imaginary indulgences and looking for ways to set himself on a symbolically progressive direction.

Over the course of the next year, Dante Gabriel indeed steeled himself for the task of achieving some sort of tangible symbolic position in the world, insofar as he felt that this goal was necessitated by the material requirements of love and marriage. Under the pressure of this requirement, he ceased to write poetry, virtually giving it up for fourteen years. As he said, he had to "giv[e] up poetry as a pursuit" because it conflicted with his artistic ambitions; he could not write, for writing meant that he would not paint (Letters, 214). He knew that he had to paint to become "ready to be a worthy husband and father"—that is, to settle himself down and enrich himself (Marsh, DGR, 134). While the material and emotional basis of a conflict within Rossetti between poetry and painting in the 1850s is patent in these letters, the sonnets of this period shine further light on a psychological conflict playing out in Rossetti, between the imaginary and symbolic elements of the self. These sonnets reveal how Rossetti at this point in his life saw the kind of imaginary love relationship that had become central to his existence as an obstacle to the symbolic practice of poetry, and he saw dabbling in poetry, his means of expressing imaginary desire, as an obstacle to the symbolic requirements of marriage. Overall, because Rossetti had not found a way to coordinate imaginary passion with symbolic control, the poetry of this period depicted such passion as a burden rather than as the ultimate symbolic stimulation that he would later find it to be.

Rossetti's "Holy Sonnets": The Transfiguration of Narcissism

Not until the years following 1868 did Rossetti begin to expand the means of his poetic craft so that it could anatomize the very problems of narcissistic attachment that earlier had paralyzed it. This was the period in which he became to some degree intimate with Jane Morris,[12] and although the sonnets of this period—like Rossetti's earlier sonnets, when he was most enraptured with Siddal—treat love as an exclusive and unifying absorption in the other, they do so in a way that is far more aesthetically accomplished and tonally integrated. In "Nuptial Sleep" (1869), for instance, Rossetti borrows tricks from paintings such as *Paolo and Francesca da Rimini*, using symmetrical imagery to evoke the narcissistic delights of extreme interpersonal passion. He thus describes how after the speaker and his lover sever a kiss that had unified them, they remain connected like "married flowers to either side outspread / [f]rom the knit stem" (6–7). The sensuality of this description of a postcoital division was taken as shocking at the time and was one of the spurs to Robert Buchanan's condemnation of Rossetti, in a review of 1871, as reprehensibly "fleshly." As Buchanan wrote, "Nuptial Sleep" "put[ ] on record . . . the most secret mysteries of sexual connection, and that with so sickening a desire to reproduce the sensual mood, so careful a choice of epithet to convey mere animal sensations, that we merely shudder at the shameless nakedness"; he went on to judge the effect "simply nasty" (1332). From a later perspective, however, the sonnet is seen as an early exponent of high aesthetic stylization, a graphical method of representing natural objects as interlocking forms that would be most readily observed in the design of William Morris and the drawings of Aubrey Beardsley. Thus, what Buchanan saw as a too-literal expression of mingling flesh is, in retrospect, actually a highly abstract rendition of flesh that contains narcissistic passion within aesthetic formality and thus introduces the symbolic order's function of "regulation" (Lacan, SII, 55).

In "Nuptial Sleep" the confusion of faces and flowers persists through the high-colored portrayal of the two lovers' "burnt red" mouths "fawn[ing] on each other" (6–8) and into the sestet, where the lovers sink like exquisitely coordinated mer-creatures "lower than the tide of dreams" and then rise "up again, through gleams / [o]f watered light" (11–12). Not all of the danger of imaginary excess in this picture is formally tamped down, however. A hint of morbidity is captured in the expression of how on their way up to the surface the lovers must penetrate a layer of "dull drowned waifs" that suggests that such a degree of imaginary overwhelming has proven fatal to others. In addition, some concern for the fate of the beloved arises as the speaker wakes before her, and it seems momentarily possible, as she lies still, that she has likewise succumbed to her immersion (14). Yet this moment at which the symmetrical style breaks down and the sonneteer is finally split off from his beloved also contains the suggestion of a new ethical bearing, for only upon waking from the imaginary rapture does the speaker attain the sobriety to distinguish and wonder at the other as a separate person, converting what Lacan calls "primary love" into "genital love," where one "acced[es] to the reality of the other as a subject" (SI, 212). In "Nuptial Sleep," we can thus see the achievement of a new aesthetic voice that allows Rossetti to maximize the resources of imaginary indulgence and symbolic control. The pursuit of beauty allows Rossetti to elevate to a symbolic principle the imaginary passion that always thrilled him, rather than having to diminish or flee prematurely from it.

One of the most aesthetic of Rossetti's love sonnets of this period is "Silent Noon" (1871), which consists largely of a tableau of a picturesque love nest. Amid a radiant pastoral landscape of "golden king-cup fields with silver edge," lovers are immersed in "visible silence, still as the hourglass" (5, 8). The beauty that surrounds them has the effect of making the time they spend together assume the perfection and permanence of art. Rossetti keeps up the illusion of aesthetic permanence in the sestet, with an image that famously introduces the static character of art into life: "Deep in the sun-searched growths the dragon-fly / Hangs like a blue thread loosened from the sky: / So this wing'd hour is dropt to us from above" (9–11). This complex image first transforms a natural insect into an aesthetic detail and then deploys the latter as an abstract figure for the permanence of lovers' time. The sonnet finally borrows the Keatsean paradox of silent music as it celebrates the "inarticulate hour / [w]hen twofold silence was the song of love," thus showing that the Rossetti speaker does not fear the inarticulacy rendered by the "close-companioned" imaginary experience but is able to revel in the silence imposed on the individual expressive organ with the confidence that this silencing will ultimately be an inducement to an integrated expression (13–14).

In other ways besides aesthetic stylization, Rossetti in the sonnets of this period deploys the resources of the symbolic order to perfect imaginary passion. Most brazenly, he does so by describing the effects of imaginary desire in sacred terms. Rossetti's version of this strategy varies from Dante's in that the transport of erotic love for Dante is a precursor to heavenly love that is finally purged so that he can follow his spiritualized beloved into heaven, whereas for Rossetti, the transport and the ascent happen simultaneously. Thus, Rossetti's sonneteer announces in "Heart's Hope" (1871) that it is at the same moment that he cannot tell "[t]hy soul . . . from thy body, nor / [t]hee from myself" that he also can no longer tell "our love from God's" (8), generating a wholly subjective version of religious apotheosis. The same effect transpires in "The Kiss" (1869), when the speaker claims to become "a god" in the course of the kiss and thereby to achieve "desire in deity": he alludes to the Orpheus myth invoked in the octet to invoke a classical sense of deity that neither Dante Alighieri nor Christina Rossetti would credit but that nonetheless projects a sacramental context onto the speaker's love (12, 14). Lingering in the order of the imaginary drives as well as in the classical tradition, Rossetti radically adjusts the value structure of Dante, "find[ing] his good" in his precursor's "bad," as well as "choos[ing] to know damnation" as the precursor defines it in order to "explore the limits of the possible" within that condition, in the terms of Harold Bloom (21). Rossetti thereby works out his role as "Dante of the darkness" that he had defined as his identity in 1861.

Rossetti's way of framing such an exploration of Dante's darkness is, in sum, his decision to use his writing to perpetually inhabit the sphere of the passions rather than to rise above them, and in those passions to find new symbolic resources proper to their glorification. In "Heart's Hope," the speaker accordingly likens the form of the sonnet to the "sea which Israel crossed dryshod"—the site of a kind of miracle that allows one to maintain speech despite immersion in speechlessness (4). Another sonnet that remarks metatextually on the ability to derive language directly out of passion is "The Love-Letter" (1869), in which a letter received from the beloved is described as being practically an issue of her body: it is "warmed by her hand and shadowed by her hair / [a]s close she leaned and poured her heart through thee," as well as a "[s]weet fluttering sheet, even of her breath aware" (1–2, 5). For the rest of the sonnet, the speaker continues to yoke ineffable feeling to communicable expression, calling the letter a "smooth black stream that makes [the letter's] whiteness fair" and juxtaposing the letter's "silent song" and the "soul" it "disclose[s]" (4, 6–7). The sonneteer does acknowledge that writing forged in this relation to passion is ever so slightly alienated from it, as he shows in the image of the beloved holding the letter up to her bosom so that "her breast's secrets peer[ ] into her breast," thereby implying that these are not identical (8, 11). However, just as Lacan holds that the symbolic order perfects the experiences of the imaginary order (SI, 141), so too does the sum effect, for Rossetti, of the transmutation of passion into language seem to be one of enhancement. The sonneteer fantasizes that in the course of writing the letter, the beloved's "eyes raised an instant, her soul sought / [m]y soul" (12–13), an apt description of an imaginary encounter that leads to a symbolic elevation, as this "sudden confluence" gives the beloved "[t]he words that made her love the loveliest" (13–14). In this suggestion that love attains its most beautiful form through words, Rossetti gives his ultimate endorsement to the symbolic process of writing about imaginary love from a position of enthrallment to it.

Despite the sonneteer's ability to render private passion into transmissible language, he reveals himself to be still faced with the problem of preserving the imaginary root of his relation to the other from the "degradation" to which relations founded in that order necessarily succumb, according to Lacan (SII, 263). Many of the sonnets that Rossetti places toward the middle of the sequence accordingly contain references to the inevitable loss of the beloved, as time takes its toll on imaginary love despite all of the symbolic measures deployed to stabilize it. "Severed Selves" (1871) displays the inevitable undoing of this intimacy in aesthetic terms: the lovers' living "dream" of love has become "attenuated" and "faint as shed flowers" (14). The lovers still mirror each other, but now at a grave distance: if in "Nuptial Sleep" their "bosoms sundered" remained enthrallingly close (5), now the closeness is only hypothetical: they are "[t]wo bosoms which, heart shrined with mutual flame, / [w]ould, meeting in one clasp, be made the same" (6–7). Notably, the love that is hardest to sustain through the ravages of life is one that lacks a palpably social form of symbolic ballast, such as marriage, which Lacan refers to as the essential symbolic "pact" that preserves imaginary relationships from degradation (SI, 174). As the sonneteer observes in "Secret Parting" (1869), there is a fragility to relations between "those for whom the roof of Love / [i]s the still-seated secret of the grove" where neither "spire may rise nor bell be heard therefrom," signifying that it has received no consecration in a church (12–14). The lovers kiss soulfully, but they are simultaneously aware of "how brief the whole / [o]f joy, which its own hours annihilate": a prospect that makes the kiss "thirstier" but no more nourishing (5–7). In these later sonnets, Dante Gabriel joins Christina in portraying narcissistic love as tragic, because it is susceptible to decay and bound to death. Yet because he can imagine nothing of a higher value to replace it, indulging aesthetically in its doomed prognosis remains the most attractive option. Additionally, even if love suffers degradation in Dante Gabriel's works, lovers never do; they hold nobly through the pangs of loss to become elevated into tragic figures of no little dignity.

The frailty of the imaginary relation is fully explored in the *Willowwood* sequence, a series of four iconic poems that appears roughly at the center of *The House of Life* and in a sense offers an encapsulation of the trajectory of the whole sequence. The four sonnets of the *Willowwood* sequence are based on the story of Narcissus, though adjusted to reflect the conditions of what Freud calls secondary rather than primary narcissism—the narcissism of those who "sexual[ly] overvaluate" others who remind them of their lost or ideal selves, as opposed to those who overvaluate themselves ("Narcissism," 88–90). The speaker of the sonnets thus becomes absorbed not in his own image in the pool but in the image of his lover, experiencing a condition of illusory mirroring in the other that is the essential experience of secondary narcissism. While critics reading these sonnets have frequently portrayed this event of mirroring as "sterile" and "solipsistic,"[13] secondary narcissism within Freudian theory is generally framed as neither of these but instead as the fundamental basis of the relation to the other, which produces the subject's first and most intense experience of expansion beyond the boundaries of the self and thus contains the potential for fertility and intimacy. As Steven Bruhm argues, narcissistic attraction "shuttles between the register of sameness ([s]he is what I am . . .) and difference ([s]he . . . give[s] me a sense of self)" and thus exceeds any definition as solipsism.[14] In short, while these critical accounts of Dante Gabriel Rossetti's narcissism tend to conclude that the speaker of the *Willowwood* sonnets cherishes a gratifying image of the self in the mistaken belief that he is loving an other, it is truer to say that the speaker cherishes the other with an inordinate intensity because of how she is mistaken for the self. The psychoanalytical condition of secondary narcissism is not that of getting away with solipsism—of keeping the ego safe from the other—but rather of letting it become too unsettled by the other, as one is "jammed by . . . [the] deceiving and realised image of the other" (Lacan, SII, 54).

Rossetti first displays this sense of an unsettling mistake of perception in "Willowwood I," when the speaker sees the other's "lips rising" in the pond to meet the reflection of his own (1.14). This first appearance of the face has been taken as a wishful illusion—in Stephen Spector's words, it is a "vision of the beloved . . . conjured up by the speaker's memory" (Spector, 456). But close observation reveals that the speaker of the *Willowwood* sonnets does not will this image of the other to appear to him; rather, her appearance occurs as a spontaneous transformation of the reflection of the angel sitting across from the speaker, a reprisal of Dante's embodied spirit of Love. Thus, we can gather that the reflection is produced and ratified by Love and is a disturbing event that happens to the speaker and that he has to respond to, like an instance of falling or refalling in love. Additionally, there is no sign in the sonnet that the image of the other that appears in the pond is a "vision," in the sense of being some sort of internally generated mirage that has no correspondence with a real living being. What this image instead appears to be is a highly persuasive illusion generated by the specular structures inherent in the imaginary order whereby an absent other is experienced as present and overlapping with the self.

The occurrence of this illusion can be understood through Lacan's account of how consciousness of objects in general passes them through the distorting, mirrorlike ego, which "[re]locates in an imaginary space [an] object which . . . is somewhere in reality" (SII, 46). As Lacan goes on to demonstrate in his optical schema for the theory of narcissism (fig. 8), a system of mirrors can reflect a bouquet of flowers to appear in a vase that is actually in a different place, such that the "imaginary vase which contains the bouquet of real flowers" is an analogy for the deceptive function of the ego, which reflects disparate objects so that they seem to be conjoined (SI, 79). In such a way, we can understand the angel Love as a figure for the distorting ego, which displaces the beloved so that she seems to be present and in imaginary proximity with the sonneteer's innermost being.

In the *Willowwood* sonnets, Love accordingly permits a deceptive intimacy with the other as the speaker "swe[eps] the spring" with his foot, disturbing self-other boundaries and allowing the two lovers to share a "soul-wrung implacable close kiss" (1.8, 2.11). This kiss has been dismissed as a "phantom kiss" . . . [because] of course [the speaker] kisses his own imaged lips" (Miller, "Mirror," 339). But there would be no pathos of loss in "Willowwood I" if Rossetti's speaker were simply kissing himself: the emotional effect of the poem lies rather in the effect of a brief intimacy heightened through a precarious sense of proximity. As the sonneteer complains, his problem is not that he is fundamentally

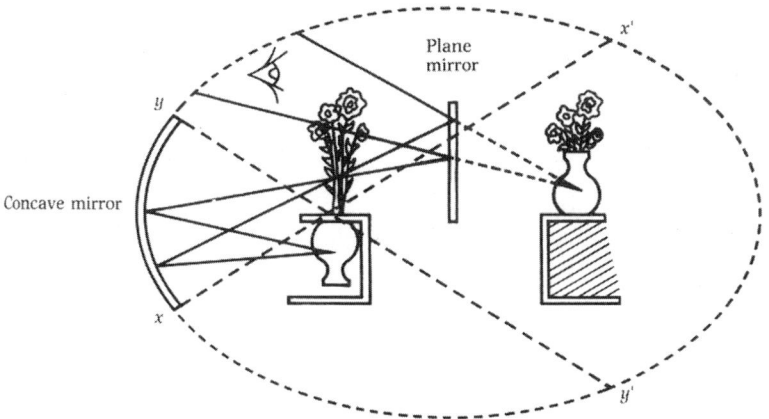

FIGURE 8. Jacques Lacan's optical schema for the theory of narcissism. From *The Seminar of Jacques Lacan, Book 2, The Ego in Freud's Theory and in the Technique of Psychoanalysis*, by Jacques Lacan, translated by Sylvia Tomaselli. Copyright © 1978 by Les Editions du Seuil. English translation copyright © 1988 by Cambridge University Press. Used by permission of W. W. Norton and Company.

alone at Willowwood, but that he is with his lover in a way that is so unstable that it permits them to be together "for once, for once, for once alone," in a contact so deceptively intense that they will both be forever haunted by the lost promise offered in that momentary illusion (2.13).

Subsequently, the wood surrounding the pool teems with "mournful forms" of the couple in their infinite span of loss: "shades of . . . days" of "soul-struck widowhood " (2.6–8). Dante Gabriel, like Christina, uses gothic imagery to depict the aftermath of imaginary captivation. While the gothic fate suffered by Christina's characters presents imaginary passion as a sinister haunting that never should have been, however, Dante Gabriel's wraiths tend to be victims of a happiness that ended too soon. Nonetheless, love for both writers has a tragic hue insofar as it reminds the subject of his deepest, most primordial loss, which each author reflects by invoking the landscape of a devastated maternal order. Just as Christina paints her ghostlands as womblike spaces that swallow up her narcissistic characters into an infinite regression, so too does Dante Gabriel's Willowwood loom before the speaker in "blood-wort burning red," a lurid maternal image that likewise displays a sense of the fatality of imaginary indulgence (3.9–10). Too much immersion is a cause—or a mask—of death, we see, as the beloved "drown[s]" away from him, "as gray / [a]s its gray eyes" (4.6–7).

But the narcissistic landscape of Willowwood also signals the possibility of renewal, as the song Love sings of "death's sterility" is one in which "the new birthday tarries long" but is nonetheless expected to come (2.3–4). In the fourth sonnet, there are some indications of how this new day will replace the hell of unsatisfied imaginary desire with a heaven in which the subject's desire becomes stabilized and spiritualized in the symbolic order—though not in the style of courtly love, in which erotic love for the other transmutes into a metaphor for divine love for the other. As in "The Landmark," the speaker counteracts his narcissistic paralysis by turning the pond into a source in which he can quench his spiritual thirst, taking "a long draught of the water where she sank, / [h]er breath and all her tears and all her soul" (4.9–10). When he does so, he comes to feel "Love's face / [p]ress[ing] on [his] neck with moan of pity and grace, / [t]ill both [their] heads were in [Love's] aureole," and he is party to a sublime elevation (4.13–14). The water can be understood as an instance of what Lacan calls the *objet petit a*: that "privileged object, which has emerged from some primal separation" that the subject may desire in the stead of the imaginary other (Four, 83). Because the subject's desire is channeled metonymically, Roland Barthes explains, the most insignificant object can seem to be "consecrated" through contact with the beloved.[15] This metonymic passage of meaning notably occurs in the symbolic order, making use of the logic of signification to attribute to something associated with the desired other an inordinate degree of value or charm. In the final lines of "Willowwood," Rossetti allows the pool, infused with the value of the beloved who had sunk into it, to baptize him with an utterly personal consecration whereby the speaker comes to be neither alone nor narcissistically unified with the beloved but unified with Love itself. The source of the speaker's sublime salvation thus is a source invested with the qualities of the unique other.

The *Objet petit a* in the Later Sonnets

The *objet petit a* accordingly has a key relationship to the subject's power of signification, prompting it and supporting it. As the "object cause" of the subject's desire, it becomes an instigator of the subject's signifying activity, arousing a metonymic chain that helps him break through the silence-inducing trance instilled by imaginary desire (Lacan, Four, 168). Thus, while the fate of one who lives in Willowwood at first seems to be the paralysis of the "mute" and "dumb" ghosts who haunt it, such a fate is bypassed when the *objet petit a* opens up a linguistic field of metonymic associations through which desire may roam. Several of the sonnets in *The House of Life* written after the composition of the *Willowwood* sequence in 1869 further indicate how by concentrating the speaker's drive on the unique qualities of the other, the *objet a* stimulates a chain of signification that sustains ephemeral imaginary love by relocating it within the symbolic order.

The speaker of "Heart's Hope" describes sonnet writing as an exploration through the "difficult deeps of Love" that can be navigated only if he can succeed in accurately discovering the right words to convey his personal experience—a "key of paths untrod" (2). If he finds within his "one loving heart" truthful words or "evidence" about his love, he will be able to generalize this evidence so that it will have universal meaning, and "to all hearts all things shall signify" (1–3). "Heart's Hope" is one of Rossetti's most metatextual sonnets, evoking the practice of fitting ideas to a "poor rhythmic period" to make them as appreciable and beautiful to the other as possible (5). The delicate process of allowing the *objet petit a* to initiate language is, meanwhile, reflected in Rossetti's persistent humility as to the poet's role in the process. The speaker of "Heart's Hope" does not impose meaning on his beloved but instead carefully and painstakingly derives meaning from his relation to her. Unable to envision what meaning he will find, he is able to describe only the qualities this meaning will have. It will be "[t]ender as dawn's first hill-fire, and intense / [a]s instantaneous penetrating sense / [i]n Spring's birth-hour, of other Springs gone by" (12–14). In other words, it will be an elusive meaning reflectable only in the instantaneous, unforeseeable associations that his experience of his beloved prompts him to make. The sequence of similes at the end of "Heart's Hope" is less a serious attempt to portray the beloved's qualities than a trope that shows how meditating on her stimulates the flow of signification.

In "Heart's Compass" (1871), likewise, the sonneteer shows that he has given up entirely on capturing the beloved in an image and is instead relying on the liquidity of signs to convey her elusive essence. He first meditates on the other as a site of sublime meaning: "Sometimes thou seem'st not as thyself alone, / But as the meaning of all things that are" (1–2). He goes on to compare the physical presence synesthetically to music and rapturously to the transcendent heavens: her "unstirred lips are music's visible tone"; her "eyes the sun-gates of the soul unbar / [b]eing of its furthest fires oracular;— / [t]he evident heart of all life sown and mown" (5–7). In this last line, the sonneteer gravely conveys the centrality of the beloved other to all life, at which point her extraordinary value sets the sonneteer wondering, "Is not thy name Love?" Here, Rossetti fully expresses the confounding effect of the *objet a*: on the one hand the beloved object is "separable" from everything else—she is particular—while on the other hand she represents the totality of his lack and therefore must be equivalent to everything that he requires to supplement himself.

Rossetti's final image in "Heart's Compass" for expressing the effect of the beloved is one of his most ambitious:

> Yea, by thy hand the Love-god rends apart
> All gathering clouds of Night's ambiguous art;
> Flings them far down, and sets thine eyes above;
> And simply, as some gage of flower or glove,
> Stakes with a smile the world against thy heart.
>
> (10–14)

The beloved grows through this imagery to a colossal size, both spiritually and physically. After becoming the vehicle by which the Love-god defeats the forces of darkness, she stands forth as the guardian of light, her eyes above permanently dispersing them and her heart nestling the world securely against itself. The surprising brutality of this final image, in which the beloved must be stabbed near the heart to undertake this world-saving function, expresses Lacan's concern that the massive compensations that the drive seeks through the *objet petit a* must do a kind of violence to the other: "I love you, but because I love in you something more than you—the *objet petit a*—I mutilate you" (*Four*, 268). In this case, however, the violence seems of a salutary kind, produced in the continual disintegration of the other's specific image so that she can signify for the speaker the wealth of that for which she stands.

In particular, the violence directed against the beloved bearer of the *objet petit a* is not the violence of the fetish, which generalizes her into a preset object. There is, in these treatments of the beloved, a distinct contrast with the use of the fetish, which in Rossetti's case sought out and produced the replication of certain generic attributes in the feminine other. Žižek has explained that the difference between the *objet petit a* and the fetish is that while the *objet petit a* is of the symbolic order and receives its charms through its symbolic association with a distinct other, the fetish is of the imaginary order and thus takes root in a fixed, transferable image.[16] We have seen how Rossetti lapsed into the use of the fetish in his later portraiture, and he could be accused of the same in several sonnets in *The House of Life*. Signs of such fetishism are particularly evident in Rossetti's rare contributions to the *House of Life* sonnets from the mid-1860s, when he was fully absorbed in his painting career. "Body's Beauty" (1867) and "Soul's Beauty" (1866) indeed comment on two paintings he was working on at the time, *Lady Lilith* (1868) and *Sibylla Palmifera* (1870). As the generic character of the sonnets' titles suggest, there is no suggestion that the women described in the sonnets are real persons known by the speaker in distinct relationships; rather, they are universal archetypes of the *femme fatale* and goddess projected onto figures with appropriate, readily fetishizable features. "Body's Beauty" thus features "golden hair" and carries "rose and poppies" (14, 9) while "Soul's Beauty" has "flying hair and fluttering hem" (11). These figures are fetishistic in the sense that any woman who expressed the attributes could imaginatively suggest these qualities, thereby functioning as vehicles of drives with regard to which they are "of no importance," to cite Lacan's phrase for the object of a fetish (*Four*, 168).

The extraordinary phallic value these women assume in the speaker's mind is, moreover, not derived from the particularity of his relationship to them but is instead projected upon them and is an index not of his love but of his insecurity in the symbolic order, which both drives him toward castration and makes him experience terror at the prospect of it. "Soul's Beauty" thus figures the highest beauty as an immensely powerful woman whose "eyes . . . draw" a man in her service "to one law," causing the speaker to follow her in every way and to tremble as he praises her (5–8). "Body's Beauty" figures a lower, more sensual form of beauty who also "[d]raws men" but does so with a fatal craft, a "bright web she can weave" that is actually the medium of their deaths (7–8). While Rossetti obviously intends the reader to discriminate between the value of the forms of beauty these two women represent, in both cases their allure resides in how they overpower the subject and force on him the destiny that he will live out, thus saving him from the agency and indeterminacy of his desire. Each of these figures allows the speaker to "stage his castration," to borrow Žižek's phrase for the goal of fetishism, and thus to evade the responsibility of a genuine symbolic relationship with the other (102).

If these two sonnets, like the pictures they echo, act as fields for the fetishistic projection of libidinally relieving archetypes, a much larger proportion of the love poems in the *House of Life* sequence show the speaker to be pressing beyond the generic appreciation of the fetish toward the particular appreciation of the *objet petit a*—which, as an element of the other that receives its value in a relationship, is always singular rather than universal and eccentric rather than typical. In "Her Gifts" (1872), the speaker accordingly emphasizes that he is above all attracted to those features of his beloved that are distinctive and even paradoxical—that is, to her unique style, expressed in her bearing that combines "[h]igh grace, the dower of queens" with "some wood-born wonder's sweet simplicity" (1–2). In this poem, the speaker first aims to capture the other by trying to describe the various parts of her body. However, the other's physical presence is so distinctive that he can only capture the effect on him of her physical attributes by making them suggest a kind of infinite value. His praise is therefore for her mouth, "whose passionate forms imply / all music and all silence," and her glance, which is "like water brimming with the sky," a reflecting pool that engenders a sense of infinite expansion in him (6–7, 3). Whatever he enjoys in her exhibits the qualities portrayed by Lacan as belonging to the *objet a*, of expressing a fullness that the actual features of the beloved could hardly contain (Lacan, Four, 268). Another feature of the *objet petit a* is that, unlike the fetish, which has a broadly transferable and exchangeable character, the *objet petit a* could belong to no other person. It is, moreover, a part of the other that no one else would value, since as a feature of the subject's jouissance—his private surplus enjoyment—it is by definition useless.[17] One Lacanian explanation of the *objet petit a* is that it is an *agalma*, a term from Plato meaning either "an offering to the gods or a little statue of a god"—because it is "a precious object hidden inside a relatively worthless box" (Evans, 125). In "Her Gifts," the sonneteer aptly registers that his enjoyment of his beloved's attributes reflects the play of wholly personal drives by claiming that he enjoys them especially as he names them, "as tongue may tell them o'er" (13). He also seems to overtly resist the image-worshipping function of the fetish by insisting that the beloved's most special feature is ultimately "her name"—the most singular, arbitrary, and immaterial attribute of her personhood, which "means more" than any imageable element of her (14).

Another sonnet that seems overtly to exchange the regime of the fetish for that of the *objet petit a* is "Love's Baubles" (1870). Here, an equivalent personage to Dante's angel Love receives generically fetishistic gifts— "slight wanton flowers and foolish toys of fruit" from numerous ladies (2). The flowers and fruit, with their "cluster and curled shoot[s]," are obviously thinly veiled representations of female anatomical charms, signalled in the profuse and overcompensating fashion that Rossetti adopted in his most fetishistic paintings, as discussed in chapter 5. The spectacle of these fetishes bores and embarrasses the male beholder, who describes how they "savour of sleep" and "seem . . . like shame's salute" (7–8). But when his own lady is bidden by Love to provide the same gifts, all of the disfavor on them falls away, and they become endowed with transcendental beauty, such that "at her touch they shone / with inmost heaven-hue of the heart of flame" (11–12). Thus, the speaker expresses that when the other is genuinely and personally beloved, the physical body is gracious rather than sinful: "[W]hen the hand is hers / Follies of love are love's true ministers" (13–14). Rossetti thereby differentiates between the generic and fetishized female body and the body of one's own lover, the personal and distinctive appreciation of which as an *objet petit a* is complementary to the highest form of love.

Even one of Dante Gabriel Rossetti's sonnets that praises the beloved's attributes in a somewhat formulaic fashion refuses to make any overt—and potentially fetishistic—description of the beloved's physical image. "Mid-Rapture" (1871) is, in particular, a poem about the difficulty of describing someone with whom one is genuinely in love. We are told in the sestet that the poem is an attempt at description in a moment during which the beloved's gaze "absorbs within its sphere / [the speaker's] worshipping face, till [he is] mirrored there / [l]ight-circled in a heaven of deep-drawn rays" (10–12). This incident, like the final one in the *Willowwood* sequence, elevates narcissistic rapture into a tableau of transcendence, though in this case the source of the sanctifying aureole is the beloved's own gaze. It is in this moment when the two lovers are interfused on multiple levels that an attempt at describing the features of the other is made. All the sonneteer can manage to do, however, is convey their effects: her voice "[i]s like a hand laid softly on the soul"; her hand "is like a sweet voice to control / [t]hose worn tired brows it hath the keeping of" (4–8). The circularity of the sonneteer's comparison of hand to voice and voice to hand engenders a vertigo that suggests that an objectifying perspective upon the beloved is impossible at such close proximity. Essentially, nothing specific emerges about the attributes of the beloved's body, other than that they support the speaker's love, as the body of the beloved as a whole becomes the adored *objet petit a* that fills in whatever is lacking in his being.

Ultimately, this lack in the self that is exposed in the signifying process around the *objet petit a* opens up the speaker to a dialogue in which the beloved other can fill in her own meanings. Accordingly, three later sonnets—"Equal Troth" (1871), "Youth's Antiphony" (1871), and "A Day of Love" (1870)—supplement the sonneteer's improvisatory meditations upon the beloved with conversations that confirm her reality as a subject, herein presenting a challenge to Spector's criticism that "the beloved never exists as another consciousness" in *The House of Life* (458). In "Equal Troth," the speaker begins by describing the beloved fetishistically as "garlanded" and "on a throne," and he wonders "how should [he] be loved" as he loves her, because he lacks her gifts (2–6). She is human enough to respond, however, and rebukes him for "doubt[ing] her love's equality," whereupon the sonneteer, duly chastened, admits that what deserves the most praise is her "heart's transcendence" (that is, the efflorescence of her subjectivity) rather than his "heart's excess" (the qualities that he hyperbolically projects upon her) (9–10, 12–13).

"Youth's Antiphony" is another sonnet that contains a dialogue between two lovers that suggests a new mature ability in Rossetti to value linguistic exchange above private effusion:

> 'I love you, sweet: how can you ever learn
>   How much I love you?' 'You I love even so,
>   And so I learn it.'
>
>   (1–3)

The sonneteer comments that lovers are "happy," whom "words as these / [i]n youth have served for speech the whole day long" (9–10). While such play could be taken as escapism, Rossetti suggests that it is actually a vehicle of transcendental grace, as through such conversation the lovers' boundaries of self are overcome in a way that perfects the effect of imaginary mirroring: "Love breathe[s] in sighs and silences / Through two blent souls one rapturous undersong" (13–14). This transcendence is, however, far more sustainable than the enthrallment of the imaginary gaze, lasting "hour after hour" instead of lapsing into decay as soon as it occurs. "A Day of Love" similarly demonstrates how lovers can benefit from transforming imaginary mirroring into mutual symbolic dialogue. After evoking the "echoing space" of time when the beloved is not, it portrays a syncopated rhythm between lovers' silences, during which "things forgotten call" to them, and speech, in which they "speak[ ] of things remembered" (13–14), thereby evoking the persistence of primordial lack while simultaneously displaying the means for bridging this lack through dialogue. The circuitry in which absence is filled in by presence through conversation reflects Lacan's logic of the signifying drive, which closes on the *objet petit a* of meaning that is nonetheless "simply the presence of a hollow" (*Four*, 180). At the same time, it shows how the language with which lovers circle that hollow is a basis for intense pleasure and connection.

Given that so much meaning can be derived from the relationship with the beloved, it should not come as a surprise when sonnets such as "Without Her" (1872) describe a world utterly deprived of value because the other is absent, for as Barthes points out, "the metonymic object" associated with the beloved can also be "an absence (engendering distress)" (173). This sonnet imagines a shadowy realm where the beloved's objects that persist after she is gone assume a nightmarish quality. "Her glass without her" is a pool "blind of the moon's face," as its surface robbed of her reflection is incapable of forming any image (1–2). "The heart without her" entails so bleak a deprivation that the speaker inquires of his "poor heart . . . what word remains ere speech be still," conveying that the act of signification hangs by a thread (9–10). Yet even here the signifying impetus of the *objet petit a* provides some consolation for the beloved's absence, insofar as the poem continues on for four more lines. Even though she is gone, the empty heart that she has left behind persists in wandering "barren ways and chill / [s]teep ways and weary" (10–11). Loneliness is among the oldest motives for poetry, and Rossetti's suggestion here of the persistence of the poetical drive beyond the presence of the beloved bears similarity to Lacan's account of the *objet petit a* as an "object of weaning" through which the subject gracefully lets go of the specific other by "symboliz[ing]" for himself "the central lack of desire" (Four, 104–5). Though such a sublimating activity is bound to be melancholy, it nonetheless allows the subject to sustain language and thus to contest the lack of desire by producing ever new instances of discourse and meaning.

"Change and Fate," the second part of *The House of Life*, affirms how the symbolizing drive that love spawns can outlive it and assume different functions, as the sonnets in this part treat subjects as diverse as religion, art, work, and death. While the later sonnets—with titles such as "Death's Songsters" (1870), and "Newborn Death" (1868)—have won *The House of Love* a reputation for morbidity, these sonnets are those in which the speaker fulfills the trajectory of the *objet petit a*, allowing the subject to wean himself from the lost other through a sublimatory process of producing meaning out of lack. "Barren Spring" (1870), for instance, reflects on the arrival of spring to the speaker who feels himself to be past its fecund pleasures. The sonnet is saturated with melancholy as he reflects on how spring can only fail to charm one "whose life is twin'd / [w]ith the dead boughs that winter still must bind" (6–7).

At the same time as it conveys an affect of sterility, however, it is profuse with vivid vegetable imagery through which the sonneteer conveys the incongruity between his inner winter and the outer spring. A crocus is a "withering flame" to him, a "snowdrop, snow," and an apple-blossom is redolent with the unhappy significance of nascent temptation (9–11). The condition of sterility thus becomes a source for imaginative fertility, and his inner winter is a blank background upon which he improvises a bouquet of decadent poetic figures. He finally reaches for the traditional Christian symbol of the lily as a figure for resurrection, proposing that his process of condensing meaning out of lack will be complete when "on the year's last lily stem / [t]he white cup shrivels round the golden heart" (13–14). The sonneteer thus gently conveys faith that the evacuation of life's splendor leaves behind an ultimate kernel of significance. This significance, in turn, might be either the Christian revelation or another form of revelation rooted in the speaker's poetic imagination, which, having projected despair on the landscape of hope around him, retains the ability to elicit from the now-wasted landscape the promise of a greater hope.

Regardless of whether "Barren Spring" makes a final bid for Christian salvation, the sonneteer indicates at the very end of *The House of Life* that he turns toward the saving grace of love for his ultimate consolation. The last sonnet in the sequence, "The One Hope" (1870), begins by portraying later life as a condition of terminal disappointment, in which "vain desire at last and vain regret / [g]o hand in hand to death, and all is vain" (1–2). Given such bleakness, the speaker is questing after some thing that will soothe him through this ravaging. Perhaps, he muses, this consolation will be a sublime peace: some "stream long unmet" in which the soul will finally "[s]toop through the spray of some sweet life-fountain" (6–7). But the speaker is not relying on such a discovery, and during the interval of uncertainty, he wonders what in the meantime can soothe the "unredeemed wan soul in that golden air" (11). The sonneteer determines that the thing must be nothing "alien" but rather something close to the intimate life of the subject: a privileged "word" that is the "one name" of the "one Hope" (12–13). William Michael Rossetti provides helpful guidance in a note claiming that "the one Hope's one name" was intended to be taken as "the name of the woman supremely beloved on earth" (DGR, 501). As we have seen in "Her Gifts," for Rossetti the name of the beloved is the ultimate *objet a*—an arbitrary sign that is nonetheless the nexus of all associations, forming a network of presence that covers the void at the heart of the subject's being. As a concentrator of meaning, it is equivalent to the Christian "word" and is available to those for whom love comes more easily than Christian revelation. Although this sonnet does not contend that the symbolic meanings provided through *eros* necessarily beat those derived from Christian *agape*, it does propose that the gleanings of love are available to the modern individual to help him cover over the gap in him left by the default of more-traditional sources of meaning.

At the end of *The House of Life*, the Rossetti sonneteer thus encounters no equivalent to the "wonderful vision" of magnificence that Dante Alighieri finds at the end of his sequence (*Vita Nuova*, 128). For Rossetti, heaven looms not as a certain vision but as a tantalizing poetic image, a mere possibility that the soul may "at once in a green plain . . . cull the dew-drenched flowering amulet" ("The One Hope," 7–8). In a sense, however, the speaker has already culled this amulet, in his final gesture of calling upon his beloved's name. It is his reward at the end of a love affair conducted with emotional courage that, long after the immediate presence of his beloved has been withdrawn, he retains, inviolate, the talisman of her name to hold onto as a lifeline. Rossetti thus proves the possibility of a secular redemption of the lover through symbolic means, through the course of which an intimacy grows that is not grasping or paralyzing, as imaginary love tends to be, but is able to bear and even to make use of the spaces between the self and the other, providing the lover with symbolic stimulation and stabilization. In short, the solution that Rossetti lays out in *The House of Life*—though less rapturous and secure an achievement than the one Dante performs in *La Vita Nuova*—resembles something like the fruits of an ordinary, successful love affair.

five

Hysterical Desire in Dante Gabriel Rossetti's Narrative Poems and Portraiture

> The gaze operates in a certain descent, a descent of desire, no doubt. But how can we express this? Modifying the formula I have of desire as unconscious—*man's desire is the desire of the Other*—I would say that it is a question of a sort of desire *on the part of the Other*, at the end of which is the *showing*.
> —Jacques Lacan, *Four Fundamental Concepts of Psychoanalysis*

DANTE GABRIEL ROSSETTI'S painting *Beata Beatrix* (1864) renders the moment in *La Vita Nuova* after Dante has found out that Beatrice is dead and describes in a canzone how "wonderfully out of the beautiful form / [s]oared her clear spirit" (*Vita Nuova*, 116). The illustration presents Beatrice with an expression of rapt beatification on her face that Evelyn Waugh described as exhibiting "consummate delicacy and beauty" (fig. 9).[1] The intense affect with which *Beata Beatrix* is laden can perhaps be attributed to the conditions of its composition: Rossetti first modeled Beatrice on his late wife, Elizabeth Siddal, and later regarded the completed version as a memorial to her (Surtees, 93). After Siddal died, Rossetti was struck with the idea of painting Beatrice with her eyes closed, and the touching gesture has a paradoxical effect of increasing the viewer's connection rather than obstructing it. Although in this regard Beatrice is not properly available to an "imaginary relation of the specular state" in the strict Lacanian sense, the painting nonetheless puts the viewer in the position of witnessing Beatrice's private narcissistic rapture and so grants him a position of intense intimacy with her (SI, 171). That the viewer is the exclusive witness of Beatrice's passion is guaranteed insofar as the other subjects in the painting, Dante and the angel Love, are depicted as standing behind her so that they cannot see her expression. The viewer who is implicitly the sole beholder of Beatrice's passion

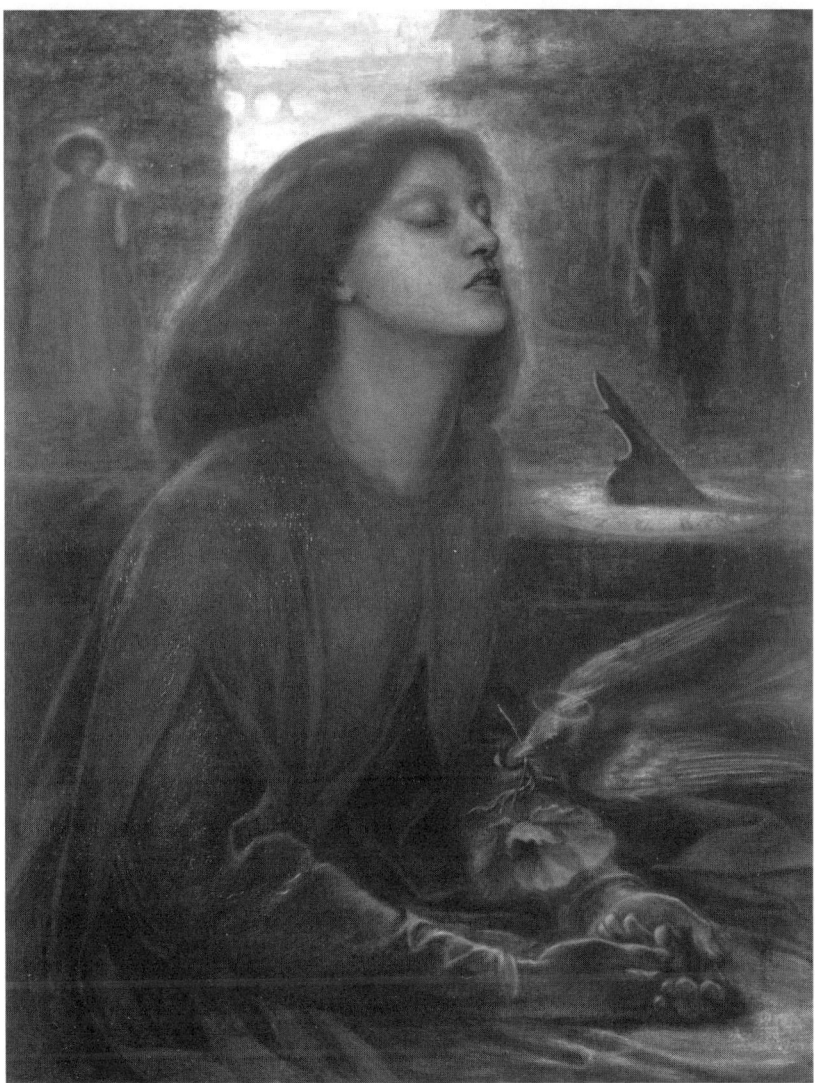

FIGURE 9. D. G. Rossetti, *Beata Beatrix* (c. 1864–70). Oil on canvas, 86.4 x 66.0 cm. Tate Gallery, London. Photo credit: Tate, London / Art Resource, NY.

at the moment of transcendence may accordingly feel his own rapture called out, just as the closed-eyes lovers in Rossetti's *Paolo and Francesca de Rimini* mirror each other in their narcissistic reverie.[2] What Kristeva calls a "merging apotheosis" of narcissistic love, in which boundaries between subject and object blur, is thus prospectively induced between the viewer and the subject of the painting (*Tales*, 3).

But while Rossetti used the above means to render his portrayal of Beatrice wrenchingly intimate, he had another requirement upon him as well—to confirm that Beatrice was genuinely experiencing the holy transformation indicated in the title by indicating the presence on the scene of a divine power who can bequeath blessedness. Rossetti's challenge in *Beata Beatrix* was thus not only to let the viewer see Beatrice's transformation but also to dramatize the presence of a supreme symbolic agency who looks beneficently upon Beatrice from a specular position that towers over that of the viewer. This agency is the supreme desirer of whom Dante writes toward the end of the *Paradiso* when he acknowledges that God appreciates Beatrice even more than he does: only her "Maker" knows "the complete" joy of her beauty (30.20–21). Similarly, Rossetti makes reference to God in his sonnet "Vain Virtues" (1869) in describing virgins as attractors of "God's desire" while they remain pure (11). These reflections by Dante and Rossetti upon an Other whose desire dwarfs that of men are in keeping with Lacan's theory that when one views a painting, one desires the object not only for oneself but also on behalf of the Other who stands behind the painting and casts his "gaze" upon it (Four, 115). As Lacan elaborates, this desiring gaze of the Other is graphically signaled in a painting by the imprint of a gleam of light somewhere in its field, so that the effect of standing before a painting is of being caught amid a powerful beam shining upon the painting's subject, and in turn, upon oneself (Four, 97). Explaining Lacan's theory, Copjec reasserts that the determining gaze in art does not belong either to the viewer or to the artist but to an Other behind the image.[3] The viewer who stands in front of the painting can experience the sensation of being in the sight line of the Other, who is normally "turned back on itself, absorbed in its own enjoyment" (Copjec, 36), but may be attracted by the painting to look in the same way that God is attracted by Beatrice. The viewer of a painting accordingly anticipates a "showing" of the Other, which in the case of *Beata Beatrix* is signaled through Rossetti's illumination of Beatrice with a dawning luminosity that casts her head in a halo (Lacan, Four, 115). This apprehension of such a showing does not negate the viewer's appreciation of the subject but augments it; for as Kristeva explains, love can be experienced as a "gleaming reflection [off of the beloved Other] of the One, which the soul watches and loves" (*Tales*, 111). This is the kind of love that occurs when the lover agrees to be "inserted in a function" within the symbolic order in exchange for forfeiting his primary, imaginary libidinal attraction toward an object—the exchange that underlies Lacan's theory of painting and has been described as the fundamental bargain of the symbolically subjected individual (MacCannell, 125). Like Dante, the viewer of a blessed object such as Beatrice is promised his own version of sublimation within the symbolic order, or at least the sensation of it.

Beatrice's role in the picture may in turn be characterized in terms of Lacan's concept of the "lure," which the painter provides the viewer so that he will be able to "trap" the gaze that he may not be able to attract on his own merits (Four, 101). The medieval artist who produces icons "play[s] with those things, in this case images, that may arouse the desire of God"; in the same way, Rossetti plays with Beatrice (Lacan, Four, 113). The way that the object in the painting acts as a lure is specifically elaborated by Rossetti in two elegiac sonnets he wrote in 1868, while worried that he might be going blind and consequently might lose the ability to paint. In "Newborn Death," art is described by him as a feminized entity "whose eyes were worlds by God found fair": an expression that indicates how he conceived of his artistic skill as that of being able to depict images that could gratify the pleasure of an abstract divine Other (10). The desire to solicit a different sort of Other is indicated in the sonnet "The Portrait" (1868) from The House of Life, as the painter-speaker, after having completed a painting of a woman, effuses, "Let all men note / [t]hat in all years / [t]hey that would look on her must come to me (12–14). The statement serves as the admission by the artist of his dependence on the woman's image to attract the attention of those men of "all years" that he requires to achieve fame, a classical and secular form of symbolic transcendence. These two descriptions of how the artist can devise a painting as a lure construct a brief catalogue of the different types of gazes that Rossetti evoked within the two stages of his career: the early "Art Catholic" phase, in which he affected a medieval style and sought a numinous ideal, and the later phase that distinctly reflects Classical Renaissance influences and values. The two sonnets of 1868, meanwhile, suggest continuities between these two phases of his career, in which Rossetti sought to attract the Other on behalf of himself—and, implicitly, his viewers—through the virtuosic extension of a feminine form.

The Lacanian concepts of the gaze and the lure helpfully augment the range of critical tools available for understanding the complex dynamics of Rossetti's paintings. Critics have previously noted that Rossetti's portraits of beautiful women not only appeal to the individual libidos of their viewers but also accommodate them to the symbolic structures they inhabit. Griselda Pollock, for instance, depicts Rossetti's paintings of women as "screen[s] across which masculine fantasies of knowledge, power and possession can be enjoyed" (123). Herbert Sussman similarly describes Rossetti's art through the concept of homosociality (*Masculinities*, 25), which Eve Kosofsky Sedgwick defines as the exchange of women by men to "maintain[ ] and transmit[ ] patriarchal power" (21). Both of these critics suggest that the gaze upon women that is encouraged by these paintings can be understood as an element of this homosocial bond, linking men together in a shared pleasure and possibly in an implicit exchange.[4] Indeed, one of Rossetti's interests in painting pinups such as *Bocca Baciata* (1859) during the 1860s seems to have been to gratify a circle of friends who also exchanged mistresses (Marsh, *DGR*, 253–59). However, insofar as Sedgwick's version of homosocial desire entails a patriarchal network in which power flows naturally among men, use of this concept is limited in the case of Rossetti, whose art tends to reflect more-obscure quests for psychic security and spiritual integration. For this reason, a conception of desire that is more broadly reflective of Rossetti's motives for painting is that of "hysterical desire," which Lacan defines broadly as the desire to "sustain the desire of the father" (*Four*, 38).[5] If homosocial desire describes a means for the exchange of power among actual men, hysterical desire more accurately characterizes the symbolic function of a work such as *Beata Beatrix*, which aims to provide the viewer with proximity to a phallic power so stupendous that it could never be assumed by any real individual. Hysterical desire also helps to characterize the asymmetrical dynamics of desire in secular contexts where the relevant symbolic Master is an abstract body of humanity that can endow symbolic acceptance, the aspiration to which engaged Rossetti at various times and to various degrees over the course of his life and that matched the interests of the middle-class clientele of his later portraits. It meanwhile draws attention to the ultimate futility of both of these campaigns of inclusion for a certain kind of male subject, who is bound to feel anxious and excluded despite all of his measures to seek security and acceptance.

The dynamics of hysterical desire in Rossetti's career are indicated not only in the various phases of his painting career but also, and more explicitly, in some of his major narrative poems. Rossetti initially articulated a hysterical dynamic of desire between men and women in his narrative poems that solicited the gaze of an Other beyond the scene of the poem's action: this includes the God that blesses the "blessed damozel" and the community of implicitly learned men to whom the speaker of "Jenny" orates his monologue. In his paintings, Rossetti went on to experiment with graphically reflecting the position of the genders in relation to the gaze of the Other through his manner of positioning his figures and his use of light. Subsequently, however, he left behind his idealistic Art Catholic practice, which pursued God's gaze, and developed a more lucrative practice of sensual portraiture in a Renaissance style that was particularly attractive to the nouveau-riche industrialists from the north of England. He arrived at a paradox, however; despite Rossetti's insistence on making use of the female figure for various symbolic ends, his paintings simultaneously go to great lengths to emphasize the individual identities and subjectivities of the women they feature. A signature drawing within Rossetti's career, *Mary Magdalene at the Door of Simon the Pharisee* (1858), seems to suggest that the viewer must cultivate an individual and personal relation to the subjects of art to benefit from the grace that they extend, insofar as this grace engages the imaginary level of the subject as well as the symbolic level.

Phallic Anxiety in the Narrative Poems

In the first decade of his artistic career, Rossetti conceived the majority of his narrative and dramatic poems, including "The Blessed Damozel" (1847/1850), "Jenny" (1848–59/1870), "The Bride's Prelude" (1848/1881), and "The Staff and Scrip" (1852/1856). One feature shared by these poems is a tendency to cast the central male figure as a hysterical male who is burdened by a sense of inadequacy and highly concerned with a Phallic Other beyond the scene whose favor they are either driven to, or barred from, attracting. This conspicuously castrated quality of the early protagonists contrasts notably with the sensually and philosophically assured speaker of most of the *House of Life* sonnets—particularly the later sonnets, in which Rossetti's mature recipe for integrating the imaginary and symbolic drives involves a brazen defiance of preexistent norms. This shift from Rossetti's early male protagonists to his later ones exemplifies what Kristeva has called writing's propensity to "inscribe[ ], not the original-paternal law, but *other* . . . illegal, paradoxal, heteronymic" laws (*Desire*, 113).

But nowhere in the *House of Life* sequence can we find the depiction of a male protagonist who is as cowed and resourceless as the speaker in "The Blessed Damozel," Rossetti's first published poem. This poem emulates Dante Alighieri's *Commedia* by figuring a moral hierarchy between a fallen man and the woman who strives to save him. The damozel is evidently a version of Beatrice, as she prays for God to raise up her lover so that she and her beloved can "bathe . . . in God's sight" in "deep wells of light"—an apt characterization of the luminosity of the divine gaze (76–78).

As he regrets, he has "close lips that knew not prayer" and is concerned that they cannot offer the necessary praise to God despite it being their will to do so; something within his nature blocks such an orison (100–101). Rossetti elaborates this obstacle in the speaker even more fully in his 1870 revision of the poem, where the speaker confesses that there is little chance that

> . . . God [will] lift
> To endless unity
> The soul whose likeness with thy soul
> Was but its love for thee[.]
> (99–102)

In this later version, Rossetti knowingly highlights the difference between Dante and the speaker of *The Blessed Damozel*. Love in this instance is not expected to redeem the singer; the mirroring process of narcissistic desire is of no use in the effort, as it was for Dante in initiating his redemption.

The absolute barrier to heaven for the speaker of "The Blessed Damozel" may be in place because he is more fallen than Dante; alternatively, he may be subject to a more inexorable and less forgiving symbolic order than Dante's. The evidence in the poem suggests that the second interpretation is more apt: the speaker's metaphysical destiny—if he is right about it—is already fixed and, unlike Dante's, will unfold independent of any efforts he makes at reform. No reason is provided for the lover's conviction of inevitable damnedness, given that he is made to seem, at the very least, a decent fellow. At the end of the poem, when he "hear[s] [his damozel's] tears," his apparently greater worry about her disillusioned hopes than his eternal suffering speaks well of his generosity as a lover (150). The man's sensation of how the damozel's "hair / fell all about my face" may lead us to infer that he will be damned for a sexual transgression (21–22). But it takes two to enact such sins, and the man mentions no woman with whom he has been involved other than his damozel, who has nonetheless attained heaven and does not seem to be a paragon of purity. While in heaven, the damozel's tone is desirous—more like that of a Francesca than a Beatrice—as she moans for her lost love: "I wish that he were come to me" (67). The narrator's description of how "her bosom must have made / [t]he bar she leaned on warm" further suggests that the damozel is a particularly earthy type (45–46). This suggestion is confirmed by the speaker's tendency to depict her in images of fertility, with her hair "yellow like ripe corn" (12) and a group of handmaidens endowed like harvest goddesses surrounding her: "Cecily, Gertrude, Magdalen, / Margaret and Rosalys . . . with bound locks" (107–9). These images of the damozel may be the fancies of the narrator, but even so, they suggest that he believes her to be both sexual and essentially redeemed—seemingly in contrast to himself, whose fallen desire is portrayed through a symbol of sterility: "the autumn fall of leaves" (23). All in all, the cosmos in "The Blessed Damozel," which appears to glorify female desire and convict male desire, seems more cruel in its justice than the cosmos of Dante's *Commedia*, where the male and female lovers Paolo and Francesca at least receive the same punishment for the same infraction.

A possible reading of the metaphysical condition outlined in "The Blessed Damozel" is suggested by Kristeva's description of a subjective logic of interiorized purity and impurity at the root of Christianity, according to which sin is "a matter for the subject himself to decide" (*Powers*, 118–19). According to such a logic, even if the male lover in "The Blessed Damozel" has committed no special sexual transgressions beyond those prospectively shared with the damozel, he may still be more sinful than she is, if he feels himself to be. Insofar as "The Blessed Damozel" seems to make the lover's damnation a matter of his own conviction rather than any apparent objective transgression, it blurs the same boundary between religion and psychology that Kristeva finds St. Paul blurred when he claimed that "to him that esteemeth anything to be unclean, to him it is unclean" (Romans 14:14, in Kristeva, *Powers*, 119). Lacan similarly contends that the sense of sin is essentially subjective, residing in the subject's individual unconscious, where "the structure of [his] desire" interpenetrates "the structure of the law" that he individually holds (*Four*, 34).

In particular, the "The Blessed Damozel" portrays a distinctly Victorian syndrome of masculine anxiety and sexual guilt, whose ubiquity in that period has been observed by social historians.[6] In Dante Gabriel's case, it was probably exacerbated by conditions in the Rossetti household. Within the Rossetti family, Dante Gabriel's mother echoed this Victorian unease with male sexuality in Christian terms, expressing a general "distaste for lust as a matter of masculine appetite" and perhaps thereby imparting to Dante Gabriel the sense of automatic male damnation that is evoked by "The Blessed Damozel" (Marsh, *DGR*, 200).[7] Even if Dante Gabriel was intellectually agnostic, as D. M. R. Bentley finds him to have been,[8] his general habits of idealization likely would have prepared the conditions for an interiorized sense of sin—given how the service of any ideal leads to the development of "projective mechanisms and obsessive rituals" to preserve some sense of a sacred sphere, according to Kristeva (Powers, 58). In general, nonbelieving Victorians tended to sustain an ideal of purity by idealizing notions such as "woman"—which they constructed as angelic.[9] "The Blessed Damozel" reveals how one consequence of this Victorian habit of idealizing femininity was the commensurate de-idealization of masculinity. Despite the archaic tone of this poem, therefore, its presentation of male desire as permanently lower in spiritual rank than that of an unexceptional damozel seems hysterical in a peculiarly Victorian manner, as it characterizes the precarious symbolic condition of the Victorian male. It also emblematizes how Victorian men such as Rossetti, who felt themselves to be deprived of traditional opportunities of sublimation, began to turn to interpersonal love as a compensatory source of value.[10] In the end, the benefit the man receives from the damozel is not a direct symbolic success that she formally helps him obtain but the love she inspires in him, which ennobles him even if it does not save him.

Another of Dante Gabriel Rossetti's poems that revises the structure of romance in keeping with Victorian conditions is "Jenny." The dramatic monologue of "Jenny" is spoken by a young man who, after a night of dancing, ends up in the room of a prostitute; as she sleeps, he forfeits any carnal intentions and instead analyzes her condition and that of prostitutes in general. With its oscillation between tones of liberality and condemnation, "Jenny" is highly ambiguous in its position on sin. Amanda Anderson discusses how, in the speaker's presentation of the prostitute Jenny, he induces a textual "instability between fallenness and conventional purity,"[11] for instance, by referring to the prostitute as "[p]oor shameful Jenny, full of grace" and thus setting her on the same plane as the Virgin Mary and by describing how she sleeps with a "lamp . . . / [l]ike a wise virgin's" (18, 315–16). Not merely ironic, these allusions sustain the paradox about female sexuality that Rossetti establishes in "The Blessed Damozel," in which the damozel is simultaneously saturated by desire and blessed. The speaker accordingly presumes very little out-and-out sinfulness in Jenny, supposing only the presence of asexual vices such as vanity and materialism that he guesses to be the contents of her "grim web" of dreams (342). He further proposes that Jenny's dreams—and, by implication, her soul—are no different from those of ordinary girls such as his "cousin Nell," who is similarly "fond of dress, and change, and praise" as well as "love" (185–90). Indeed, because of Jenny's lack of distinguishing marks of sin, the speaker concludes that the most significant context of her punishment is social rather than metaphysical: she has been cast into "man's pitiless doom," which is its own "lifelong hell" (244–45).

Even as the speaker minimizes Jenny's sexual sin, however, he violently condemns the sexual sin of the male sex, repeatedly turning from his chivalrous analysis of the conditions of Jenny's fall to a severe chastisement of male desire. Murray Roston observes that the image of the fallen women in Victorian art frequently acted as "a personification of [man]'s failure to attain" his moral ideals and consequently served as a sign of "male guilt."[12] In a similar way, when the speaker looks at Jenny, he declares that "the woman almost fades from view," revealing a broader "cipher of man's changeless sum / [o]f lust" (277–79). For Jenny's situation he blames the "hateful[ ]" actions of "man,"

> Who spares not to end what he began,
> Whose acts are ill and his speech ill,
> Who having used you at his will,
> Thrusts at his side.
>
> (83–87)

The emphasis on male viciousness in "Jenny" is not an incidental aspect of the poem but an essential one; William Michael Rossetti recollects in his note on the poem that the poem grew, in part, out of a fragment about male lust that Dante Gabriel wrote in 1847 that persists in the final form of "Jenny," in which the speaker muses that it is "like a toad within a stone / . . . there since the earth was curs'd" (282–83).[13] The speaker who analyzes Jenny in morally ambivalent terms sustains this unambiguous conviction of masculine damnedness throughout the poem, ultimately pleading, "how atone, / Great God, for this which man has done?" (241–42). The sudden mention of God in the monologue of this young libertine meanwhile exemplifies the tendency toward religious idealization that persists in the psyches of even Dante Gabriel's most cosmopolitan characters.

In an especially theoretical section of "Jenny," moreover, the speaker shifts from a metaphysical analysis of the sense of sin to a semiotic one that anticipates the theories of Lacan. He observes that the "Paphian," or wanton "Venus," still "seems / [a] goddess," indicating that women may exhibit desiring bodies and remain uncompromised in the symbolic order

(362–63). In contrast, men must not expose their genitals, lest they seem to lack power: "Priapus" must be hidden "to the waist" so that "whoso look on him shall see / [a]n eligible deity" (366–68). In this strikingly perceptive comment, the speaker points out that male lust is troublesome not only because of the damage it does to women such as Jenny but also because its exhibition reveals the fact of male dependency and, hence, male castration. This condition of masculine power is also explored by Lacan, who notes that the phallus can "play its role" as a sign of power "only when veiled," for then it appears as a "sign of latency" with the potential to act ("Phallus," 288). In the ancient mysteries of Greece, Lacan adds, the exposure of the penis invoked a "demon of shame" whose role was to "strike the signified"—the penis—to maintain the mystique of the phallus as a "signifier": a cause of desire rather than an effect of it. Rossetti's speaker likewise seems to be ashamed of the exposure of his desire, insofar as it threatens to expose his genitals in the condition of being merely a "cause of desire" and thereby to reveal his distance from the condition of phallic power.

Perhaps partly not to expose himself in this way, the speaker ends his visit to the prostitute's chamber without the usual consummation but nonetheless leaving some coins in Jenny's hair, a gesture of payment that he claims to carry out because he is "ashamed of [his] own shame" (381). But there is a further and broader transaction captured in this gesture. The payment of Jenny has been taken by some critics as a measure by the speaker to dominate and possess her.[14] But there is no clear expression of power in this payment, which substitutes for sexual domination rather than enacting it. Moreover, this gesture elicits feelings of unease, rather than grandiosity, in the speaker. The gesture of putting "golden coins" amid Jenny's "golden hair" may accordingly be analyzed in terms of the logic of the fetish—as equivalent to the money shot in pornographic films where the male porn star ejaculates onto the body of the woman, which signifies not so much his command over the woman but the submission of his personal desire to the viewer's fantasy (340–42). In this light, we may recall how Slavoj Žižek analyzes the fetishistic gesture not as asserting a claim of power over an other but rather as exhibiting submission to an Other: it is a "staging of castration" whereby the subject relieves anxiety regarding his desire by enacting that desire according to a preconceived discursive code—in this case, that of capitalist payment (104). As a poem about prostitution, "Jenny" is accordingly also about the prostitution of the artist who seeks to excite the interest of the Other not only on behalf of himself but also on behalf of his readers or patrons. In chapter 3, I discuss how Rossetti explained his switch from identification as a painter to a poet because his verse, "being unprofitable, has remained unprostituted" (in Gaunt, 106–7). Rossetti thus acknowledged that commercial popularity for an artist involves a form of prostitution, whereby he leaves off the gratification of his own desire and learns how to create the fantasies that will arouse the desire of the abstract Other on behalf of his readers, just as a literal prostitute must do for her clients. Lacan similarly describes how the painter's work takes on value in the market when it offers to those who "g[i]ve the artist a living" the dialogue with the Other that they seek, through the selection of an appropriate gaze (Four, 111–12). In this regard, what the speaker's shower of gold ultimately symbolizes is the payment by the Other that the speaker is hoping to receive for his poem. The solution to male shame, it would appear, is to fully submit oneself to one's castration, by subordinating one's desire in some fashion—here, in a capitalistic one—to the desire of the Other.

We can see the speaker of "Jenny" enacting such a submission in a different context when, after he experiences shame, he states that he is going to embark on a quest to cleanse his soul through "thoughts" that will seek "a far gleam" and clear "a dark path" (386–87). In the case of the speaker, one might question whether it is properly a religious quest that he has in mind, given that the reference to "thoughts" is distinctly intellectual and could refer back to the academic context grounded early in the poem, where the speaker describes the room "full of books" that he normally inhabits, which has been keeping him from Jenny's room (23). The speaker also indicates that the monologue expressed inside Jenny's parlor is intended for some sort of learned community beyond it when he mocks himself as to "what use" his thoughts are in the presence of a sleeping prostitute, thereby implying that the monologue's true audience may be elsewhere (297). To a great extent, the monologue partakes of the quality of an academic prolusion, in which the speaker argues with himself about how far he may take his rhetorical conceits. For instance, the speaker describes Jenny through an extended metaphor of ravaged flowers, then cuts himself off because his analysis has overreached: "Nay, nay, mere words" (121). Through what David Riede describes as the speaker's "verbal pyrotechnics, his learning, his wit," he seems to indicate that his analytical fiat is directed toward an abstract audience beyond the frame of the poem, before whom he could redeem his desire through intellectual achievement (106).

In this sense, the speaker offers his reverie upon "Jenny" as a lure to these abstract Others, who, if they find it engaging, may allow him to trade his problematic desire for a positive evaluation—an intellectual sublimation particularly necessary for this speaker, who has no idea of how to "atone" in the religious sense, as he acknowledges (241). As Lacan would have it, the need to engage the approval of an Other is central to the subject's construction of desire in the symbolic order. Here our desire is never a direct reaching for simple objects, as our need is, but has a "paradoxical, deviant, erratic, eccentric, even scandalous character" ("Phallus," 286). The speaker of "Jenny" accordingly reveals that his desire is not only carnal but also exhibitionistic, directed not solely toward Jenny but also toward the opportunity to show off his good conscience regarding her. Additionally, it makes use of the lure of Jenny herself, an impetus that explains the curiously mixed tone of "Jenny," whereby the speaker alternates between condemnations of his desire for Jenny and references to her in lascivious imagery that seems intended to arouse that very desire in the Other, such as his depiction of her "wealth of loosen'ed hair / [her] silk ungirdled and unlac'd / [a]nd warm sweets open to the waist" (47–49). Although the speaker of "Jenny" has been described by Robin Sheets as a client of pornography, it is more precise to describe the speaker as a purveyor of high-toned pornography who combines salacious representation with intellectual sublimation in the same way that the painters Raphael and Leonardo that the speaker references pictured beautiful women "to men's souls" (238).

Ultimately, however, a reading of "Jenny" as a symbolic exchange in all of these ways does not fully encompass its complex dynamics. One more thread in the monologue asserts the necessity to regard Jenny with intersubjective human love. The speaker indicates an element in "Jenny" that exceeds her usefulness as an offering to the Other when he wonders "what [she's] thinking of" (58) and acknowledges that her thoughts, like his, might seek their own "far gleam" (385). A little earlier in the poem, this empathy in the speaker leads him to "[l]et her sleep" (332), an action that leads to a dawning sense of ethical intuition within himself, as "somehow in [him]self the dawn / [a]mong stirred clouds and veils withdrawn / [s]trikes greyly on her" (330–32). This concern for Jenny as an individual further leads the speaker to experience his deepest shame and consequently his most profound intersubjective openness. After he deposits the coins in Jenny's hair, he regrets having mocked her in such an impersonal manner, and he turns toward her "poor face" more fully (380–81). He goes on to consider the thoughts that may function inspirationally "in her life" as they do in his, plants a chaste kiss upon her, and utters one of the only genuinely interpersonal lines in the poem: "Good-bye, my dear" (302–8). In these gestures that involve a turning toward Jenny's face and a recognition of her hidden thoughts, the spirit of connection with the other that is founded in the imaginary relation is revived, allowing the speaker to overcome the most objectifying and alienating aspects of the symbolic relation to the Other. This connection with and care for Jenny's soul—however brief its action within the poem—is, in turn, the field that seems to open up the prospect of genuine grace for the narrator, who witnesses this young prostitute not merely through the eyes of a bitter john or social judge but with those of a compassionate lover and artist. As in the case of "The Blessed Damozel," the hysterical subject in his pursuit of symbolic redemption cannot bypass the relationship to the other, although at times when he is experiencing intense insecurity, it would appear that he aims to.

Some additional features of the hysterical male subject are explored in "The Bride's Prelude," a narrative poem that further formulates the ambiguous position of the artist's desire hinted at in "Jenny." In this narrative, a young bride named Aloÿse confesses to her sister Amelotte that she has been seduced, made pregnant, and abandoned by her fiancé, whom her brothers are belatedly forcing her to marry to alleviate the family's bankruptcy. The dynamics of a judging light are fully expressed in the poem's evocation of this morally complex situation, which is full of chiaroscuro details signifying the approval and withdrawal of the gaze; it is "a world of mirrored tints minute," in the words of the narrator (45). Aloÿse, who feels the weight of her transgression, tends to retreat into the shade from a "sun shed[ding] judgement-fire" (822–23). The virginal bridesmaid, Amelotte, meanwhile, "laugh[s] into the air / [w]ith eyes that [seek] the sun" (6–7). The fiancé, Urscelyn, is a figure of darkness, appearing in Aloÿse's narrative at night, when he undertakes his seduction.

At the same time, Urscelyn is a peculiarly Rossettian demon lover, not entirely without redeeming qualities: as a knight he is supposed to have a "stout heart," and like the speaker of "Jenny," he is a scholar widely "praised / [f]or letter-lore" (252–58). In the manner of an artist, Urscelyn plies a trade that gives him access beyond his symbolic circle, acting as a doctor who entices the higher-status Aloÿse with a promised cure for her illness. While his seduction is portrayed as unforgivable in the poem, it is simultaneously qualified by a depiction of his anxious condition as a man. Urscelyn stands outside the order of power and privilege in which Aloÿse belongs because he is only marginally related to her family, "[bearing] our shield, but barred athwart" (255). He thus has no legitimate access to the aristocratic Aloÿse, which perhaps offers a slight justification for his roundabout attack on her. An understanding of Urscelyn as a marginal man is further heightened in an interpretation of his barred family crest through Lacan's schemata of the barred subject. Lacan's primary notation for the subject is a barred "s," in which the bar signifies the subject's castration, through which he discovers his secondariness "in relation to the signifier" (Four, 141–42).[15] Like Lacan's subject, Rossetti's Urscelyn lacks real phallic power and must obtain what he desires through art—in its senses of professional skill and of trickery alike. Confirming Urscelyn's false claim to power is his name, which Rossetti seems to have etymologically contrived from the Greek and Latin roots for Ur-scelus, or "Criminal Tail," further implying that the character's phallic prerogative is unsound. Urscelyn is thus in this sense, too, an artist figure, residing outside the sphere of privilege, intruding upon it surreptitiously, and, once inside, rendering a violence to the privacy of its women. The consequence is that, as with so many of Rossetti's figures, he must reside in the shadow, perpetually evading the illumination that would show up his castration.

The situation in "The Bride's Prelude" ends inconclusively, with Aloÿse awaiting Urscelyn full of dread and the intention of bitter revenge (499–500). It is suggestive that Rossetti published the poem in an incomplete form, never adding the second part, in which he had planned to have Urscelyn killed in a duel. By not completing this poem, Rossetti was not required to either symbolically confirm the castration of this contentious male figure or to place him within the scene of burning guilt in which Aloÿse abides. Given Rossetti's comments about exposure in "Jenny," we may imagine that this erasure allowed Rossetti not to represent Urscelyn—and his desire—directly. By never appearing in the action, Urscelyn remains an absence shadowed on the scene of actions, like the artist who forms a "stain" on his paintings, to use Lacan's term (Four, 97). Insofar as it preempts Urscelyn's appearance, "A Bride's Prelude" gives a preliminary sense of the dynamics of the gaze in Rossetti's later portraits, which tend to bypass the depiction of men and bestow all value and meaning onto women and their faces.

"The Staff and Scrip" is the last major narrative poem that Dante Gabriel Rossetti initiated, and the one that constructs the most overt triangular tableau between a male artist, a woman, and a judging Other. Rossetti based "The Staff and Scrip" on a tale in the *Gesta Romanorum*, a medieval collection of Latin stories characterized by their morals, but he gave the tale an entirely original meaning through his interpolations and changes

(*Works*, 649n). The original story follows the relationship between a pilgrim and the lady he pledges to assist, whose lands are being harried by an evil duke. In return, the pilgrim asks the lady to keep his staff and scrip, symbolic of the Christian pilgrimage and the Christian Word, but the lady discards these items and so becomes an exemplar of spiritual corruption (Ferguson, 181). Rossetti's version of "The Staff and Scrip" transforms it into a different sort of moral fable, about a man who sacrifices life and love in exchange for the artistic and spiritual inspiration that a woman can provide. In Rossetti's version of the fable, the lady is a queen; the queen does not discard, but keeps, the staff and scrip, proving her faith to the pilgrim and giving another indication in Rossetti's work of his high regard for women.

Moreover, this queen does not merely take gifts but gives them, indicating Rossetti's sense of the important role played by women in providing a route to phallic goods within the symbolic order. When the pilgrim places his staff into the care of the woman, the queen lends him "a sharp sword" (76), symbolizing Christian martyrdom (Ferguson, 182) but also conveying that service to her is what will obtain for the pilgrim a measure of phallic status. The pilgrim then suggestively kisses the sword "all bare, instead of her," perhaps to sublimate his desire for the queen into a hysterical intention to serve the Other to whom she has given him access (78–80). The other two gifts that the lady bestows on the pilgrim identify him distinctly as an artist. The first is a "green banner wrought / [w]ith one white lily stem, / [t]o bind his lance," upon which the pilgrim writes and kisses "her name" (81–85). The banner appears to be symbolic of writing, and the manner in which the pilgrim "bind[s]" the phallic lance with the banner suggests an association between artistic inspiration and symbolic pursuit. The queen's last gift is "a white shield" upon which the pilgrim "blen[ds] fair hues that sh[i]ne" to produce an image of "her face," which he also kisses (86–90). The shield doubtlessly symbolizes the craft of painting, in which the artist, like Rossetti, relies on the female face as a mystical charm by which he hopes to lure the favor of the Other. Overall, the pilgrim seems to embody the role of a hysterical artist-writer who is dependent on woman not merely for inspiration but for his means to articulate that inspiration and thereby vindicate himself within a phallic economy.

"The Staff and Scrip," like "The Blessed Damozel," also suggests that the regime of the Other is not quite just. The pilgrim dies in battle because his sword breaks "where he had kissed the blade," revealing his failure to adequately appease the Phallic Other, perhaps insofar as he had inadequately sublimated his desire (157). The theology of "The Staff and Scrip" is thus as merciless as that of "The Blessed Damozel," not allowing a man to redeem himself through decency or good works. The most troubling moment in this poem occurs when the queen, who is mourning the pilgrim, seeks consolation from the holy scrip that he left her, hoping that "letters writ to calm / [h]er soul lay in the scrip" (177–78). Instead, she finds nothing but "a torpid balm / [a]nd dust of palm" (179–80) that symbolize empty words and ashes (Ferguson, 36). This revelation of the meaninglessness of the supposedly holy text that the pilgrim had left for the queen further conveys that phallic access is elusive to a perverse degree, as it confirms that the sincere pilgrim never had any real sacred knowledge.

Nonetheless, the ballad narrator of "The Staff and Scrip" still maintains the reality of a divine Other. At the conclusion of the poem, the narrator's suddenly oracular voice charges the dead knight to "stand up . . . still armed . . . before His brow" and claim his desired queen in the form of an "imperishable peace" to which she has been transformed by their "jealous God"—to claim, that is, the sublime end for which the pilgrim had bargained (191, 203). But this consolation of peace feels hollow in the context of the poem, as to obtain it the pilgrim has had to forfeit everything he ever valued in life—not only his desire for the queen but also his writing, his art, and the glimmer of meaning that he seems to have tried to pass onward (205). The Other in "The Staff and Scrip" thus seems to be no benevolent God who guarantees meaning but rather a version of the perverse superego described in chapter 2 who "benefits from the sacrifice of enjoyment—and always at the subject's expense" (Copjec, 6).[16] As an epilogue to Rossetti's other narrative poems, "The Staff and Scrip" reinforces the merciless nature of the divine Other, who maintains a cruel and arbitrary regime over desiring male subjects.

After the 1850s, when Rossetti wrote "The Staff and Scrip" and the other narrative poems discussed above, he rarely initiated attempts to represent desiring male subjects from an external perspective in either poems or paintings, perhaps because of the consistently disturbing visions of the fates of such subjects that these works tended to evince. From the 1860s onward, he instead tended to portray the dynamics of male desire either by implication in his female portraiture or at intimate range through his sonnets. In both media, however, Rossetti generally evaded the wider scope of narrative that is opened up in these earlier poems; he thus avoided drawing further disturbing conclusions about the character of the Phallic Other who functions as what Lacan calls the "cause of desire" for the hysterical subject ("Phallus," 287).[17]

The Lure and the Light

In one of his first drawings, Rossetti produced a graphic paradigm that demonstrates how a hysterical subject tries to obtain phallic approval through the mediation of woman. This sketch of Rossetti's pictorial model for phallic access can be seen in his early *Genevieve* (1848), an illustration and revision of Coleridge's poem "Love" (fig. 10). In Coleridge's original poem, a young singer serenades a girl named Genevieve in front of a "ruined tower" topped by a medieval knight; as he sings of how that knight died to save his lady's chastity, he elicits Genevieve's sentiment and her romantic favor, so that finally,

> She fled to me and wept.
> She half enclosed me with her arms,
> She pressed me with a meek embrace;
> And bending back her head, looked up,
> And gazed upon my face.
> (84–88)

Coleridge's "Love" can be taken as a commentary on the ironies of Romantic literature, in which actual, modern masculinity is depleted like a ruined tower, but men can still associate themselves with fictitious, symbolic heroes to achieve their artistic and literal seductions. This dynamic portrayed by Coleridge thus resembles Lacan's paradigm of "display" as an element of courtship, whereby the man seeks to "identify himself with the ideal type of his sex" to make a good impression on a woman (*Four*, 193). As Lacan further explains, the male bent on seduction must "overvaluat[e]" his attributes by association, given that the phallus is "lacking in the real" and can only be appropriated through some relation to a phallic symbol (*Four*, 100–102). Coleridge's singer who inflates his masculinity is no more of an imposter than is his female counterpart, however, for Genevieve puts on what Lacan calls a masquerade of femininity ("Phallus," 290), producing crocodile tears of sentiment out of an instinct that the narrator characterizes as "partly love . . . partly fear / and partly . . . bashful art" ("Love," 89–90). Through their impostures, Coleridge's man and woman become ordinary embodiments of the normative sexuality that Lacan defines as the activity/passivity opposition

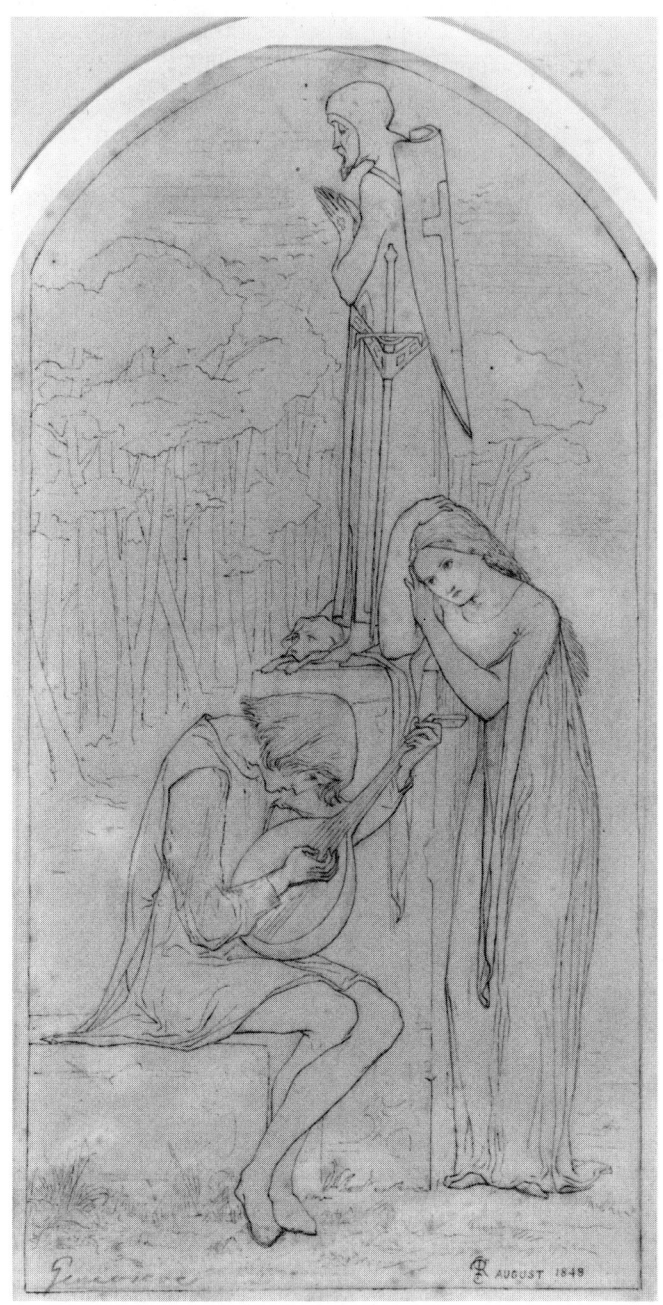

FIGURE 10. D. G. Rossetti, Design for *Genevieve* (1848). Pen and ink, 26.3 x 14 cm. Fitzwilliam Museum no. 0748. Photograph © Fitzwilliam Museum, University of Cambridge.

(Four, 193), as the singer ardently "gaze[s] upon [Genevieve's] face" while she maintains "downcast eyes" (26, 28). The couple through these means obtain their appropriate sexual and symbolic rewards without any difficulty, as the singer "w[ins] [his] Genevieve / [his] bright and beauteous bride" as handily as a knight might have done (95–96).

Rossetti's illustration of *Genevieve* swerves the material away from Coleridge's ironic account of sexual display and masquerade to produce a very different account of gender relations in the symbolic order. To begin with, Rossetti undoes many of the conventional oppositions of courtship that Coleridge's poem exemplifies. Rossetti's singer does not gaze ardently at Genevieve as Coleridge's singer does but seems absorbed in playing his lyre, while Rossetti's Genevieve does not blush coyly but dotes with majestic sympathy on the singer—not really needing to be conventionally courted, given her relative degree of power. Rossetti moreover emphasizes Genevieve's importance within the phallic economy of the poem by illustrating one of the few stanzas of Coleridge's poem that gives primary attention to her (Surtees, 7):

> She leaned against the armed man
> The statue of the armed knight
> She stood and listen'ed to my lay
> Amid the lingering light.
> ("Love," 13–16)

Rossetti has also focused his illustration on the moment in "Love" when Genevieve seems most sincere, rather than artificial as Coleridge tends to capture her, and thereby registers a shift in the tone of art away from Romantic irony concerning gender relations and toward a more distinctly Victorian reverence for the spirito-aesthetic rapture that women, in their triumphant goodness, may prompt in men. The passage illustrated also anticipates the precise value that such women would hold for Rossetti in later workings-out of this theme, which is to provide a link between ordinary, humble men and potent, abstract Others. Another change from Coleridge's depiction is that the tower in Rossetti's drawing is not ruined but is instead perfectly intact; this produces a significant change in the couple's relation to the knight, who is no longer a relic, ironically brought to life by the couple's discourse, but a living and powerful presence. The singer for his part meekly studies his instrument, seemingly to produce the sentimental effect that will illuminate Genevieve's face, in the hopes that her beauty will, in turn, help him gain the attention of the knight.

Rossetti seems also to have aged the knight, who is described in Coleridge's poem as "bold and lovely" and thus potentially identifiable with the singer. In Rossetti's illustration, the knight is portrayed as a stern father who seems to signal some degree of disapproval of the bent young singer by directing his gaze away from him. Rossetti's alternative casting of singer, woman, and knight in an order of ascending dignity and power emblematizes the hysterical structure of the gaze in Rossetti's work more generally. It also aptly expresses the thrust of hysterical desire in Rossetti's works, in which the male's desire for the woman is secondary to his need to attract the desire of the male Other, while at the same time conveying the woman's precise function within the artist's hysterical arrangement, to soften and mystify what would otherwise be an unbearable submission to the Other.

In his Art Catholic paintings, *The Girlhood of Mary Virgin* (1849) and *Ecce Ancilla Domini!* (1850), Rossetti began to express these dynamics of the gaze through a more implicit logic of light and darkness. In *The Girlhood of Mary Virgin*, Rossetti portrays the young Mary and her mother, whom he modeled on Christina and on their mother, as they embroider a potted lily that is symbolic of the unborn Christ and is being held by an angel (fig. 11). Through a window, we can see Mary's father, St. Joachim, tending vines around the roof of the house. As Rossetti biographer Jan Marsh points out, the division of labor in this painting matches the Victorian division between a feminine sphere of simple and holy activity within the domestic context and a masculine sphere of work and achievement in the greater world (DGR, 12). However, gender is more than a cultural divider in this painting; it is also a metaphysical one, as we can see from the strong differential of light that distinguishes the female figures inside from the man outside. The virgin, her mother, and the angel are all brightly illuminated by a gleam that appears to be entering the house from the front of the canvas rather than through the window at the back, given the direction of the shadows. St. Joachim, outside, is lit in far less radiant daylight hues and therefore seems to be less sanctified by the holy gaze that is blessing the iconic scene. In this regard, *Girlhood of Mary Virgin* figures an allegory of gender division within the Rossetti family, such that religion in the Rossetti household was "a female affair" sweeping up the daughters while Gabriele Rossetti and his sons tended toward agnosticism, a distinction that reinforced the more general Victorian division between female holiness and male fallenness along gender lines (Marsh, DGR, 27).

The dynamics of the gaze depicted in *Girlhood of Mary Virgin* also dramatize Rossetti's gendered metaphysics of male exclusion from the gaze of

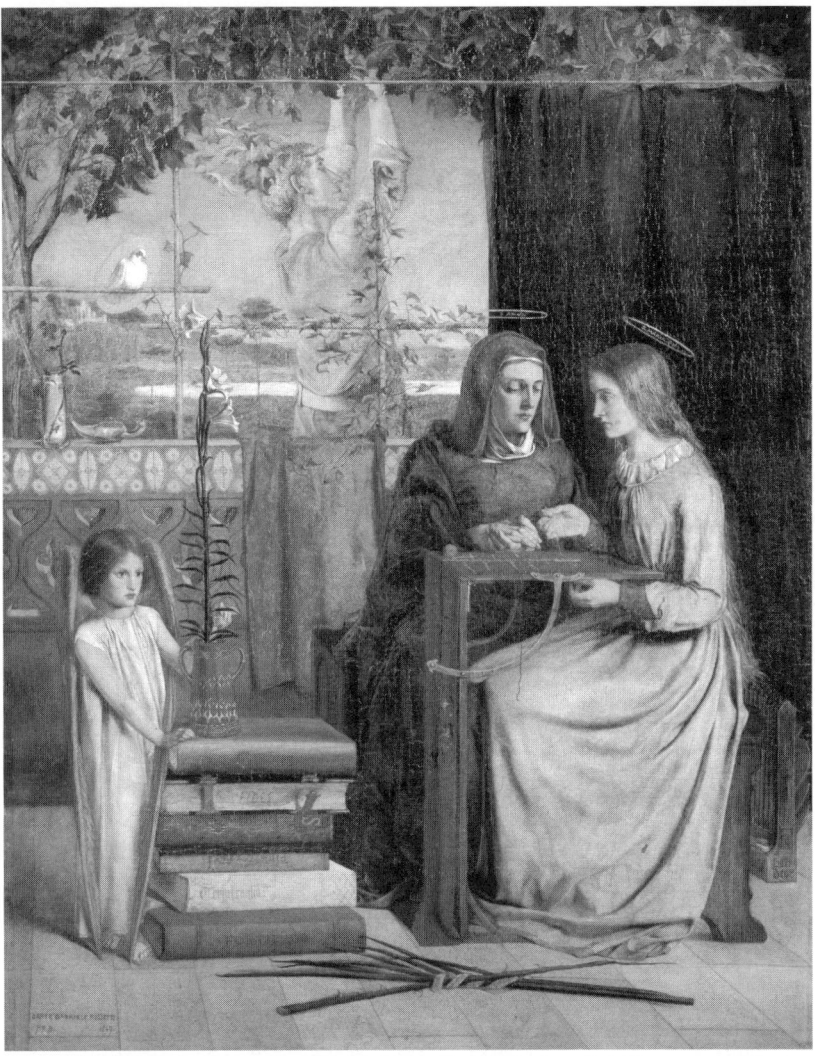

FIGURE 11. D. G. Rossetti, *The Girlhood of Mary Virgin* (1848–49). Oil on canvas, 83.2 × 65.4 cm. Tate Gallery, London. Photo credit: Tate, London/Art Resource, NY.

the Other more broadly. This drama of male exclusion is given additional content in *Ecce Ancilla Domini!*—a more complex composition that portrays the annunciation granted by the angel Gabriel to the Virgin Mary. The signature element of this painting is the lighting, which bathes the scene of *Ecce Ancilla Domini!* in a white field so conspicuous that the painting was subsequently referred to by Rossetti as "the ancestor of all the white paintings which have since become so numerous" as well as "an ideal motive for whiteness."[18] This whiteness obviously signifies the intense importance and attraction this scene holds for the Other, a suggestion affirmed in Kristeva's discussion of religious Renaissance art, where she notes that white traditionally signifies "the transcendental dominion of One" (Desire, 224). From Rossetti's perspective, however, the whiteness of Ecce Ancilla Domini! did not simply ratify the sublimity of the annunciation but produced a harsh glare on the painting that he acknowledged in his reference to the painting as a "blessed white eye-sore" (Letters, vol. 1, 124). Rossetti's description recalls Lacan's observation of the potentially blinding effect of the gaze when it condescends to "show[ ] itself to a subject," which Lacan suggests is comparable to when one is confronted with an excessively bright light and "screws [one's face] up in a well-known grimace" (Four, 94).

In the case of Ecce Ancilla Domini! the glaring effect of the light seems, moreover, to be tied to its representation of a phallic encounter whose sexual implications can never be fully suppressed, and which Rossetti has not restricted himself from suggesting. In his portrayal of the annunciation, he depicts Mary retreating into the corner of her bed, shrinking away from the angel Gabriel, whose foreshortened appearance emphasizes his virile muscularity in contrast with her smallness, as David Sonstroem has observed (37). The angel's phallic intentions are further reinforced by the many sexual objects that surround the virgin, including an erect embroidery stand and a sconce above her head that seems to symbolically combine a staff and grail. The combined effect of these pictorial nuances is to telegraph the forcefulness, and possibly even the mercilessness, of the divine will.[19] Within this scene of light, Rossetti has planted a dark area that suggests the voyeuristic viewer's shameful shadow on this holy but glaring scene. As Lacan explains, in addition to indicating the presence of the Other's gaze in the zone of maximum luminosity, the painter also evokes the shadow of the viewing subject who blocks that gaze in a dark spot in the painting that Lacan variously and interchangeably calls "the screen," "the stain," "the spot," and "the hole" (Four, 96, 108–9). Rossetti has accordingly interrupted the light in one area of Ecce Ancilla Domini! by placing a blue curtain in the corner directly behind Mary. This curtain shades the point in the picture where the glare would otherwise be most fierce, thereby allowing the viewer to see the object upon which the gaze's eye is riveted, "mak[ing] the milky light retreat . . . and allow[ing] the object it concealed [i.e., Mary] to emerge" (Four, 108). But the hole that permits the visibility of the scene also suggests that the viewer of this scene is somehow guilty—because of either

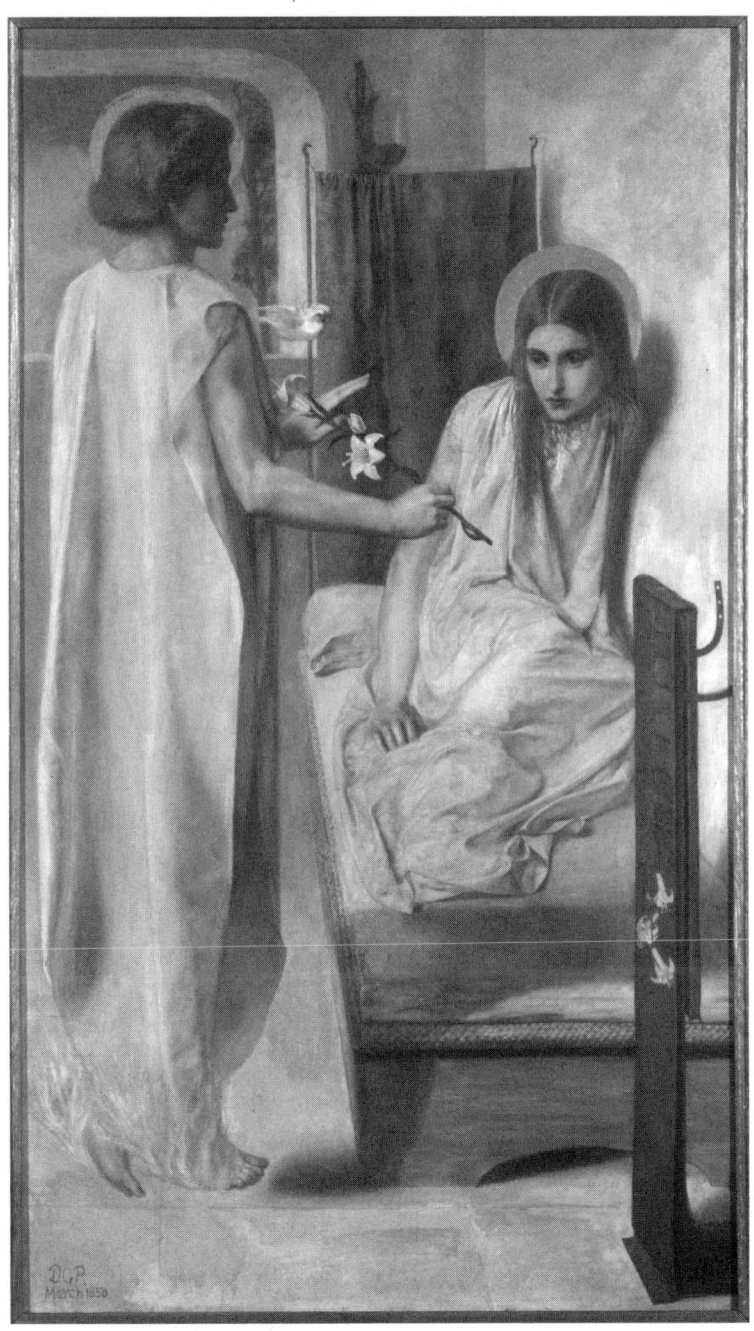

FIGURE 12. D. G. Rossetti, *Ecce Ancilla Domini!* (1849–50). Oil on canvas, 72.4 × 41.9 cm. Tate Gallery, London. Photo credit: Tate, London/Art Resource, NY.

his intrusion or the sexual inferences he is drawing—pointing to the way in which the gazing Other intimidates the viewer with the supremacy of its desire and its power to reinforce the subject's castration through techniques such as humiliation and shame. Rossetti's most famous Art Catholic paintings thus ultimately reveal the same ruthless nature of the Other that can be seen in such Art Catholic poems as "The Blessed Damozel," in which the man is damned while his woman remains bathed in the divine light. In the same way, paintings such as *Girlhood of the Mary Virgin* and the forcefully entitled *Ecce Ancilla Domini!* evoke a tyrannical God who jealously claims all feminine beauty for his own pleasure and either exiles or intimidates their menfolk as well as the implicitly male viewers of the paintings in which the women feature. At the same time, these violent scenes hold obscure gratifications for the viewers. As we have seen, the most fetishistic—and thus, presumably, phallic—imagery is pleasing to the subject insofar as it permits him to dramatize his castration and thereby assume a secure place within a symbolic order beyond the demands of his desire (Žižek, 102). In this way, Rossetti's Art Catholic dramas serve a peculiarly hysterical and self-flagellating form of visual pleasure—one that would be reprised in even his most ostensibly licentious art.

Hysterical Desire in Portraiture

After 1858, Rossetti as a painter shifted away from holy subjects toward distinctly secular ones, generally preferring to paint not illuminated virgins and blessed ladies but more-compromised women from the annals of myth and literature whose faces demonstrate a characteristic mixture of seductiveness, melancholy, and ennui. Critics tend to describe this shift to more-luxurious subjects in Rossetti's works in implicitly judgmental terms, highlighting the intrusion of mercenary motives.[20] But while such readings tend to emphasize differences between Rossetti's earlier and later paintings, analysis of these paintings through Lacan's theories of art reveals significant continuities in Rossetti's art between the two eras. If the divine Other retreats in these later paintings, he seems to be replaced with an array of secular Others with commensurate cultural power, who lay similarly unquestionable claims to the desirable objects that are portrayed. In particular, the contexts of several of Rossetti's portraits of the mid-1860s, such as *Fair Rosamund* (1863) and *Helen of Troy* (1863), reflect specific backgrounds of powerful, jealous men. Rosamund was the concealed mistress of Henry V, and Surtees proposes that the cord held by her right hand is "tighten[ing] as her royal lover approaches" (81), thus indicating through the composition that his regal arrival is at hand for what Lacan calls a "showing" (Fair, 115). The titles of both Rossetti's *Bonifazio's Mistress* (1860) and the later, unrelated *Fazio's Mistress* (1863; fig. 13), based on a courtly poem by Fazio Degli Uberti (1326–60) of Renaissance Florence, likewise hint at an adulterous situation supervened a culturally powerful husband who could wreak some violence against an intruding or voyeuristic viewer in the same way that the jealous god of *Ecce Ancilla Domini!* could.

This model of desire foregrounded in Rossetti's portraiture, in which the object is a high-born married or contested lady, expresses continuity

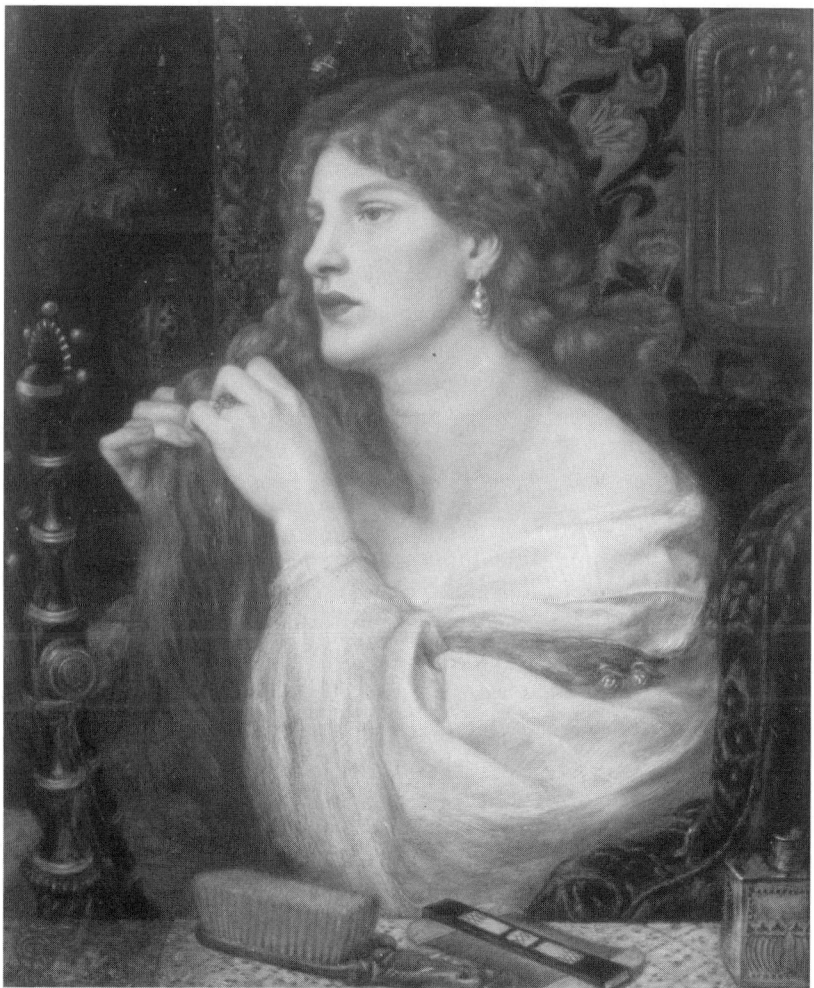

FIGURE 13. D. G. Rossetti, *Fazio's Mistress* (1863–73). Oil on mahogany, 43.2 x 36.8 cm. Tate Gallery, London. Photo credit: Tate, London/Art Resource, NY.

Dante Gabriel Rossetti's Narrative Poems and Portraiture

with the structures of medieval courtly love, which, as Kristeva has described, "aims at completion and remains an adultery" (Tales, 280). In Rossetti's portraiture, as in the records of courtly love, the adulterous situation seems to hold special appeal for culturally marginal male subjects—or "vassal[s]" in Kristeva's terminology (Tales, 280)—insofar as it offers opportunities for them to compensate for their shortfall of symbolic capital by entering the field of the Other's desire through a woman who has access to that field. As Lacan elaborates in his study of courtly love, "the inaccessibility of the object is posited as a point of departure" for a mode of art that allows the subject to solicit a "sign of the Other as such" (SVII, 149, 152). This implied structure relationship perhaps also goes some way toward explaining the typical expression of dissatisfied sensibility upon many of Rossetti's female subjects' faces during the 1860s, as it suggests the quality of lack that underlies the function of the courtly lady, whom Lacan describes as that of a "vacuole" through which the presence of the Other will be transmitted (150). The ladies' longing expressions also provide a space of fantasy for the implied viewer or owner of the painting to fill, as he conceives himself as a candidate for satisfying the lady's ungratified desire and thus imaginatively justifies his precarious presence in her boudoir.

That the role of the man who encroaches upon a powerful husband's symbolic terrain by way of his wife belongs particularly to the artist, moreover, is suggested by Rossetti through his writing of the short story "St. Agnes Intercession" (1850/1904), as well as in his illustration of this story, *Bonifazio's Mistress*. The kernel of "St. Agnes of Intercession" is the tale of a lady from an apparently important family who dies while modeling for her lover (Surtees, 76n). Rossetti was apparently fascinated by this concept, having claimed at the time of painting *Bonifazio's Mistress* that he had been turning it over in his mind for eight years. By painting his dying mistress, the artist might imagine himself capturing the higher-status woman's symbolic capital as it leaves her body, giving an implication of spiritual voyeurism that would be played out more fully when Rossetti composed *Beata Beatrix* in 1864. While in the story the lady is supposed to have perished of natural causes, the decontextualized drawing of *Bonifazio's Mistress* cannot help but imply a relationship between the act of painting and the woman's death, thereby suggesting that the artist's vampiric incursion upon the lady's symbolic terrain can have nefarious consequences, as it unambiguously does in the "Bride's Prelude."[21] In both of these examples, the male protagonist's desperation to lure the gaze of the Other to himself initiates a fatal dynamic.

In other paintings as well, Rossetti signals the background presence of jealous husbands or lovers through his arrangements of light and dark zones. Some of the paintings, such as *Woman Combing Her Hair* (1864), are lit craftily through a reflected window, which suggests the imminent arrival of the husband or at least the likely route of his approach. Others, such as *Helen of Troy* (1863), *Venus Verticordia* (1864), *Monna Pomona* (1864), and *Morning Music* (1864), are illuminated more boldly from the front and like *Ecce Ancilla Domini!* thrust the viewer into the dangerous path of castration by an Other who is looming. This form of triangulation places the artist or viewer in front of the painting in the position of furtive lover or shameful voyeur—a role that contains mixed pleasures, providing for a momentary triumph of access, a titillating threat of discovery, and finally, a prospect of symbolic relief through castration. This last prospect—that the paintings promise castration—is suggested insofar as several of these front-lit paintings from the mid-1860s are particularly fetishistic, surrounding the depicted women with fierce symbols of phallic violence that give content to the implied threat of a showing by the Other. *Venus Verticordia*, who with her naked bosom is a figure of Eve in the garden but also of a harlot, holds an apple of temptation as well as an arrow to signify the violence that would be inflicted upon the beholder by her jealous God if the promise of the pleasure she offers up were to be taken. *Helen of Troy* similarly fingers her pendant of a torch that symbolizes the destructive fires of war, signifying the destruction that Achilles returned upon Paris and his society in exchange for Paris's presumptuous abduction of her. Moreover, as in the earlier Art Catholic works, where there is typically a God suggested beyond the frame of the painting, the implicit threat of castration is always part of jouissance of the picture, which offers to the viewer a promise of momentary symbolic inflation with the attentions of the coveted woman, alongside the painful threat that his ascent will be instantly terminated and he will be plunged into peril.

This understanding of the libidinal scenario of Rossetti's portraits offers a counterpoint to a typical interpretation of his later work, which is that the women he figured are themselves castrating figures represented by a man who saw femininity as a threatening force that he wished to manage and contain.[22] The focal point for this diagnosis of Rossetti's castration anxiety tends to be *Lady Lilith*, a fetishistic painting of the fatal biblical character upon whose image Rossetti inscribed the sonnet "Body's Beauty" (1867) included subsequently in *The House of Life*. The sonnet warns the reader of the persistent reign of Lady Lilith over men, as she casts a murderous spell through "the bright net she can weave" with her golden hair (5). While this painting is definitely suggestive of a male anxiety concerning feminine sexuality, there remains a question as to whether this anxiety was an especially paradigmatic formation for Rossetti, as has been proposed. Around the time Rossetti was researching the Lilith theme, he was involved in a correspondence with the poet Thomas Gordon Hake in which Rossetti asked Hake to elaborate on the myth of the "perilous principle of femininity" (Marsh, DGR, 286). This theoretical dialogue—rather than any prolonged and paradigmatic attitude toward women—seems to have been the source for Rossetti's engendering of this painting/poem combination. The representation of women as malevolent is relatively rare in Rossetti's oeuvre as a whole; far more commonly, he portrays his women as either full of blessedness or sympathetically laden with a sensibility that betokens lack, as in *La Pia de Tolomei* (1868) and *La Donna della Finestra* (1879). As Riede has pointed out, even the namesake figure in *Lady Lilith* does not look terribly fatal, striking one as yet another of Rossetti's melancholy and languid women—albeit with a mirror. The mirror she holds does suggest that Rossetti's Lilith presents a danger to the subject owing to her extravagant primary narcissism, which can form a trap of lovelessness for the hapless male suitor; such a feline capacity is, however, a far cry from wielding genuine phallic power over him.[23]

Far from agreeing that the paintings of the 1860s reflect some new attitude toward women, I therefore propose that insofar as they treat women as the favorites and lures of a castrating male Other, they are continuous with the function that Rossetti attributes to women in his Art Catholic mode. In other ways, too, there seems to be a relative degree of continuity between the psychodynamics of the two moments. Although Jerome McGann suggests that the later stage of Rossetti's art expresses a "disillusion[ed]" quality that is fundamentally different from the idealistic quality of his earlier phase of painting (*Game*, 346), a Lacanian perspective reveals that Rossetti's later painting is in thrall to the same hysterical principle of desire that seeks the easing of masculine symbolic insecurity in the earlier works. Insofar as there is a move toward de-idealization in these later paintings, it seems to be reflective of a shift in Rossetti's conception of where the ideal abided—within a Dantesque conception of divine holiness or within a secular condition of social inclusion.

Moreover, while this shift plausibly reflected an adjustment in Rossetti's personal sense of value as he grew more materialistic and less in thrall to his initial quasi-religious ideals and scruples, it also shows him aiming to gratify a particular Victorian audience whose sensibilities had likewise developed in this direction. Referring to Freud's theory of the artist,[24] Lacan reiterates that a painter's work has social value insofar as he is capable of "vary[ing] the selection of a certain kind of gaze" in keeping with his "morality"—that is, in keeping with the symbolic priorities of the time (Four, 101). As Lacan elaborates, "if a creation of desire, which is pure at the level of the painter, takes on commercial value . . . it is because its effect has something profitable . . . for that part of society that comes under its influence" (Four, 111). Lacan interprets Freud's notion of artistic profitability as meaning that the painter produces an elevating and Apollonian effect on the mind of his constituents through his manipulation of the gaze, which essentially pacifies the beholder's drives by "encourag[ing] renunciation" (Four, 111). In other words, when a viewer apprehends an aptly suggested Other in the background of a painting, he will relinquish his aggression against that Other and submit himself to it. For Lacan, this dynamic is beneficial to the social orderliness and cohesiveness of society insofar as it renders people willing to accept the castration of their desirous and aggressive selves, to which they are in any event bound as symbolic subjects.

In the case of Rossetti, the morality underlying his selection of the gaze was definitely in flux. Although he was originally in thrall to the Catholic morality of his upbringing, which subjected him to a merciless God, he seems to have gradually given himself over to the morality of his materialistic Victorian milieu, which allowed him as an artist to seek a certain precarious form of class inclusion at the mercy of a privileged cultural Other. In this regard, he ended up selecting a gaze that not only sustained for him the hysterical enjoyments he had always craved but also did a certain kind of social work. The evolution of his morality in this direction was, however, gradual. Rossetti's first sensual painting, *Bocca Baciata* (fig. 14), was painted for George Boyce, a friend who sustained a "mock rivalry" with Rossetti for a number of women, such as his model Fanny Cornforth (Marsh, DGR, 253–59). The traffic in women between Rossetti and Boyce is apparently what instigated Boyce to commission *Bocca Baciata*—"kissed mouth"—which was modeled on Cornforth and led a fellow painter to comment that Boyce "will I expect kiss the dear thing's lips away" (quoted in Surtees, 80). Rossetti also sold Boyce many of his other sexual-toned paintings, including *Bonifazio's Mistress, The Farmer's Daughter* (1865), *Belcolore* (1863), and *The Merciless Lady* (1865), revealing the momentary dominance of homosocial dynamics in his art. Ultimately, however, it was when *Bocca Baciata* favorably impressed his dealer Ernest Gampart that Rossetti began to devise the specifically "Venetian" manner

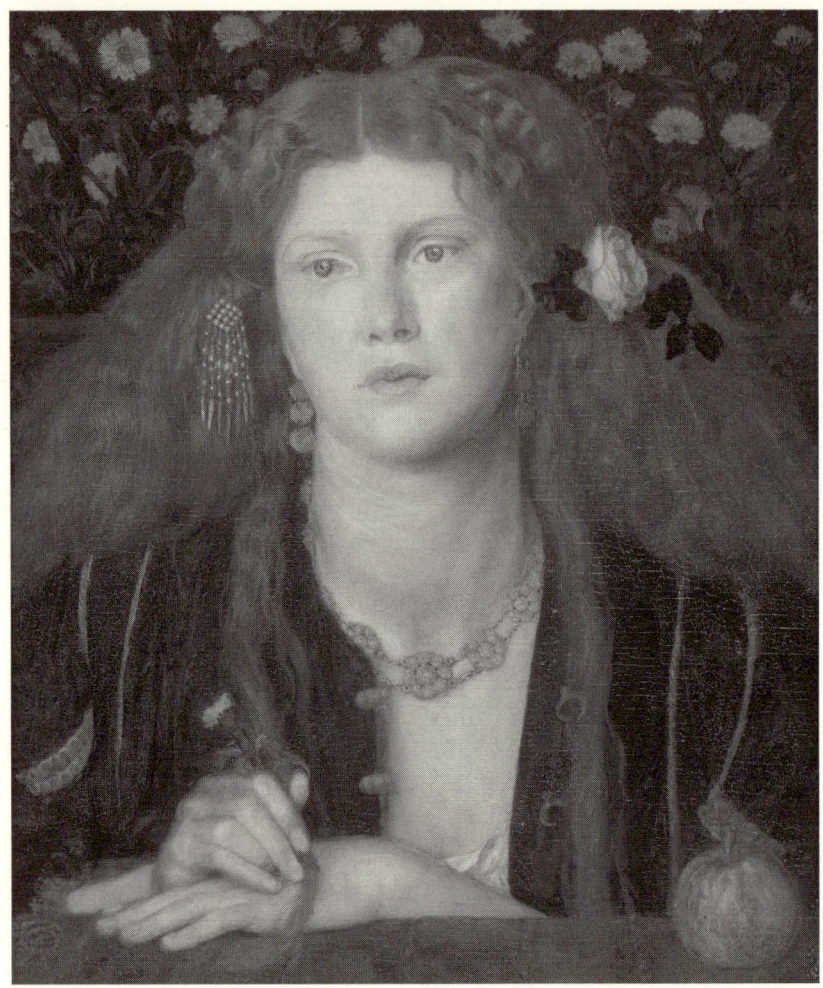

FIGURE 14. D. G. Rossetti, *Bocca Baciata*, 1859. Oil on panel, 32.1 x 27.0 cm (12 5/8 x 10 5/8 in.). Museum of Fine Arts, Boston, Gift of James Lawrence, 1980.261. Photograph © 2008 Museum of Fine Arts, Boston.

of his later work (Marsh, *DGR*, 270). In developing this later mode of portraiture, Rossetti immensely exaggerated the decorative qualities of the *Bocca Baciata*, which is actually fairly undramatic in its arrangement of the model's features and modest in the ornamentation of her person.

Given how the Pre-Raphaelite Brotherhood he had founded had initially opposed the artificiality of Renaissance art, Rossetti had to increase the level of ornament and stylization in later portraits to "bridge the gap between his artistic genius and the vulgar taste," as Riede has suggested

(20). In this regard, Rossetti effectively castrated his artistic desires to obtain an implied patronage, acknowledging his greater need for cultural and material acceptance from an abstract Other that could offer it. An increasing dependence on his dealers throughout this period caused him to swerve away from "the creation of larger, more elevated subjects," Surtees observes, noting how on occasions when Rossetti proposed such subjects, he was generally rejected by his dealers (276).[25] In exchange, Rossetti developed a luxe style of feminine portraiture that was particularly agreeable to attracting the "textile magnates, shipowners, brewers, bankers and the like" that constituted the new art clientele in England (Marsh, DGR, 275).

A number of critics have studied what it was about Rossetti's paintings of the 1860s that appealed to this group of nouveau riche industrialists and merchants. According to such accounts, Rossetti's industrialist clients particularly enjoyed the languid and florid atmosphere of his later stylized paintings, the collection of which allowed them to distinguish themselves from the rest of their pragmatic class by fashioning themselves as "passionate lover[s] of beauty" (MacLeod, "Art," 340). William Gaunt has further observed that Rossetti's romanticism provided industrialists with a "refuge from industry, from the machine" (65). He accordingly quotes the patron Thomas Dixon musing rapturously that Rossetti's paintings reflected "the life which I long for, and which to me never seems realisable in this life" and "produce[d] on the mind such a vague and dreamy sensation, approaching as it were the Mystic Land of a Bygone Age" (Gaunt, 65).

Given that this moment of Rossetti's career is considered to have been strongly influenced by Renaissance portraitists such as Titian,[26] Lacan's account of the operation of the gaze in Renaissance art can be considered particularly helpful for understanding the appeal of Rossetti's later art to this industrialist constituency. While Lacan does not talk about portraiture as such, he does observe that the military murals of the Renaissance period referred to the gazes of "those persons who, when the audience are not there, deliberate in the hall" (113). In a similar way, Rossetti's Venetian-influenced portraiture of the mid-1860s such as *Fazio's Mistress* and *The Blue Bower* (1865) could have succeeded in evoking the implicit gaze of a ruling class of fathers and husbands, transposed from the Renaissance to the Victorian period, thereby permitting an ascendant Victorian class of industrialists to imaginatively penetrate the nobility's private milieu.[27] Along the same lines, Sussman has observed that the same Victorian industrialists who "married into the landed gentry [and] bought ancient country houses" also "took pride in acquiring Italian Renaissance paintings and richly colored Pre-Raphaelite art."[28] One might note that all of these types of acquisitions would have allowed the artworks' owners to insert themselves imaginatively within spheres of uncontested aristocratic privilege, where, incidentally, the painting of women's portraits did assume an explicitly homosocial function of advertising daughters for marriage. This motive of allowing industrialist consumers to intrude upon the sphere of aristocratic privilege aptly demystifies the "vague and dreamy sensation" that Rossetti's patrons, such as Thomas Dixon, obtained from Rossetti's art. The suggestion of a "golden, dim dream" inspired by his paintings was thus not especially inherent in the forms or even in the contents of the paintings but instead arose from the access that they seemed to provide to a traditionally aristocratic domain of leisure and beauty.

At the same time, one would have to conclude that the access to privilege that Rossetti's paintings seemed to offer was largely illusory, given that wealthy industrialists—unlike their contemporaneous noble counterparts—remained bound to work for their money. The illusory nature of this ascendance is perhaps visible in one of Rossetti's special pictorial habits, which was to layer his gorgeous costumes on models who featured physiognomies that were perceived as lower class, as Susan Casteras points out in her observation that critics often condemned his figures' "coarse[ ]" and "common[ ]" bodies (30). Such an effect—by which Rossetti may have subliminally signified the possibility of class mobility—also reinforces the barriers against it, for the implication of Casteras's argument is that the nobility would never have claimed these women as their own. In this regard, the merging of the classes that seems to have been promised through the purchase of Rossetti's art was a purely fictitious one. Moreover, the hysterical structure of the gaze that dominates them, according to which these women are manifestly other people's wives and mistresses as well as lures for a threatened castration, suggests that the middle-class ambitions reflected in these paintings were complemented by a middle-class willingness to have these ambitions thwarted and to reinforce a status as castrated within the hierarchical structure of English society. Thus, while Raymond Williams has observed that industrial capitalism in the mid-Victorian period invented a mystified notion of culture to counteract its dehumanizing practices and provide consolation for a lapsing religious faith, the response of industrialists to Rossetti's paintings of the 1860s suggests that mid-Victorian aesthetic culture may have also had the effect of easing class antagonisms.[29] By placing middle-class industrialists in the line of the aristocratic gaze they coveted, these paintings would have at once made class barriers seem more permeable than they were in reality and also subdued any violent feelings that those of the middle class may have felt toward the privileged class by encouraging the renunciation of a campaign to displace the elites of society.

The Exceptionality of Mary Magdalene

As we have seen, there were side effects to the assumption of commercial value by Rossetti's art, as the courting of this value pushed aside Rossetti's ability to explore the scope of his personal desire. As Gampart insisted that he continue to repeat his most saleable formulae—"innumerable 'visions of carnal loveliness with floral accessories,'" as Rossetti called them (Marsh, DGR, 275), Rossetti found his increasingly popular artistic vocation at odds with his more personal expressions and came to dislike the commercial quality of his work (McGann, "Betrayal," 345). His contempt for his patrons' stupidity and gullibility—he referred to the Yorkshire merchant John Mitchell as "a cad" and to Frederick Craven of Manchester as a "stupid enthusiast"—suggests that he felt frustration at the "prostitution" of his aesthetic practice on behalf of less-sensitive individuals (Marsh, DGR, 275). Perhaps part of the problem was that, to Rossetti, the feminine figure was never exactly circumscribed to a vision of carnal loveliness. As we have seen, Rossetti at his best was not inclined to stereotype. Earlier in his career, he sustained the possibility that the prostitute Jenny has redemptive thoughts and that carnal women such as the blessed damozel could be found in heaven. Even in his later career, Rossetti's most sensually portrayed women are never reducible to their physical appearance; as McGann has noticed, one of Rossetti's persistent strengths as an artist is his animated, sensitive faces, such that even his most symbolically determined paintings of women are "revelations of embodied soul" and "scene[s] of wonderment, inexhaustibly interesting" that exceed the meanings they seem designed to convey (Game, 119–20).

This empathic effect of depth and individuality in his paintings seems to extend to a consistent premise of poems such as "The Blessed Damozel" and "Jenny," as well as the later House of Life sonnets, that a requirement for obtaining grace through the aegis of women is that one must not merely make use of their fetishistic value but also see and love them individually, thereby maintaining some opening for the imaginary level of the subject that underlies his powerful one-to-one connections with others. Kristeva has correspondingly noted that Dante is paradoxically only able to perceive divine presence through Beatrice because he passionately loves her, because although the meaning he seeks is sublime, it is simultaneously "internal to the luminous refractions of the narcissistic world" (*Tales*, 294). This counternarrative is sustained through the painstaking craft and empathic tone of Rossetti's portraiture, which holds out the possibility that if one's perspective on the depicted women does not reduce the women to vehicles of the kinds of stereotypical repetition that the market favors, one may forge some sort of valuable personal meaning through one's connection to these women.

The most eloquent expression of this possibility within Rossetti's art can be seen in a drawing he composed in 1858, at the cusp of his emergence as a popular painter. *Mary Magdalene at the Door of Simon the Pharisee* is based on the New Testament account of how the prostitute Mary Magdalene had "seven demons" expelled from her by Jesus and subsequently became one of Jesus's foremost disciples and witnessed the resurrection (Mark 16:9). This parable thus proves what Rossetti seems in moments to evince in poems such as "Jenny," which is that circumscribing a person's spiritual status in a stereotypical manner is foolish because opportunities for grace can be found in unexpected places. In his drawing of Mary Magdalene, Rossetti raises the possibility that a viewer of his art who is not merely attuned to her carnal loveliness may observe the spiritual potential even in a figure of a sinner. Rossetti's highly detailed illustration presents Mary Magdalene, a Rossettian beauty with flowing hair and longing eyes, being solicited by a clamoring crowd (fig. 15). As Rossetti described in his 1869 sonnet of the same name, the crowd mobs her for her beauty, demanding, "'Why wilt thou cast the roses from thine hair? / Nay, be thou all a rose,—wreath, lips and cheek" (1–2). The crowd is thus thrown into distraction by Mary Magdalene's most stereotypical Rossettian fetishes of femininity—her flowers and her hair—and they try to fix her with these fetishes. Meanwhile, they throw crude sexual offers at her, suggesting that Mary "come thou there" where "this delicate day of love we two will share" (3–5). The consequence of the mob's fixation upon Mary Magdalene's beauty is that they fail to see what is actually illuminating her features with such radiance: the face of Jesus Christ looking at her over the heads of the crowd from Simon the Pharisee's window and emanating a brilliant halo. *Mary Magdalene* thus graphically displays how a glimpse of the Other may be caught through the grace of any woman, if one is attentive enough to notice what she is catching in her own glance. Notably, the drawing's heroine is one of the few women in Rossetti's mature period whose eyes are focused on

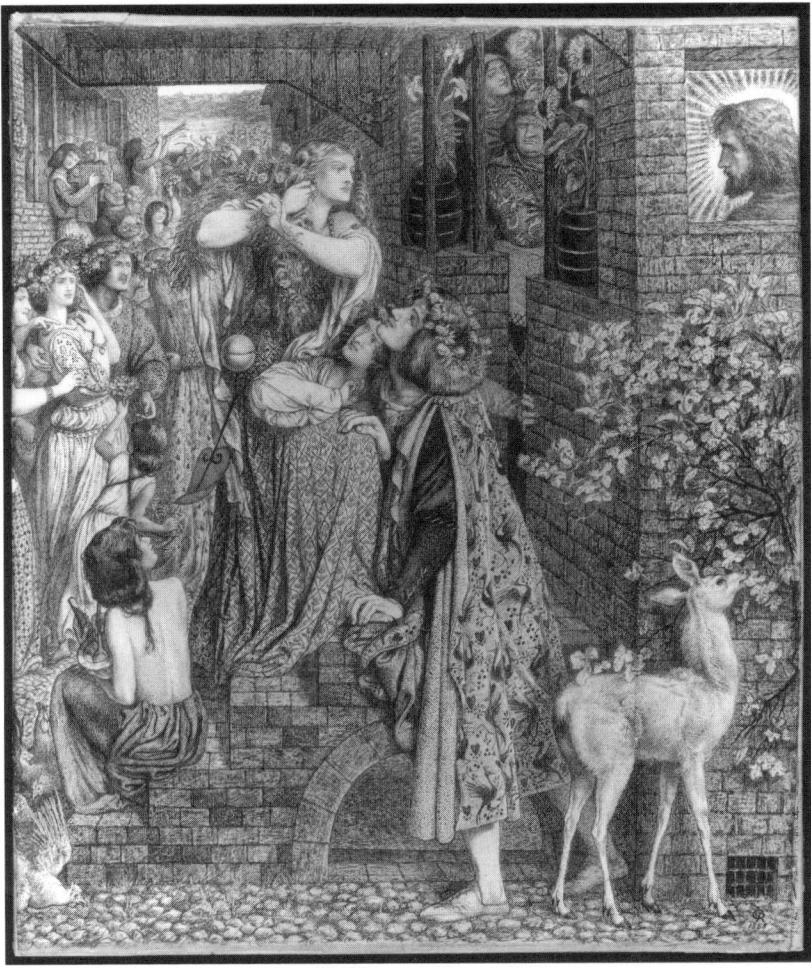

FIGURE 15. D. G. Rossetti, *Mary Magdalene at the Door of Simon the Pharisee* (1858). Pen and Indian ink on paper, 50.8 x 45.7 cm. Fitzwilliam Museum no. 2151. Photograph © Fitzwilliam Museum, University of Cambridge.

a point within the frame, rather than on some obscure point beyond or past the viewer.

This portrayal of a beautiful, ostensibly sinful woman who is, in fact, looking at Jesus must more broadly qualify our assumptions as to where the obscure glances of so many of Rossetti's women lead. *Mary Magdalene*, for instance, offers an alternative to J. Hillis Miller's account of what Rossetti's women are looking at, when he suggests that these women are either narcissistically contemplating themselves or else are looking for a "missing man" who "will not come" (334, 344). This woman contemplates neither herself nor a missing man, but a holy man who cannot be seen from the mob's perspective: the "Bridegroom's face / [t]hat draws [her] to Him" ("Mary Magdalene," 9–10). By implication, though we might not see it, the figures of Rossetti's other portraits may equally be looking towards an Other who is holier than we would have guessed based on the symbolic presentation of these figures. Drawn on the cusp between Rossetti's Art Catholic and Venetian periods, and at once a painting of a holy lady and a sinful lady, *Mary Magdalene* unifies these diverse eras and modes of Rossetti's art, warning against any severe grouping of Rossetti's sinful ladies apart from those of his women who are visibly spiritual. *Mary Magdalene* thus offers another symbolic route for the viewer that is in keeping with the individual attention to the other granted through the mediation of the *objet petit a*, as described in chapter 4, as it demands that the glance of a woman in a painting be individually scrutinized for the chance that she has found out an unexpected power of redemption behind the frame.

At the same time, in his drawing's insistence that one might have to look beyond the immediate content of a scene to understand where the subject is looking, Rossetti the artist might have sought the same regard for himself—insofar as his position as a "prostitute" who subordinates his desires to those of the Other parallels that of Mary Magdalene's. With this painting, Rossetti thus outlines a defense of the popular artist who may sell damnable wares but could nonetheless remain capable of signaling a higher redeeming force. Alert viewers must likewise be attentive to the glance of the artist, the drawing says, lest one fail to glimpse the heights at which he gazes.

Conclusion

> Beyond the seas we know, stretch seas unknown
>   Blue and bright-colored for our dim and green;
>   Beyond the lands we see, stretch lands unseen
> With many-tinted tangle overgrown;
> And icebound seas there are like seas of stone,
>   Serenely stormless as death lies serene.
>   —Christina Rossetti, *Later Life*

> Some prisoned moon in steep cloud-fastnesses,—
>   Throned queen and thralled; some dying sun whose pyre
>   Blazed with momentous memorable fire;—
> Who hath not yearned and fed his heart with these?
> Who, sleepless, hath not anguished to appease
>   Tragical shadow's realm of sound and sight
>   Conjectured in the lamentable night? . . .
> Lo! the soul's sphere of infinite images!
>   —Dante Gabriel Rossetti, "The Soul's Sphere"

CHRISTINA ROSSETTI AND DANTE GABRIEL ROSSETTI, as members of a singular Victorian moment and heirs of an intersecting array of cultural literary influences, managed to weave richly colored Pre-Raphaelite tapestries of art and letters that are at the same time highly intricate maps of the workings of desire. In the Rossetti oeuvres, literary and pictorial forms double as protopsychoanalytic codes in which the Victorian desiring subject is revealed in all of his or her division as well as in his or her glory. Through the development of aesthetic products that refract unwieldy unconscious forces into beautiful and revealing spectra, both Rossettis undertook the project that would be set out by Freud as that of clinical psychoanalysis of colonizing obscure fields of id with intelligible edifices of ego. The Rossettis did not merely craft these edifices out of private motifs and fantasies but gave shape to Lacan's idea of the symbolic order as a network from which all projects of symbolization necessarily draw. The two siblings accordingly sculpted a recognizable and shared range of cultural motifs from classical, biblical, and Romantic sources to articulate the tug of instinctual compulsions and the self's projects to transcend these. From such sources, Rossetti art derived both its demonic character—Christina's lurid underworlds, Dante Gabriel's shadowlands—and its holy tints—its radiant aureoles and crystalline expanses. From such sources, the Rossetti siblings also extracted their imagistic vocabulary for the earthy realms in between—the florid gardens and vertiginous pools that contain abysses of unfathomable and dangerous bliss.

Over time, in the course of mapping out of these landscapes of myth that double as conditions of the psyche, both Rossettis came to know themselves. We can see this in how they increasingly shaped these cultural materials into deliberate and satisfying expressions of their personal vistas. Thus, in Sonnet 23 from *Later Life*, Christina uses a sublime scene to give lucent form to the most abstract form her faith would take, picturing "seas unknown / [b]lue and bright-colored" (1–2) as the unintelligible zone of the Other: that pole of our desire that Lacan also calls "the Thing" that orients our sublimation and that "is impossible for us to imagine" (SVII, 125). Likewise, in "The Soul's Sphere/52" (1873), one of Dante Gabriel's later contributions to *The House of Life*, he portrays the value to him of sources of illumination that are always growing more obscure—a "dying sun" and a "prison'd moon"—but that at least are ready-to-hand, banked within his personal imaginative repertoire, "the soul's sphere of infinite images" (1–2, 8). In these two examples, we can glimpse the convergence in the Rossettis' aesthetic and ideological projects, both dependent as they were on metaphysical constructions of landscape and of light to convey their quests for ultimate values. We can also see divergences in how they plotted the chiaroscuric Pre-Raphaelite landscapes of their progresses. For Christina, light was purgative but benevolent, and the stations on her route formed a boundless linear sequence to an ultimate luminosity. For Dante Gabriel, the stations amounted to a series of aesthetic installations to be circulated among in a perpetual connoisseurship. Here the light had to remain dim, witnessed as it was primarily reflected off of the figures of beautiful women.

The Rossettis in their separate projects meanwhile affirm a certain suspicion that, in the mid-Victorian period, illumination properly fell upon the sphere of women—an imbalance not merely aesthetic but also metaphysical, given how, as discussed in chapter 5, the gleam of light is expressive of the gaze of the Other. In these terms, while Christina had the symbolic confidence to put herself in the line of the light, Dante Gabriel designed triangular arrangements to throw some light of the gaze back upon himself, finding its direct glance an eyesore. This contrast between Christina's attraction to the light and Dante Gabriel's dread of it appears to be grounded in a broader chiasma of gender developments in mid-Victorian England that granted Christian female subjects the courage to approach luminous realms of divine holiness through practices of sublimation while deterring men from such pursuits. This Victorian turn of events is especially interesting given that sublimation is typically presented as a masculine prerogative within psychoanalytic theory, with Freud's most developed example being that of Leonardo da Vinci, and Lacan's being that of the courtly troubadours along with Dante Alighieri.[1]

A reason for the typical gendering of sublimation as a masculine pursuit may be found in a gloss that Lacan makes on Freud's exposition of the concept of sublimation. A viable route of sublimation, as Lacan explains, consists of a socially established practice for disdaining the libidinal claims of most objects at the same time as it "raise[s] [one] object . . . to the dignity of the Thing" (*SVII*, 112). While Freud conspicuously dwells on the psychic benefits of sublimation as the achievement of a "way out" from ego demands ("Narcissism," 95), Lacan emphasizes that the criterion that actually links together and distinguishes instances of sublimation is their generation of a product that brings "social recognition" to its producer (*SVII*, 107). We can understand why this aspect of sublimation would be central for Lacan insofar as he understands all signification as occurring within a symbolic grid in which subjects find their place; in this regard, the insertion of the subject into the symbolic field is what compensates her or him for renounced ego demands. Because there have been many more types of discursive and artistic activity that have brought social recognition to men than those that have brought equivalent recognition to women, it seems probable that the kind of libidinal stability specifically associated with sublimation has, in general, been more accessible by the former than the latter.

Curiously, however, in the mid-Victorian period, the most prominent and hallowed Christian routes of sublimation were favored practices for the female sex at the same time as they were deemed to be unviable and unattractive among men. During this period, as Christ-like qualities such as passivity and self-sacrifice increasingly overlapped with the Victorian expectations of femininity, Christianity's practices of symbolic self-purification and seeking after redemption came to seem feminized, or disposed for women.[2] That Jesus was seen as the ultimate exemplar of women's virtues is suggested by the treatment of the figure by Pre-Raphaelite artist Holman

Hunt, who constructed "The Light of the World" (1853), his famous portrait of Jesus, using female as well as male models (Sussman, *Masculinities*, 125–26). A phenomenon of increasing numbers of women publishing pious texts simultaneously caused the feeling to take root that, in the words of Archdeacon Harris, "there is no higher form [of Christianity] than that of a highly educated devout English woman."[3] This belief that women were especially suited to Christian virtues emerged concurrently with the establishment of convents of different denominations in which Victorian spinsters were challenged to reprise the medieval practices of Catholic nuns by exchanging their sexual feelings for "ideal-love in the religious sense" and generally pursuing "self-conquest."[4]

As we have seen, Lacan contends that the quest for spiritual goals does not in itself meet the psychoanalytical definition of sublimation, which also requires the production of some culturally valued product. But as Mary Arseneau has recently portrayed at length, the Anglo-Catholic sisterhoods, as well as the informal female communities that circulated around the Tractarian churches of the mid-Victorian period, presented a significant context for the aesthetic practices of female religious poets such as Christina Rossetti.[5] Although Christina did not join an Anglo-Catholic sisterhood, there are ample signs that she saw herself as an auxiliary to their projects: for instance, in how she particularly addresses women in her devotional writings and promotes "sisterhood" at the end of *Goblin Market*, a position generally taken to refer to the work of Anglican sisterhoods in rescuing fallen women.[6] Meanwhile, Christina simultaneously pursued a more general relevance for her work within the aesthetic culture at large, as we can see in her decisions to print her secular and her religious poetry side by side in the same volumes. Lacan's redefinition of sublimation as the simultaneous pursuit of both of these aims—recognition by both the Other and the community—helps to explain the indivisibility of spiritual and aesthetic agendas in her writing.

Christina Rossetti's writing arguably meets the standard of sublimation in another sense as well, insofar as in it she moves deliberately beyond the hazards of idealization that Peter Cominos sees permeating the ascetic practices of Victorian women, whereby women were encouraged to stream libidinal desire toward the idealized image of Jesus (159). In his Freudian reading of this phenomenon, Cominos proposes that the expectation of innocence placed upon Victorian women prevented them from recognizing the libidinal origins of their religious impulses, leading to widespread neurotic repression. As discussed in chapter 1, Christina seems to recognize this same danger; although at times her work does show her speakers diverting libidinal drive toward a divine object, she eventually completes the circuit of sublimation by reshaping that drive into a properly symbolic impetus for metaphysical and ethical investigation. We can see the symbolic potency of her work particularly well in the later sonnets of the *Later Life* sequence, where she reflects on the kernel of "emptiness" at the heart of the numinous that for Lacan centers all sublimatory energies in art (*SVII*, 130). Christina describes the human pursuit of the divine as passing over a vast, empty space between earthly and heavenly existence: "[L]ifeless tracts of sand, which intervene / Betwixt the lands where living flowers are blown" (23.7–8). Her tone is melancholy as she speaks of the "wide vacuity of hope and heart" that inevitably frames her emotional existence, distorted as it is by her immersion in temporal unreality (25.6, 25.10). But she nonetheless keeps up her fortitude to solicit a "sign of the Other" across this field of emptiness (Lacan, *SVII*, 152), as she finally asks to see unveiled "Death who art not death"—a brazen bid for a glimpse of presence within the heart of the void (26.14).

Here, as elsewhere, Christina Rossetti shows how her renunciation of earthly substitutes for "the Thing" allows her to develop a powerfully exclusive relationship with her Other. Although her Other is undeniably phallic, she shows in such discursive displays that she requires no male priest or conspicuously male anthropomorphic form to mediate her relation to it. Indeed, while Christina's feminist credentials are in many respects poor, her insistence on progressing autonomously toward her Other represents a distinctive feminist achievement, and one through which her female readers perhaps benefited. Martha Vicinus has argued that the authority and high status that women within Anglican sisterhoods achieved permitted their symbolic development in previously unavailable directions: "The Anglican sisterhoods were . . . among the first to insist upon a woman's right to choose celibacy, to life communally, and to do meaningful work. . . . [They consequently] empowered women, validating women's work and values in a world that seemed materialistic, godless, and male" (83). Although Vicinus puts the emphasis on the symbolic benefits of the community work that the women in these sisterhoods practiced, the discursive activities that circulated in these communities offered symbolic benefits, allowing women to climb the ranks of the Christian cosmic hierarchy and to accrue a commensurate degree of symbolic status. Perhaps, too, such discursive forms of empowerment rallied confidence in Victorian women for other forms of incursion into masculine prestige.

Meanwhile, at the same time as women such as Christina Rossetti were benefiting from opportunities for sublimation, men such as Dante Gabriel Rossetti were apparently being obstructed from them. As discussed in chapter 3, Dante Gabriel initially held out some hope of pursuing a courtly path of sublimation in emulation of Dante's medieval style. Although Dante Gabriel consistently suggested through his speakers that the obstacles to such a path emerged primarily from his own character, which lacked the steadfastness of courtly love's path of renunciation, the times themselves also militated against such a pursuit. As Lacan insists, courtly discourse—like the discourse of sublimating desire toward the divinity that Christina Rossetti expounded—is fundamentally one of "holding back, of suspension, of *amor interruptus*," whereby one refuses to allow the drives to attach themselves to any real content (*SVII*, 163). The writer of a courtly discourse must accordingly seek after the same aesthetic goal of registering "emptiness" as any other venturer on a sublime quest, in his case by worshipping a lady who is so utterly inaccessible in her perfection that desire on the libidinal level attenuates to make way for gratification on the symbolic level (152). The lady whom the courtly lover worships with his full vocabulary of extravagant praise accordingly functions as a coded screen for an unrepresentable phallic presence, whereby "a blessing or salutation [from the lady] is for the courtly lover . . . the sign of the Other as such" (152)."[7] Since the Renaissance, Lacan argues, this capacity for representing the lady as an insubstantiality so that she can act as a screen for the Other has been extinguished (112); Kristeva agrees that courtliness has been revived in more recent centuries "only as an impossible, if baleful, ideal" (*Tales*, 296).

A sense of how the courtly pattern of sublimation through an idealized female object had become unviable by the nineteenth century is reflected upon by Dante Gabriel Rossetti in his early short story "Hand and Soul" (1849; in *Collected Writings*, 47–58). In this piece, he portrays a young English traveler in Italy who is struck by the quiet merit of a painting of a simply clothed woman by a minor thirteenth-century painter named Chiaro di Messer Bello dell' Erma. The traveler learns that Chiaro's subject was a female angel who had appeared to him, producing the sublime effect "that the first thoughts he had ever known were given him as at first from her eyes, and he knew her hair to be the golden veil through which he beheld his dreams" (53). This woman teaches Chiaro the virtues of aesthetic and spiritual sincerity and so becomes the guide to a spiritual sublimation in which desire itself is the vehicle of holy ascent, as it was for Dante Alighieri. The angel instructs Chiaro that he will know that a subject is ratified by God by seeing that "his flame is upon it for a sign"; as he grows sensitive to this sign, the angel advises, God will "learn to hold communion with thee, and at last own thee above him" (55)—an indication of the heights of symbolic prestige available to one who renounces his libidinal relation to the object on behalf of its ability to pass to him a sign from the Other.

Notwithstanding the immense blessing that this painting receives at the time of its conception, in Dante Gabriel Rossetti's story it is completely overlooked by what are Victorian-age visitors to the gallery. The curator ignores it, involved as he is with his collection of sensuous Guido de Renis. The young art students fail to notice it, endeavoring as they are to copy a presumably buxom Raphael (58). The painting is thus stranded amid other cultural distractions, its winsome, ideal subject having failed to sustain an impression over the succeeding centuries of art with their accretion of ornamented, material females. In Dante Gabriel's depiction of how this painting of an idealized and numinous object fails to attract favor in his time, "Hand and Soul" indicates his recognition that a pure and sincere rendering of a lady as the ethereal screen of a divine presence would have brought an artist no social recognition in the nineteenth century, and perhaps also his intuition that measures for investing ladies with the earthiness and personality that we have seen Dante Gabriel cultivating were necessary to convey the dynamics of his age.

It is possible that Dante Gabriel Rossetti even sensed what theorists of Victorian masculinity have since articulated: Victorian codes of desire tended to militate against male practices of restraint and renunciation in art as in life, instead legislating procedures of expenditure and consummation. In particular, what was approved of in the spheres of political economy, sexuality, and art was a condition of a "regulated flow," as Herbert Sussman describes (*Masculinities*, 132). James Eli Adams similarly observes the prevalence of a critical consensus in the Victorian arts that "equate[d] sexual with artistic potency," whereby male enterprise, like capital, was to be thriftily husbanded and then conspicuously discharged under favorable circumstances.[8] Within this context, performances of effacing the body for idealized aims tended to engender irritation in the Victorian period, as critics, for instance, referred to medieval artistry as "sexually neurastheni[c]" and tended to view early Pre-Raphaelite presumptions to reproduce the medieval atmosphere of austerity and purity as similarly unmasculine (*Masculinities*, 84). At the time, even the idea of a brotherhood of painters aroused sexual anxieties, as Sussman observes

(*Masculinities*, 139). Given the symbolic pressure toward masculine flow and discharge within the capitalist economic models that also commanded male sexuality and art, an artistic or poetic practice of courtly sublimation that cultivated the virtues of *amor interruptus* would plausibly have been difficult for a man to sustain. To have produced unearthly inaccessible ladies in this age of realism would, in turn, have been to render oneself perverse as well as irrelevant. One can trace this tension between ideality and concreteness in Dante Gabriel Rossetti's early verse. In "The Blessed Damozel," for example, the speaker's suggestion that the damozel exerts a "bosom's pressure" testifies to the inability of the speaker to sustain the degree of reserve necessary to render her as a courtly image (1850 edition, 51). Similarly, the speaker of "Jenny" cannot elevate his subject above her compromising circumstances into a Magdalene, however much he gestures in this direction. Instead of being courtly lovers, these fellows are sites of Victorian duality, alternating between spiritual aspirations and all-too-earthy circumstances, and there is consequently no seed of sublime redemption enwrapped in their desire, as there is for Chiaro—only, at best, the compensatory rewards of an all-too-human love.

While Dante Gabriel Rossetti's failure to represent a courtly ideal of sublimation is a source of much of the charm and tension in his work, it did exact a neurotic toll that is evident in the anxiety permeating his work of a lost masculine grandeur. In the Victorian period, the ideal of manhood more generally fell under extreme pressure as men were required to continually find new places for themselves amid shifting hierarchies and labor arrangements (Adams, *Dandies*, 5–6). Nostalgia for an inalienable manhood was expressed by Victorians such as Thomas Carlyle and Alfred, Lord Tennyson, and can likewise be seen in Rossetti's sketch of Coleridge's "Love," where he portrays the condition of the contemporary male as perpetually subordinated to a past phallic ideal. Additionally, Rossetti seems to have lived his own life in perpetual homage to the luminary Dante, whose direct access to the phallic God through a route of sublimation was unavailable to him. Even the women whom Victorian men idealized could not help them emerge from this reduced condition, for these women's functions were to soothe them rather than to elevate them, according to the ideologies of the time that stringently organized gender into what Mary Poovey has called an "oppositional economy."[9] According to this economy, the suspicion that male sexuality was especially susceptible to corruption was as firm as the conviction that female sexuality was oriented toward purity.[10] Accordingly, in his iconic poem of domestic idealization, "The Angel in the House" (1854), Coventry Patmore holds that while a wife "succeeds with cloudless brow, / [i]n common and in holy course," her husband "fails, in spite of prayer and vow / [a]nd agonies of faith and force" (5.1–4). The inflexibility of this division between male and female spiritual potential can be seen in Rossetti's graphical representation of *The Blessed Damozel* in his painting of 1878, in which the frame enforces the division between the symbolically trapped man and his sublime damozel—the former with his hands reaching upward as though they are bound, the latter expressing a visage that is melancholy but radiant.

The violently intruding frame in *The Blessed Damozel* serves as an apt representation of the polarizing cultural conditions that determined Christina Rossetti's and Dante Gabriel Rossetti's senses of their respective symbolic potential, whereby Christina as a virginal "damozel" found the heavens conditionally open to her, while Dante Gabriel experienced the humiliation of a spiritually diminished scope, even while he pitched his eyes aloft. To be sure, this mid-Victorian conjunction of ascendant femininity and obstructed masculinity represented by Dante Gabriel and Christina was temporary, swiftly giving way to other gender formations. The time when men were barred from forms of sublimation within the Christian tradition began to pass even in the 1860s, as churchmen such as Edward Bouverie Pusey and writers like Charles Kingsley devised a "muscular Christianity" that emphasized practices of redemption that did "not exalt the feminine virtues to the exclusion of the masculine."[11] More broadly, the Christian tone of Victorian life fell off over the course of the Victorian period, opening up other symbolic options for male artists. Aestheticism and modernism liberated male writers and artists into a new phallic confidence through which they could pursue vistas of symbolic purity unburdened from anxiety about sin. The suffragettes and the New Women disdained the ambivalent forms of power that could be achieved within the patriarchal bounds of Christian asceticism, seeking a larger sphere of action and throwing off self-mortifying sexual restrictions.

Nonetheless, Christina Rossetti and Dante Gabriel Rossetti at midcentury remain fascinating specimens as they exemplify a fleeting moment in which masculine inaptitude for the available form of symbolic sublimation was matched by feminine avidity for it—a unique form of power reversal within a broader patriarchal context. Although the power gained and lost in such symbolic shifts is abstract, it is nonetheless real; for as Joan Copjec has suggested, the subject's freedom lies precisely in the forms of resistance that he is wily enough to mount against the pure regime of the pleasure principle. As Copjec puts it, there are significant "historical effects [in] the fact that men and women often act to avoid pleasure, to shun . . . [material] goods," in order to escape from the constraint of being utterly "motivated by self-interest" (68, 96). Copjec acknowledges that some of these forms of resistance—which she defines as being the basic indices of the psychoanalytical subject—may be ascetic and morbid. Nonetheless, she holds that given that we are all symbolic subjects "for whom pleasure cannot function as an index of the good, since the [good] is lost to [us]," it is in our ability to face how we are compelled by this reservoir of lost good that we find our ethical bearing as subjects (87). In this regard, a psychoanalytical moment in which a woman laid claim to the discursive tools to brazenly explore her relationship with the Other—while a man, bound to an economy of discharge, was captive to the dissatisfying repetitions of pleasure that the Other set out for him—is distinctly incongruous with our general ideas about the gendering of power and castration and is worth attending to, even if it was only a moment.

Notes

Abbreviations

CR   Christina Rossetti
CR   Jan Marsh, *Christina Rossetti: A Writer's Life*
DGR Dante Gabriel Rossetti
DGR Jan Marsh, *Dante Gabriel Rossetti: Painter and Poet*

Introduction

1. All quotations of CR's poems are taken from *The Complete Poems of Christina Rossetti*, ed. Rebecca W. Crump (Baton Rouge: University of Louisiana Press, 1979); and all quotations of DGR's poems are taken from *Dante Gabriel Rossetti: Collected Writings*, ed. Jan Marsh (London: Ellis, 1911; Chicago: New Amsterdam Books, 2000). Years given in parentheses represent the date of writing, followed, when relevant, by the date of publication.

2. As the online *Rossetti Archive* entries on *The House of Life* explain, DGR's sonnet sequence went through a series of publishing incarnations, notably an early publication of 16 sonnets in the March 1869 issue of *Fortnightly Review* and a more complete publication of 50 sonnets in his *Poems* (London: F. S. Ellis, 1870), which some readers find to be the most coherent version of the sequence. In this volume, I draw upon his most comprehensive version of the sequence, which numbered 101 sonnets and was included in his *Ballads and Sonnets* (London: F. S. Ellis, 1881). See Jerome McGann, ed., *Rossetti Archive: The Complete Writings and Pictures of Dante Gabriel Rossetti; A Hypermedia Archive* (http://www.rossettiarchive.org/index.html).

3. Loy Martin, *Browning's Dramatic Monologues and the Post-Romantic Subject* (Baltimore, MD: Johns Hopkins University Press, 1985), 25.

4. Jacques Lacan, *The Seminar of Jacques Lacan, Book II: The Ego in Freud's Theory and in the Technique of Psychoanalysis, 1954–1955* (New York: Norton, 1991), 26 (cited in the text as SII). In referring to the psychoanalytic subject, I use the male pronoun generically and in chapters on DGR, and the female pronoun in chapters on CR.

5. Jacques Lacan, *The Seminar of Jacques Lacan*, Book I, *Freud's Papers on Technique*, 1953, 1954 (New York: Norton, 1991), 13 (cited in the text as SI). For Freud's theory of the life and death instincts, see *Beyond the Pleasure Principle* (1920, New York: Norton, 1989), 47–50.

6. Julia Kristeva, *Desire in Language* (New York: Columbia University Press, 1980), 116. Kristeva's characterization of the symbolic order as the force of law that constrains the desire of the subject's "body" somewhat simplifies Lacan's orders of the imaginary, the symbolic, and the real, whose interaction is discussed further later in the introduction. Kristeva's "desire of the body" that repels symbolic subjectification actually seems most similar to Lacan's and Freud's concept of "the drives," which are experiences of bodily libido located in what Lacan calls "the real"—the category of unmediated being that both terrifies and compels the subject through its sublime unspeakability. In contrast, the term *desire* in Lacan's terminology is often used to figure the cravings of the subject insofar as they are always already in the process of being mediated by language and thereby of being submitted to the approval of the symbolic Other.

7. Juliet Flower MacCannell, *Figuring Lacan: Criticism and the Cultural Unconscious* (Lincoln: University of Nebraska Press, 1986), 125.

8. James Eli Adams, "Victorian Sexualities," in *A Companion to Victorian Literature and Culture*, ed. Herbert F. Tucker (Malden, MA: Blackwell, 1999), 130.

9. Wendell Stacy Johnson, *Sex and Marriage in Victorian Poetry* (Ithaca, NY: Cornell University Press, 1975), 39.

10. See Joan Copjec, *Read My Desire: Lacan against the Historicists* (Cambridge, MA: MIT Press, 1994), 18–30.

11. With respect to the question raised by Elizabeth Wright and others as to whether psychobiography is a trustworthy critical method, I would argue that in the case of the Rossettis the majority of the texts are lyrical writings that align fairly readily with biographical incidents, thus warranting some degree of personal interpretation. Many others repeat motifs and themes that so penetrate the writers' lyrical content that they invite investigation as developments of the lyric material. The main danger raised by Wright is that the critic might underestimate the author's consciousness by giving too much credit to unconscious operations and thus underestimating the author's power over their symbolic materials. In general, I have attempted to avert any such reductiveness. See Elizabeth Wright, *Psychoanalytic Criticism: Theory in Practice* (London: Methuen, 1984), esp. 38–45.

12. Many historians of Freud have observed that his psychoanalytic theory has roots in the Romantic period insofar as his approach is concerned with liberating stifled emotions and exposing obscure elements of human nature. See, for instance, Lionel Trilling, "Freud and Literature" (1940), in

The Liberal Imagination (New York: Viking, 1950), 35; Harry Trosman, "Freud's Cultural Background," in *Freud: The Fusion of Science and Humanism: The Intellectual History of Psychoanalysis*, edited by John E. Gedo and George H. Pollock (New York: International Universities Press, 1976), 50.

13. Jacques Lacan, *The Seminar of Jacques Lacan*, Book VII: *The Ethics of Psychoanalysis, 1959–1960* (New York: Norton, 1992), 321 (cited in the text as *SVII*).

14. Sigmund Freud, "The Uncanny," in *The Standard Edition of the Complete Psychological Works of Sigmund Freud*, vol. 17 (1919), trans. and ed. James Strachey (London: Hogarth, 1955), 240–41.

15. See Ekbert Faas, *Retreat into the Mind: Victorian Poetry and the Rise of Psychiatry* (Princeton, NJ: Princeton University Press, 1988), 199. Faas in particular attributes this poetic motif to "Swinburne and his circle," a grouping that plausibly includes both Rossettis. DGR was close friends with Swinburne and was paired with him by Robert Buchanan for the "sickly self-consciousness" of the two men's poetry. Jan Marsh, *Dante Gabriel Rossetti: Painter and Poet* (London: Weidenfeld and Nicolson, 1999), 401 (cited in the text as DGR). CR was not a libertine like the men, but poems such as *Goblin Market* have always been seen as suggestive of hidden sexual meaning, even by her brother and editor William Michael Rossetti. See Marsh, *Christina Rossetti: A Writer's Life* (New York: Penguin, 1995), 233 (cited in the text as CR).

16. Marsh, CR, 55.

17. The term was ascribed in "The Fleshly School of Poetry: Mr. D. G. Rossetti," the devastating *Contemporary Review* article of 1871 by Robert Buchanan, reprinted in *The Broadview Anthology of Victorian Poetry and Poetic Theory*, ed. Thomas J. Collins and Vivian J. Rundle (Peterborough, ON: Broadview, 1999), 1329–40.

18. See Jenny Bourne Taylor, "Obscure Recesses: Locating the Victorian Unconscious," in *Writing and Victorianism*, ed. J. Bullen (New York: Longman, 1997), 137–79; Janet Oppenheim, *"Shattered Nerves": Doctors, Patients, and Depression in Victorian England* (New York: Oxford University Press, 1991).

19. Unpublished interview quoted in Trilling, "Freud and Literature," 54.

20. Jerome McGann, *Dante Gabriel Rossetti and the Game That Must Be Lost* (New Haven, CT: Yale University Press, 2000), 6 (cited in the text as *Game*).

21. Julia Kristeva, *Powers of Horror* (New York: Columbia University Press, 1982), 208 (cited in the text as *Powers*).

22. Examples include Christine Wiesenthal's account of the gaze in "Regarding Christina Rossetti's 'Reflection,'" *Victorian Poetry* 39, no. 3 (2001): 389–406; and J. Hillis Miller's account of the way in which narcissistic desire gives way to castration anxiety in DGR's writing and portraiture in "The Mirror's Secret: Dante Gabriel Rossetti's Double Work of Art," *Victorian Poetry* 29, no. 4 (1991): 333–59 (cited in the text as "Mirror").

23. The most famous example is provided by Sandra Gilbert and Susan Gubar in *The Madwoman in the Attic: The Woman Writer and the Nineteenth-Century Literary Imagination* (New Haven, CT: Yale University Press, 1979), in portraying Christina Rossetti as masochistic and identifying her with the heroine of her eponymous short story "Maude," who, they argue, has a "need for the constraining cross inflicted by a patriarchal God" (353).

24. Antony H. Harrison, *Christina Rossetti in Context* (Chapel Hill: University of North Carolina Press, 1988), xvi–xvii (cited in the text as *Context*). Kathleen Blake similarly professes that she is "wary of post-Freudian doctrine" for use with Christina Rossetti. See Blake, *Love and the Woman Question in Victorian Literature: The Art of Self-Postponement* (Totowa, NJ: Barnes and Noble, 1983), 11 (cited in the text as *Love*).

25. Ellen Handler Spitz, "A Critique of Pathography: Freud's Original Psychoanalytical Approach to Art," in *Essential Papers on Literature and Psychoanalysis*, ed. Emanual Berman (New York: New York University Press, 1993), 254–57.

26. For psychoanalytic criticism of CR that draws upon Irigaray and Cixous, see Barbara Garlick, "The Frozen Fountain: Christina Rossetti, the Virgin Model, and Youthful Pre-Raphaelitism" in *Virginal Sexuality and Textuality in Victorian Literature*, ed. Lloyd Davis (Albany: SUNY Press, 1993), 105–28; Margaret Reynolds, "Speaking Unlikenesses: The Double Text in CR's 'After Death' and 'Remember Me'" in *The Culture of Christina Rossetti: Female Poetics and Victorian Contexts*, ed. Mary Arseneau, Antony H. Harrison, and Lorraine Janzen Kooistra (Athens: Ohio University Press, 1999), 3–21. Wiesenthal's "Regarding Christina Rossetti's 'Reflection,'" meanwhile, borrows from Butler as well as Lacan.

27. See Griselda Pollock, *Vision and Difference: Femininity, Feminism and the Histories of Art* (New York: Routledge, 1988).

28. Norman Kelvin, in "Dante Gabriel and Christina Rossetti: A Pairing of Identities," *Victorian Literature and Culture* 32, no. 1 (2004): 239–59, has begun the process of understanding "the gap between the[ ] respective questing" of CR and DGR (254). In addition, David Clifford and Laurence Rouissillon's *Outsiders Looking In: The Rossettis, Then and Now* (London: Anthem, 2003), is a new volume of essays that investigates qualities shared among the members of the Rossetti family, including their cosmopolitan outsider status in London.

29. See, for instance, Alison Chapman, "Defining the Feminine Subject: D. G. Rossetti's Manuscript Revisions to Christina Rossetti's Poetry," *Victorian Poetry* 35, no. 2 (Summer 1997): 139–56; Gail Lynn Goldberg, "DGR's 'Revising Hand': His Illustrations for Christina Rossetti's Poems," *Victorian Poetry* 20, no. 3–4 (Autumn–Winter 1982): 145–59; Antony H. Harrison, "Epistolary Relations: The Correspondence of Christina and Dante Gabriel Rossetti,"

Journal of Pre-Raphaelite Studies 4 (1995): 91–101 (cited in the text as "Epistolary"). Harrison observes that lifelong correspondence between CR and DGR shows their relationship was "often as mutually supportive as it was competitive," as they commented on each others' works and assisted in the commercialization of these works ("Epistolary," 96).

30. Critics are in disagreement as to the extent of continuity between Kristeva and Lacan. Elizabeth Grosz, in *Jacques Lacan: A Feminist Introduction* (New York: Routledge, 1990), finds Kristeva "dutiful" (150), while MacCannell criticizes Kristeva for arriving at "a very different destination from Lacan" because she is too "mystical" (*Figuring Lacan*, 28). I find that Kristeva generally sustains Lacanian root concepts while elaborating them in rewarding directions, in particular in her readings of cultural products in *Tales of Love* and *Powers of Horror*.

31. *Jouissance* is Lacan's term for a kind of pleasure that, insofar as it challenges the boundaries of the self in its intensity, verges on pain. See definition of "Jouissance" in Dylan Evans, *An Introductory Dictionary of Lacanian Psychoanalyis* (New York: Brunner-Routledge, 1996), 91–92.

32. See Jacques Lacan, "The Mirror Stage as Formative of the Function of the I" (1949), in *Ecrits: A Selection* (New York: Norton, 1977), 1–7 (cited in the text as "Mirror").

Chapter 1: The Transcendental Tendency in Christina Rossetti's Poetry of Love and Devotion

1. Julia Kristeva, *Tales of Love* (New York: Columbia University Press, 1981), 154–55 (cited in the text as *Tales*).

2. See Harrison, *Context*, 89; Colleen Hobbs, "A View from 'The Lowest Place': Christina Rossetti's Devotional Prose," *Victorian Poetry* 32 (1994): 409–23 (cited in the text as "View").

3. See Harrison, *Context*, 54, for a discussion of how Pre-Raphaelite art in general aimed to integrate the impulses of eros and agape.

4. Dante Alighieri's *Divine Comedy* is cited throughout this volume as *Commedia*, with the individual books likewise referred to by their Italian title in the text. In general, Dante's *Commedia* is another text in which spiritual passion is indistinguishable from the amorous impulses of the subject, as the beloved Beatrice whom Dante met in the streets of Florence becomes a "figure" of "the whole sacramental principle," according to translator and explicator Dorothy L. Sayers in her note to canto 30 of *Purgatorio* (311).

5. Kristeva also observes the imaginary trope of specularity in the Christianity of twelfth-century mystics, who believed that one can find one's own image in God, given that God created man in his image (*Tales*, 160–61).

6. Sigmund Freud, *Civilization and Its Discontents* (1930), trans. and ed. James Strachey (New York: Norton, 1961), 11.

7. Sigmund Freud, "On Narcissism: An Introduction" (1914), in *The Standard Edition of the Complete Psychological Works of Sigmund Freud*, vol. 14, *Art and Literature: Jensen's Gradiva, Leonardo da Vinci and Other Works*, trans. and ed. James Strachey (London: Hogarth, 1957), 146–58 (cited in the text as "Narcissism").

8. Sigmund Freud, "Leonardo da Vinci and a Memory of His Childhood" (1910), in *The Penguin Freud Library*, vol. 14, *Art and Literature: Jensen's Gradiva, Leonardo da Vinci and Other Works*, trans. and ed. James Strachey (Toronto: Penguin, 1985), 164 (cited in the text as "Da Vinci").

9. Lacan, *SVII*, 125. Lacan indicates that he is less optimistic than Freud about the ultimate capacity of the subject for complete sublimation (91) and less convinced of the benignity of the attempt, proposing that expressions of the sublime "point to the field of destruction" (217). Nonetheless, in identifying sublimation as the ultimate end of all symbolic activity as well as the goal of the death drive (217), Lacan normalizes subjects such as Christina Rossetti in whom the impulse toward the sublime and the death drive are unusually strong.

10. See definition of "The Thing" in Evans, *Introductory Dictionary*, 204–5.

11. Marsh, for example, describes "Confluents" as "a gossamer lyric heralding the influence of the new Aestheticism" (CR, 428–29).

12. For more on CR's pursuit of a divine lover, see Dolores Rosenblum, "Christina Rossetti's Religious Poetry: Watching, Looking, Keeping Vigil," in *Victorian Women Poets: A Critical Reader*, ed. Angela Leighton (Cambridge, MA: Blackwell, 1996), 114–30 (cited in the text as "Religious").

13. Grosz, *Jacques Lacan*, 40.

14. For more on CR's spiritual warning poems, see Harrison, *Context*, 96; Mary Arseneau, "Incarnation and Interpretation: Christina Rossetti, the Oxford Movement, and *Goblin Market*," *Victorian Poetry* 31, no. 1 (1993): 79–93. Arseneau sees CR's poems about the delusions and dangers of erotic desire as continuous with the broad category of CR's poetry in displaying how one "who is not tempted by the empty promise of material things ... can indeed interpret the world in a meaningful and Christian way" (91).

15. Jacques Lacan, "Subversion of the Subject and Dialectic of Desire," in *Ecrits: A Selection* (New York: Norton, 1977), 324 (cited in the text as "Subversion").

16. This reading of CR is summed up by Diane D'Amico in "Eve, Mary and Magdalene: Christina Rossetti's Feminine Triptych," in *The Achievement of Christina Rossetti*, ed. David A. Kent (Ithaca, NY: Cornell University Press, 1987), 180.

17. George B. Tennyson, *Victorian Devotional Poetry*, (Cambridge, MA: Harvard University Press, 1981), 5.

18. Raymond Chapman, *Faith and Revolt: Studies in the Literary Influence of the Oxford Movement* (London: Weidenfeld and Nicolson, 1970), 187.

19. Richard Boothby, *Death and Desire: Psychoanalytic Theory in Lacan's Return to Freud* (New York: Routledge, 1991), 13.

20. The Freudian understanding of the repetition compulsion has more than once been used to diagnose CR's formally and thematically repetitive verse in pathological terms. Gilbert and Gubar draw on negative Freudian implications of obsessive compulsive behavior when they express regretfully that CR "[took] up her pen to spend a lifetime writing 'Amen for us all,'" (*Madwoman in the Attic*, 554). Rosenblum, in "Christina Rossetti and Poetic Sequence," in *The Achievement of Christina Rossetti*, ed. David Kent (Ithaca, NY: Cornell University Press, 1987), more overtly invokes the Freudian diagnosis when she worries that collected editions of CR's poetry "reveal a poet writing under a compulsion to repeat" (133).

21. In chapter 2, I explore what do seem to be deliberately morbid expressions of the death drive in CR's gothic-inflected writing, which seem designed to contrast with these sublimatory versions.

22. In "Song," the speaker's notoriously steely command to her lover that when she is dead he should "[s]ing no sad songs" because she will be in a place where "[h]aply [she] may remember" him "[a]nd haply may forget" (15–16) has frequently been read as encapsulating an insincerely ironic or passive-aggressive complaint (1–2, 13–14); see, for instance, Susan Conley, "Rossetti's Cold Women: Irony and Liminal Fantasy in the Death Lyrics," in *The Culture of Christina Rossetti: Female Poetics and Victorian Contexts*, ed. Mary Arseneau, Antony H. Harrison, and Lorraine Janzen Kooistra (Athens: Ohio University Press, 1999), 260–84. But the poem can also be read as a sincere response to the limits of love and life, consistent with CR's ongoing eschatological representation of death as a place beyond earthly limitations.

23. Sigmund Freud, *The Ego and the Id*, trans. Joan Riviere, ed. James Strachey (New York: Norton, 1960), 7 (cited in the text as *Ego*).

24. Jacques Lacan, "The Signification of the Phallus" (1958), in *Ecrits: A Selection* (New York: Norton, 1977), 290 (cited in the text as "Phallus").

25. I am grateful to Colleen Hobbs for identifying these passages from *Face of the Deep* in which CR directly addresses the subject of gender (see Hobbs, "View").

26. Shirley Foster, in "Speaking Beyond Patriarchy: The Female Voice in Emily Dickinson and Christina Rossetti," in *The Body and the Text: Hélène Cixous, Reading and Teaching*, ed. Helen Wilcox, Keith McWatters, Ann Thompson, and

Linda R. Williams (New York: St. Martin's Press, 1990), uses Irigaray's conception of how écriture féminine is "freed from law, unencumbered by moderation" and "turbulent, non-unified" (67); Reynolds draws on Irigaray to characterize CR's writing as "distinctly feminine" and "unfettered" (17); and Armstrong finds in CR's writing a "female subjectivity" that favors "obliqu[e] and indirect[ ]" means of expression (342).

27. Jacqueline Rose, "Introduction—II," in *Feminine Sexuality*, by Jacques Lacan and the École Freudienne, ed. Juliet Mitchell and Jacqueline Rose (New York: Norton, 1985), 49.

28. Correlatively, Kristeva locates the dominance of the semiotic order primarily in the poetics of male writers such as Celine and Artaud (*Desire*, 10).

Chapter 2: The Superegoic Demon in Christina Rossetti's Gothic and Fantasy Writings

1. Lorraine Janzen Kooistra, "Visualizing the Fantastic Subject: *Goblin Market* and the Gaze," in *The Culture of Christina Rossetti: Female Poetics and Victorian Contexts*, ed. Mary Arseneau, Antony H. Harrison, and Lorraine Janzen Kooistra (Athens: Ohio University Press, 1999), 140.

2. David F. Morrill, "'Twilight is not good for maidens': Uncle Polidori and the Psychodynamics of Vampirism in *Goblin Market*," *Victorian Poetry* 28, no. 1 (1990): 1.

3. See definitions of "Superego" (200–201) and "Ego-Ideal" (52) in Evans, *Introductory Dictionary*.

4. Jean Laplanche and Jean-Bertrand Pontalis, "Fantasy and the Origins of Sexuality" (1964), in *Formations of Fantasy*, ed. Victor Burgin, James Donald, and Cora Kaplan (New York: Methuen, 1986), 20. Laplanche and Pontalis chart a middle course between Freud's seduction theory, which argues for the backdrop of a distinct event behind the fantasy (such as a "sexual approach from the adult"), and his later refutation of it, in which he saw fantasies as signs of a pre-given "sexual constitution" of the subject ("Fantasy," 17).

5. Reprinted in *Selected Prose of Christina Rossetti*, ed. David A. Kent and P. G. Stanwood (New York: St. Martin's Press, 1988), 17–51.

6. CR was similarly perceived as a spontaneous writer, with quick and natural "habits of composition," as Marsh notes, recalling William Michael Rossetti's account of how CR "scribbled the lines off rapidly enough" (Marsh, CR, 69–70).

7. According to Marsh, CR received similar religiously toned messages against self-display from her mother, who, while encouraging her daughters' achievements, chastened them to avoid "the selfish wish to shine over

others" (CR, 149). Although CR subsequently went through an adolescent stage of being a withdrawn young woman "renowned for her lack of fashion consciousness" (72), one presumes that she must have had to at least partially overcome this scruple against display to publish her verse.

8. Dorothy Mermin, *Godiva's Ride: Women of Letters in England, 1830–1880*, (Bloomington: Indiana University Press, 1993), 77. Other readers of *Maude* have similarly understood the eponymous heroine's behavior and death as essentially legislated by her prevailing symbolic order. Gilbert and Gubar are among those who read Maude's death as "dutiful" and expressing the inevitable recourse of the Victorian law against "the female sin of vanity" (*Madwoman in the Attic*, 552, 547). Similarly, Margaret Linley, in "Dying to Be a Poetess: The Conundrum of Christina Rossetti," in *The Culture of Christina Rossetti: Female Poetics and Victorian Contexts*, ed. Mary Arseneau, Antony H. Harrison, and Lorraine Janzen Kooistra (Athens: Ohio University Press, 1999), suggests that Maude embodies a "tradition of women's writing" in which poetesses were supposed to simultaneously embody "extravagant soulfulness" and a "transcendent feminine modesty" that required them to eventually stifle self-expression (286, 290).

9. William Michael Rossetti notably observes that CR was similarly "overburdened with conscientious scruples of an extreme and even a wire-drawn kind" (Marsh, CR, 39).

10. Fred Botting, *Gothic* (New York: Routledge, 1996), 116.

11. The poem "Three Nuns" was also published as a stand-alone work in CR's posthumous *New Poems, Hitherto Unpublished or Uncollected* (1896). Line numbers for the poem are cited.

12. This effect of forbidden sexuality has previously been sensed in "Three Nuns" by Harrison, who observes hints of a past sexual seduction within the first nun's narrative (*Context*, 134).

13. This imagery evokes CR's famous poem "Winter: My Secret" (1857/1862), in which the speaker similarly describes a drive for protective garments: "a shawl, / A veil, a cloak, and other wraps: / I cannot ope to everyone who taps" (10–12).

14. Susan Isaacs, "On the Nature and Function of Phantasy," discussed in Laplanche and Pontalis, "Fantasy," 23.

15. See Christine Wiesenthal, "Regarding Christina Rossetti's Reflection." Applying the gender-performance theories of Judith Butler, Weisenthal finds that CR's characters cannily evade the normative heterosexual masquerade by becoming a "black hole" to men who might gaze upon them, a gesture that she proposes allows the characters to more freely choose to "refus[e] to be a certain gender" in a normative style (394–95).

16. Kooistra similarly insists that "a woman cannot live in the world without looking and being looked at," for "these activities are essential to life, to love" ("Visualizing the Fantastic Subject," 141).

17. For example, Gilbert and Gubar read into Maude's search for a "constraining cross" proof that CR's religious practice was "masochistic" (Madwoman in the Attic, 553).

18. Apart from Morrill's analysis of Polidori's influence on CR's works, Garlick observes that CR was "fascinated by the Doppelgänger legend" and other gothic motifs ("Frozen Fountain," 4), while D'Amico observes the background of Maturin in Rossetti's writing in "Christina Rossetti: The Maturin Poems," Victorian Poetry 19 (1980): 117–37.

19. Anne Williams, Art of Darkness: A Poetics of Gothic (Chicago: University of Chicago Press, 1995), 144.

20. CR's invocation of forbidden narcissistic attachment as a mercilessly turbulent fate may be a response to DGR's illustration of the couple in his painting Paolo and Francesca da Rimini (1849–55) from the previous year. While DGR made the visages of the two partners seem to be not suffering but rather caught up in a kind of eternal rapture—an interpretation that sustains DGR's artistic interest in glorifying imaginary desire at all costs—CR refutes DGR's vision by portraying this hell of desire as one of eternal alienation. Mary Arseneau also points out this resemblance between CR's North and Dante's second circle of hell in "'May My Great Love Avail Me': Christina Rossetti and Dante," in The Culture of Christina Rossetti: Female Poetics and Victorian Contexts, ed. Mary Arseneau, Antony H. Harrison, and Lorraine Janzen Kooistra (Athens: Ohio University Press, 1999), 39.

21. In constructing an opposition between a bland southern fiancé and a potent northern seducer, CR may well have drawn on the contrast that her acquaintance John Ruskin had described three years earlier in The Stones of Venice (1853; New York: Da Capo Press, 2003), between "servile" Latinate architecture and "wild[ ]" and "rough[ ]" gothic architecture (161, 157).

22. Other critics have likewise observed this liberalizing feature of demons in CR's writing. For example, Sylvia Bailey Sherbutt, in "Revisionist Mythmaking in Christina Rossetti's 'Goblin Market': Eve's Apple and Other Questions Revised and Reconsidered," Victorian Newsletter 82 (1992), understands the goblins as "purveyors . . . of creative liberation" (41), while Nina Auerbach, in Woman and the Demon: The Life of a Victorian Myth (Cambridge, MA: Harvard University Press, 1982), proposes that demonism was another way, besides Christian transcendentalism, in which CR fueled her "dream of self-apotheosis," in keeping with the role of demons in Victorian literature more broadly to allow their authors to imagine an "essentially female" creative power (64, 101).

23. As Kristeva explains, the primal repressed is rooted in "the archaic relation to the mother" (*Powers*, 63). In her version of the Oedipal complex, the symbolic order subsequently overwrites this archaic logic of inside and outside that structures the relationship with the mother with a logic of subject and object. It subsequently abjects anything to do with that original order—including signs of the power of maternity—to mask its own "frailty" (*Powers*, 70).

24. CR's depictions of Eden as a place or time when colors were brighter accords with how Lacan describes the recollection of the primal order in dreams as signaled through "intensification of . . . colours." See Jacques Lacan, *The Four Fundamental Concepts of Psychoanalysis* (New York: Norton, 1981), 75–76 (cited in the text as *Four*).

25. Stephen Prickett, *Victorian Fantasy* (Bloomington: Indiana University Press, 1979), 21–25.

26. See Sigmund Freud, *The Interpretation of Dreams* (1900), trans. and ed. James Strachey (New York: Avon, 1965), esp. chapter 4, "Distortion in Dreams" (cited in the text as *Interpretation*).

27. Northrop Frye, *The Great Code: The Bible and Literature* (1983; Toronto, ON: Penguin, 1990), 135.

28. Quotations of the *Inferno* are taken from Dante Alighieri, *The Divine Comedy 1: Hell*, trans. Dorothy L. Sayers (Toronto: Penguin, 1955). Although Kristeva does not conspicuously refer to the *Inferno* in *Powers of Horror*, her accounts of the abject character of narcissistic transgressions in this volume seem to draw upon imagery from Dante's eighth circle of hell, which holds frauds and sexual corrupters in a lake of ordure.

29. The sun was a symbol of God in the Victorian period in particular, as discussed in J. B. Bullen, ed., *The Sun Is God: Painting, Literature and Mythology in the Nineteenth Century* (New York: Oxford University Press, 1989).

30. Terence Holt, "'Men sell not such in any town': Exchange in 'Goblin Market,'" in *Victorian Women Poets: A Critical Reader*, ed. Angela Leighton (Cambridge, MA: Blackwell, 1996), 131–47.

31. Dorothy Mermin, "Heroic Sisterhood in 'Goblin Market,'" *Victorian Poetry* 21, no. 2 (1983): 113.

32. Review in *The Academy*, December 5, 1874, quoted in *Selected Prose of Christina Rossetti*, 117.

33. The game is plausibly a satire of Samuel Smiles's *Self-Help* (1859)—a book that came to stand for the Victorian cult of self-sufficiency, which CR implicitly critiques as a manifestation of the same egoism.

34. As Julia Briggs has suggested, in "Speaking Likenesses: Hearing the Lesson," in *The Culture of Christina Rossetti: Female Poetics and Victorian Contexts*, ed.

Mary Arseneau, Antony H. Harrison, and Lorraine Janzen Kooistra (Athens: Ohio University Press, 1999), the demonic stories in *Speaking Likenesses* have a social function, and it seems true that the worst danger these demons offer is not that they ruin individual lives but that they disrupt civil relationships (218).

Chapter 3: Imaginary Oscillation in Dante Gabriel Rossetti's Illustrations of Dante

1. William Gaunt, *The Pre-Raphaelite Tragedy* (1942; London: Cardinal, 1975), 41.

2. Perhaps because of his name, DGR's relationship to Dante seems not only to have inspired DGR but also to have intimidated him. When Gabriele Rossetti's first son was born, he called his son "little Dante" and gave the baby the poet's name as his third; when DGR signed his name to the translation of Dante's *La Vita Nuova* at age 21, he reversed his initials to put the "D" first, signaling his aim to emulate this master (Marsh, *DGR*, 3, 49–50).

3. Arseneau fairly observes in her study of CR's debt to Dante that while CR developed "theocratic[s] readings of Dante's writings," Dante Gabriel Rossetti focused on "the figure of Beatrice [as] the inspiration for an exploration of the transcendent possibilities of human love" ("May My Great Love," 27).

4. Harold Bloom, *The Anxiety of Influence: A Theory of Poetics* (New York: Oxford University Press, 1973), 45, 42.

5. See Walter E. Houghton, *The Victorian Frame of Mind, 1830–1870* (New Haven, CT: Yale University Press, 1957), 86.

6. Jerome McGann, "Dante Gabriel Rossetti and the Betrayal of Truth," *Victorian Poetry* 26, no. 4 (1988): 342–43 (cited in the text as "Betrayal").

7. Sayers, in her introduction to Dante, *The Divine Comedy* 1: *Hell*, 68.

8. See Steve Ellis, *Dante and English Poetry: Shelley to T. S. Eliot* (New York: Cambridge University Press, 1978). Ellis criticizes DGR for focusing too much on Dante's early writing and consequently founding an emotional "cult of the *Vita Nuova*" among fellow Victorians that overlooked the intellectual achievement of the *Commedia* (134).

9. Freud further explains that whereas primary narcissism is characterized by "self-contentment" and a monopolization of psychic energy by "ego libido," secondary narcissism is a syndrome of excessive dependence on the other, whereby the too-loving subject has so dissipated his psychic energy in "object love" that he is driven to love someone who will stand for a personal ideal, so that he can indirectly return some ego-libido to himself ("Narcissism," 87–88, 94).

10. Ellie Ragland-Sullivan, *Jacques Lacan and the Philosophy of Psychoanalysis* (Urbana: University of Illinois Press, 1986), 35.

11. Marshall Alcorn, *Narcissism and the Literary Libido: Rhetoric, Text, and Subjectivity* (New York: New York University Press, 1994), 16–17.

12. David Riede, *Dante Gabriel Rossetti Revisited* (Toronto, ON: Maxwell McMillan, 1992), 34. Stephen Gurney, in "Rossetti: The Failure of Eros," *University of Hartford Studies in Literature* 14, no. 3 (1982), likewise proposes that by forgoing Dante's "architectonics of a comprehensive spiritual design," DGR achieves an artistic practice that records "sporadic moments of passion in the autobiography of his spirit" (114).

13. In his own life as well, DGR featured symbolic immaturity in resisting the symbolic constraints of marriage with Elizabeth Siddal for as long as possible and maintaining a longstanding adulterous relationship with Jane Morris, but there are indications of symbolic subversiveness in his regarding these women as his spiritual and intellectual soulmates. See Beverly Taylor, "Beatrix / Creatrix: Elizabeth Siddal as Muse and Creator," *Journal of Pre-Raphaelite Studies* 4 (1995): 29–41, for a discussion of how DGR encouraged and promoted Elizabeth as an artist. Also see John Bryson and Janet Camp Troxall, eds., *Dante Gabriel Rossetti and Jane Morris: Their Correspondence* (Oxford: Clarendon Press, 1976), which helps to counteract impressions that DGR merely admired Morris for her beauty with evidence that the two exchanged books and ideas about art.

14. Herbert Sussman, *Victorian Masculinities: Manhood and Masculine Poetics in Early Victorian Literature and Art* (New York: Cambridge University Press, 1995), 31 (cited in the text as *Masculinities*). DGR's most controversial representations of masculine desire occur in the sonnets of *The House of Life*, which enraged reviewers insofar as these displayed "emasculated delight in brooding over and toying with matters that healthy manly men put out of their thoughts," according to an accusatory column in the *Saturday Review* of June 1872.

15. Charles Williams, *The Figure of Beatrice* (London: Faber, 1943), 115; quoted by Sayers in Dante, *The Divine Comedy* 1: *Hell*, 118.

16. Quoted by Ellis in *Dante and English Poetry*, 123.

17. Sayers, explanatory note to canto 5 of Dante, *The Divine Comedy* 1: *Hell*, 102.

18. Ellis equally finds that DGR's representation of Paolo and Francesca exhibits "a vital attraction that is missing" from his depiction of Dante's chaste and one-sided love for Beatrice (123).

19. Dante Alighieri, *La Vita Nuova*, trans. Dante Gabriel Rossetti, in *Dante Gabriel Rossetti: Collected Writings*, 86.

20. Susan P. Casteras, "Pre-Raphaelite Challenges to Victorian Canons of Beauty," in Malcolm Warner, Susan P. Casteras, Lindsay Smith, Jerome McGann, Sara S. Hodson, and Shelley M. Bennett, *The Pre-Raphaelites in Context* (San

Marino, CA: Henry E. Huntington Library and Art Gallery, 1992), 27. Sussman agrees that DGR's anti-academic style of representing revolutionized Victorian aesthetic norms led to the permanent dissolution of "sharp definitions and valuations of art along the binaries of male/female" (*Masculinities*, 172).

21. Arrangements between the heights of subjects in DGR's paintings seem to have been quite deliberate, with DGR commenting once in a letter that "[p]roportions always bother me more than anything else"; quoted in Marina Henderson, *D. G. Rossetti* (New York: St. Martin's Press, 1973), 31.

22. Lawrence J. Starzyk, "Victorian Artistic Recursions," *Mosaic* 20, no. 2 (1987): 57–70.

23. See Antony H. Harrison, "Dante Rossetti: Parody and Ideology," *Studies in English Literature* 29 (1989): 715–61.

24. Dante's account of his dream in *La Vita Nuova* also exposes such imaginary identifications, as before Dante views the dead Beatrice, he is assailed by "terrible and unknown appearances" who call out, "Thou art dead," and so blur the boundaries between his fate and Beatrice's (*Vita Nuova*, 103). He thus "misrecognizes" his relation to the other in a way that expresses the quality of imaginary desire (Lacan, *SI*, 167).

25. Virginia Surtees provides the symbolic interpretation of the crimson angels in *The Paintings and Drawings of Dante Gabriel Rossetti (1828–1882): A Catalogue Raisonné* (Oxford: Clarendon, 1971), 44 (cited in the text as *Catalogue*); George Ferguson's *Signs and Symbols in Christian Art* (New York: Oxford University Press, 1961) is a source of Christian interpretations of the lamp (176) and the dove (16).

26. Lothar Honnighausen, *The Symbolist Tradition in English Literature: A Study of Pre-Raphaelitism and the Fin de Siècle* (New York: Cambridge University Press, 1988), 3–4.

27. In *Letters of Dante Gabriel Rossetti*, vol. 2, ed. Oswald Doughty and Robert Wall (Oxford: Clarendon Press, 1965), 899 (cited in the text as *Letters*, 2).

28. See, for example, Lynne Pearce, *Woman/Image/Text: Readings in Pre-Raphaelite Art and Literature* (Toronto: University of Toronto Press, 1991); Pollock, *Vision and Difference*; Virginia M. Allen, "'One Strangling Golden Hair': Dante Gabriel Rossetti's Lady Lilith," *Art Bulletin* 66 (1984): 285–94. DGR's fetishes were also conspicuous in his habits of attraction: Elizabeth Gaskell, who knew DGR in 1859, commented that he was "hair mad," because "if a particular kind of reddish brown, crepe wavy hair came in, he was away in a moment, struggling for an introduction" (Marsh, *DGR*, 208).

29. Sigmund Freud, "Fetishism" (1927), in *The Standard Edition of the Complete Psychological Works of Sigmund Freud*, vol. 7, trans. and ed. James Strachey

(London: Hogarth, 1953), 153. Note that a foot of Dante's that protrudes conspicuously in the direction of the cabinet in the watercolor has likewise been sheathed under his coat in the second version.

30. Žižek refers to this imaginary object as the "mother" in *Plague of Fantasies* (New York: Verso, 1997), 104, but his comment may be also generalized, I think, to others toward whom one has formed an imaginary attachment.

31. Laura Mulvey, "You Don't Know What Is Happening, Do You, Mr. Jones?" *Spare Rib* 8 (1973): 15. Mulvey apparently generalizes her link between fetishism and narcissism from Freud's account of how a man who fetishizes women's feet "represents" for himself the idea of "a woman's penis, the absence of which [he had] deeply felt" as a child, having previously "imagined [the female genitals] as male ones" (Freud, "Fetishism," 155).

32. By 1867, DGR is thought to have suffered yet another circumstance "unfavorable" to the sexual aim, as diverse illnesses impaired his "physical virility" (Marsh, *DGR*, 342). Under such circumstances in which the genital goal becomes physiologically inaccessible, one might imagine that fetishism would continue to intensify.

33. Jane Morris subsequently became the fetishistic ideal of all of the Pre-Raphaelite artists; as Henry James stated, it is impossible to know whether Morris was "a grand synthesis of all Pre-Raphaelite pictures ever made" or whether the Pre-Raphaelites' paintings were "a 'keen analysis' of her" (quoted in Marsh, *DGR*, 339).

34. See Dianne Sachko MacLeod, "Dante Gabriel Rossetti and Titian," *Art Bulletin* 68 (1986): 36–39.

Chapter 4: The Symbolic Perfection of the Imaginary in Dante Gabriel Rossetti's The House of Life

1. See Arline Golden, "Victorian Renascence: The Revival of the Amatory Sonnet Sequence, 1850–1900," *Genre* 7, no. 1 (1974): 133–47.

2. William Michael Rossetti, *Dante Gabriel Rossetti: His Family Letters with a Memoir*, vol. 1 (London: Elvey, 1895), 105 (cited in the text as *Dante*).

3. See Maria DiBattista, *First Love: The Affections of Modern Fiction* (Chicago: University of Chicago Press, 1991), 57.

4. From *Sonnets by Dante Gabriel Rossetti*, an early notebook containing DGR's fair copies of poems he wrote before 1850 and edited by William Michael Rossetti, held in the Tinker Library, Beinecke Rare Book and Manuscript Library, Yale University, and available online at http://www.rossettiarchive.org/docs/tinker.yale.radheader.html.

5. David Larg, *Trial by Virgins: Fragment of a Biography* (London: Peter Davis, 1933), 58.

6. Another critic who has famously read the *House of Life* sonnet series as redemptive is William E. Fredeman, in "Rossetti's 'In Memoriam': An Elegiac Reading of *The House of Life*," *John Rylands Library Journal* 47 (1965): 298–341.

7. For instance, Stephen J. Spector, in "Love, Unity, and Desire in the Poetry of Dante Gabriel Rossetti," *ELH* 38, no. 3 (1971), finds that toward the end of the sequence, the speaker's "personality disintegrates," and he is "unable to escape from the prison of subjectivism" (457). Similarly, Stephen Gurney, in "Rossetti: The Failure of Eros," *University of Hartford Studies in Literature* 14, no. 3 (1982), observes that the terminal sonnets "sound like nothing more than the last attempt of a shattered pilgrim" (112). Paul Jarvie and Robert Rosenberg, in "'Willowwood' Unity and *The House of Life*," *Pre-Raphaelite Review* 1, no. 1 (1977–78), find that *The House of Life* "darkens progressively, moving slowly into the painful world of the speaker's mind" (119).

8. As paraphrased by Lacan in *SI*, 141. Presumably the referenced quotation is Freud's comment that the subject "is not willing to forgo the narcissistic perfection of his childhood; and when, as he grows up, he is disturbed by the admonitions of others and by the awakening of his own critical judgement, so that he can no longer retain that perfection, he seeks to recover it in the new form of an ego ideal" ("Narcissism," 94).

9. During this period, DGR revived his art as well, recovering eyesight that he had feared was declining. His artistic rebirth culminated in the 1871 version of *Dante's Dream*, which was produced "with labor undertaken for love not lucre" according to biographer Jan Marsh, though the work nonetheless sustains his fixations on the fetish and the symbol (*DGR*, 413).

10. "Early in 1853, [DGR] drafted a characteristically convoluted sonnet ["Known in Vain"], which seems to describe the first acknowledgment of mutual feeling" (Marsh, *DGR*, 109).

11. Marsh likewise proposes that "emotional perturbation was one reason why Gabriel Rossetti . . . had [no paintings] to show in 1852" (*DGR*, 89).

12. "Undeniably, the return to verse, in the form of love sonnets, coincided with clandestine passion for Janey" (Marsh, *DGR*, 351).

13. Jarvie and Rosenberg find that the Willowwood sonnets express DGR's "sterile vision of self-love" ("Willowwood," 118); J. Hillis Miller contends that these sonnets reveal DGR's preference for a "solipsistic relation" ("Mirror's Secret," 339).

14. Steven Bruhm, *Reflecting Narcissism: A Queer Aesthetic* (Minneapolis: University of Minnesota Press, 2001), 177.

15. Roland Barthes, *A Lover's Discourse: Fragments*, trans. Richard Howard (1977; New York: Hill and Wang, 1978), 173.

16. Žižek, answer to my audience question at public talk, King's College, Halifax, November 2002.

17. Jacques Lacan, *Le Seminaire*, Livre XVII, *L'envers de la psychanalyse*, 1969–1970 (Paris: Seuil, 1991). An English edition of this volume has recently been released as *The Seminar of Jacques Lacan*, Book XVII, *The Other Side of Psychoanalysis*, trans. Russell Grigg (New York: Norton, 2006).

Chapter 5: Hysterical Desire in Dante Gabriel Rossetti's Narrative Poems and Portraiture

1. Evelyn Waugh, *Rossetti: His Life and Works* (London: Duckworth, 1928), 130.

2. I generally refer to the viewer of DGR's art in this chapter as male because of what seems to be the essential logic of the structuration of the gaze in these works, which is that the viewer is in the position of the castrated male subject. However, while the maleness of DGR's viewer is typical, it is not essential. For Lacan, both men and women are subject to the threat of castration, and though they experience this differently, both are intimidated by it to seek an "unconscious position" within a normative symbolic order ("Phallus," 281). As such, many symbolic functions seem to be shared by both genders. Accordingly, some of the wives of DGR's male patrons appear to have enjoyed the sublimity of his paintings as much as their husbands did: for instance, George Rae wrote in a letter to DGR that his wife "spen[t] half the day before [DGR's *Beloved*] as certain devout Catholic ladies had used to do before their favorite shrines in the days of old"; quoted in Dianne Sachko MacLeod, "Art Collecting and Victorian Middle-Class Taste," *Art History* 1, no. 3 (1987): 339 (cited in text as "Art").

3. Copjec herein attempts to clarify an error that she finds in "film theory" usages of Lacan, which contend that the gaze is a projection of "surveillance" that men inflict on women (16), arguing that this is a misreading of the gaze, which could never "coincide" with and empower any subject, since it "symbolize[s] the central lack of all subjects," in Lacan's words (16; *Four*, 77).

4. See Philip Culbertson's clarification of Sedgwick's concept of the male gaze in "Designing Men: Reading the Male Body as Text," in the online *Journal of Textual Reasoning* 7 (1988): "The male gaze . . . must objectify for homosociality to work. Ironically, the homosocial system can be maintained only when men avert their gaze from each other; the gaze, however figuratively, must remain focused on a woman."

5. Freud believed hysteria to be present among men as well as women despite the etymology of the term (*Interpretation*, 474).

6. Houghton observes that industrialization and scientific discovery in the Victorian period produced a male anxiety of impotence: of being "small and inconsequential, caught in the grip of huge social or physical forces" (*Victorian Frame of Mind*, 336). Adams similarly notes that the growth of capitalism in the Victorian period entailed a need for men to be dutiful rather than self-willed, which in turn induced "an unease with male sexual aggression" ("Victorian Sexualities," 129).

7. In addition to this maternal factor of repression in the Rossetti household, there may also have been a paternal one. Chris R. Vanden Bossche notes, in "Moving Out: Adolescence," in *A Companion to Victorian Literature and Culture*, ed. Herbert F. Tucker, 82–96 (Malden, MA: Blackwell, 1999), that in the Victorian period, parents began to extend their authority into a young person's teenage years—something that we can see Gabriele Rossetti doing, particularly in relation to DGR's career (see Marsh, *DGR*, 13). Gilles Deleuze and Félix Guattari further observe, in *Anti-Oedipus: Capitalism and Schizophrenia* (1972; Minneapolis: University of Minnesota Press, 1983), that the extension of family life in the nineteenth century led to "unparalleled repression of desire" (121).

8. See D. M. R. Bentley, "From Allegory to Indeterminacy: DGR's Positive Agnosticism," parts 1 and 2, *Dalhousie Review* 70, nos. 1 and 2 (1990): 71–96, 146–66.

9. Adams, "Victorian Sexualities," 129.

10. Another example of a Victorian male poet who arrived at the solution of love as a solution for spiritual discouragement is Matthew Arnold.

11. Amanda S. Anderson, "D. G. Rossetti's 'Jenny': Agency, Intersubjectivity, and the Prostitute," *Genders* 4 (1989): 103–21.

12. Murray Roston, *Victorian Contexts: Literature and the Visual Arts* (New York: New York University Press, 1997), 51.

13. In Dante Gabriel Rossetti, *The Complete Works of Dante Gabriel Rossetti*, ed. William Michael Rossetti (London: Ellis, 1911), 649n (cited in the text as *Works*).

14. See Robin Sheets, "Pornography and Art: The Case of 'Jenny,'" in *Critical Essays on Dante Gabriel Rossetti*, ed. David G. Riede (Toronto, ON: Maxwell McMillan, 1992), 155.

15. More precisely, Lacan's bar signifies the subject's split between his sense of "I" and his awareness of himself as a signifier, where he "sees himself duplicated." This split between one's being and one's symbolic identity is what Lacan calls the subject's "first split" (*Four*, 141–42).

16. The poem thus appears to be motivated by a similar intuition of the arbitrariness of paternal authority that DGR's brother, William Michael Rossetti, arrived at when he "experienc[ed] a sudden absolute perception of the Judeo-Christian deity as a cruel tyrant, and for ever reject[ed] all revealed religion" (Marsh, DGR, 26).

17. One further indication of DGR's increasing disenchantment with the divine Other can be found in a *House of Life* sonnet entitled "Vain Virtues" (1869). In this sonnet, the speaker regrets how "this and that fair deed" committed earlier in a life fail to redeem the doer for sins that he commits later (2). With the force of his imagery, which compares these sins to fallen virgins being sucked into the pits of hell, the sonneteer seems generally to indict the cruelty of the cosmic regime that would refuse to balance out a person's good and bad over the course of a lifetime when rendering its judgment.

18. In an unpublished letter of April 25, 1874, to Frederic George Stephens, quoted in Surtees, *Catalogue*, 14.

19. Apparently disavowing the effect of his own composition, DGR denies the sexually violent suggestions of the painting in a contemporaneous sonnet written on the painting's theme, "Mary's Girlhood" (1848). In the sonnet, he describes Mary as cheerful and confident rather than conspicuously vulnerable, waking "in her white bed" with "no fear" (12).

20. McGann argues that DGR came to paint works that "triumphed in and through [their] commercialism" ("Betrayal," 348), while William E. Fredeman, in "A Shadow of Dante: Rossetti in the Final Years (Extracts from W. M. Rossetti's Unpublished Diaries, 1876–1882)," *Victorian Poetry* 20 (1982), conjectures that DGR "consciously sacrificed his artistic integrity for pragmatic ends" (217).

21. Comparisons may also be drawn with CR's "In an Artist's Studio" (1856), where the artist who "feeds upon" his model's face is a double for a demon lover (9).

22. Riede, for instance, proposes that luxurious portraits of seductive women, including *Lady Lilith*, convert "the seductiveness of woman . . . into the safe and acceptable form of art" and thus keep the terrors of women "distant to keep them harmless" (109). Pollock agrees that images of powerful women in DGR's oeuvre "symbolize the castration which men fear" (16), while J. Hillis Miller likewise finds that DGR's pictures of seductive and vain women such as *Lady Lilith* produce fear of castration in the male viewer (346). Virginia Allen goes further in proposing that DGR was "obsessive" in his fear of female castration and that he specifically designed *Lady Lilith* as an attack on the "New Woman" because he was "unlikely" to have been "an

advocate of Woman's Rights" ("One Strangling Golden Hair," 22–23). But Marsh observes DGR to have been "relatively emancipated" in his relations with women and friendly with strong female artists and feminists such as Anna Howitt and Barbara Smith Bodichon (116).

23. In his figuring of a self-involved woman with a mirror, DGR anticipates Freud's idea of the "narcissistic type": a person who is dangerous not because of castrating intentions but because of supreme aloofness, which is hazardously attractive insofar as it reflects back a surplus of "ego-libido" toward people who lack it in themselves ("Narcissism," 101).

24. Lacan appears to be making reference to Freud's "Formulations Regarding the Two Principles in Mental Functioning," in *The Standard Edition of the Complete Psychological Works of Sigmund Freud*, vol. 12, trans. and ed. James Strachey (London: Hogarth, 1958), 218–26, where Freud argues that the artist is "a man who turns away from reality because he cannot come to terms with the renunciation of instinctual satisfaction which it at first demands . . . [and] becomes the hero, the king, the creator, or the favourite he desired to be" by manipulating other's fantasies in such a way that relieves their dissatisfaction as well (224).

25. *The Boat of Love* (1874), a conception on a Dantesque theme, was rejected by several of DGR's principal patrons, and *A Fight for a Woman* (1865), which portrayed no woman but only two men fighting, was rejected by Gampart because "it was likely to prove unpopular" (Surtees, *Catalogue*, 137, 103).

26. See MacLeod, "Dante Gabriel Rossetti."

27. McGann has similarly noted that in DGR's paintings, "clothing, jewelry, and an elaborate rhetoric of decoration characteristically locate the spectacular—which is to say, the social—mechanisms of sexual desire" (*Game*, 6).

28. Herbert Sussman, "Industrial," in *A Companion to Victorian Literature and Culture*, ed. Herbert F. Tucker (Malden, MA: Blackwell, 1999), 254.

29. Raymond Williams, *Keywords: A Vocabulary of Culture and Society*, rev. ed. (New York: Oxford University Press, 1983), 89. Cited by Sussman in "Industrial," 254.

Conclusion

1. See Freud, "Leonardo da Vinci"; Lacan, *SVII*, esp. section 2, entitled "The Problem of Sublimation."

2. See Sean Gill, "Ecce Homo: Representations of Christ as the Model of Masculinity in Victorian Art and Lives of Jesus," in *Masculinity and Spirituality in Victorian Culture*, ed. Andrew Bradstock et al. (New York: St. Martin's Press, 2000), 166.

3. Quoted in Martha Vicinus, *Independent Women: Work and Community for Single Women, 1850–1920* (London: Virago Press, 1985), 74.

4. See Peter Cominos, "Innocent *Femina Sensualis* in Unconscious Conflict," In *Suffer and Be Still: Women in the Victorian Age*, ed. Martha Vicinus (Bloomington: Indiana University Press, 1972), 163; see also Vicinus, *Independent Women*, 67.

5. See Mary Arseneau, *Recovering Christina Rossetti: Female Community and Incarnational Poetics* (New York: Macmillan, 2004).

6. Antony H. Harrison, "Christina Rossetti and the Sage Discourse of Feminist High Anglicanism," in *Victorian Sages and Cultural Discourse*, ed. Thaïs E. Morgan (New Brunswick, NJ: Rutgers University Press, 1990), 90. Also see Diane D'Amico, "'Equal before God': Christina Rossetti and the Fallen Women of Highgate Penitentiary," in *Gender and Discourse in Victorian Literature and Art*, ed. Antony H. Harrison (DeKalb: Northern Illinois University Press, 1992), 78.

7. Dante's triumph with Beatrice, in Lacan's view, is that he converts an image to whom he bears an initial attraction into a literary conceit that is "close to allegory" and thus can plausibly carry the freight of motivating the Florentine's metaphysical, spiritual, and political inquiries, which are his true interest (*SVII*, 149).

8. James Eli Adams, *Dandies and Desert Saints: Styles of Victorian Masculinity* (Ithaca, NY: Cornell University Press, 1995), 5–6 (cited in the text as *Dandies*).

9. Mary Poovey, *Uneven Developments: The Ideological Work of Gender in Mid-Victorian England* (Chicago: University of Chicago Press, 1988), 9.

10. Cominos, "Innocent *Femina Sensualis*," 157.

11. Kingsley is quoted by Lori M. Miller in "The (Re)Gendering of High Anglicanism," in *Masculinity and Spirituality in Victorian Culture*, ed. Andrew Bradstock et al. (New York: St. Martin's Press, 2000), 36.

Bibliography

Adams, James Eli. *Dandies and Desert Saints: Styles of Victorian Masculinity*. Ithaca, NY: Cornell University Press, 1995.
———. "Victorian Sexualities." In *A Companion to Victorian Literature and Culture*, edited by Herbert F. Tucker, 125–38. Malden, MA: Blackwell, 1999.
Alcorn, Marshall. *Narcissism and the Literary Libido: Rhetoric, Text, and Subjectivity*. New York: New York University Press, 1994.
Allen, Virginia M. "'One Strangling Golden Hair': Dante Gabriel Rossetti's Lady Lilith." *Art Bulletin* 66 (1984): 285–94.
Anderson, Amanda S. "D. G. Rossetti's 'Jenny': Agency, Intersubjectivity, and the Prostitute." *Genders* 4 (1989): 103–21.
Armstrong, Isobel. *Victorian Poetry, Poetics and Politics*. New York: Routledge, 1993.
Arseneau, Mary. "Incarnation and Interpretation: Christina Rossetti, the Oxford Movement, and Goblin Market." *Victorian Poetry* 31, no. 1 (1993): 79–93.
———. "'May My Great Love Avail Me': Christina Rossetti and Dante." In *The Culture of Christina Rossetti: Female Poetics and Victorian Contexts*, edited by Mary Arseneau, Antony H. Harrison, and Lorraine Janzen Kooistra, 22–45. Athens: Ohio University Press, 1999.
———. *Recovering Christina Rossetti: Female Community and Incarnational Poetics*. New York: Macmillan, 2004.
Auerbach, Nina. *Woman and the Demon: The Life of a Victorian Myth*. Cambridge, MA: Harvard University Press, 1982.
Barthes, Roland. *A Lover's Discourse: Fragments*. 1977. Translated by Richard Howard. New York: Hill and Wang, 1978.
Battiscombe, Georgina. *Christina Rossetti: A Divided Life*. New York: Holt, Rinehart and Winston, 1981.
Bentley, D. M. R. "From Allegory to Indeterminacy: DGR's Positive Agnosticism," parts 1 and 2. *Dalhousie Review* 70, nos. 1 and 2 (1990): 71–96, 146–66.
Blake, Kathleen. *Love and the Woman Question in Victorian Literature: The Art of Self-Postponement*. Totowa, NJ: Barnes and Noble, 1983.
Bloom, Harold. *The Anxiety of Influence: A Theory of Poetics*. New York: Oxford University Press, 1973.

Boothby, Richard. *Death and Desire: Psychoanalytic Theory in Lacan's Return to Freud*. New York: Routledge, 1991.

Bossche, Chris R. Vanden. "Moving Out: Adolescence." In *A Companion to Victorian Literature and Culture*, edited by Herbert F. Tucker, 82–86. Malden, MA: Blackwell, 1999.

Botting, Fred. *Gothic*. New York: Routledge, 1996.

Bourne Taylor, Jenny. "Obscure Recesses: Locating the Victorian Unconscious." In *Writing and Victorianism*, edited by J. Bullen, 137–79. New York: Longman, 1997.

Briggs, Julia. "*Speaking Likenesses*: Hearing the Lesson." In *The Culture of Christina Rossetti: Female Poetics and Victorian Contexts*, edited by Mary Arseneau, Antony H. Harrison, and Lorraine Janzen Kooistra, 212–31. Athens: Ohio University Press, 1999.

Bruhm, Steven. *Reflecting Narcissism: A Queer Aesthetic*. Minneapolis: University of Minnesota Press, 2001.

Bryson, John, and Janet Camp Troxall, eds. *Dante Gabriel Rossetti and Jane Morris: Their Correspondence*. Oxford: Clarendon Press, 1976.

Buchanan, Robert. "The Fleshly School of Poetry: Mr. D. G. Rossetti." *Contemporary Review* (October 1871). In *The Broadview Anthology of Victorian Poetry and Poetic Theory*, edited by Thomas J. Collins and Vivian J. Rundle, 1329–40. Peterborough, ON: Broadview, 1999.

Bullen, J. B., ed. *The Sun Is God: Painting, Literature and Mythology in the Nineteenth Century*. New York: Oxford University Press, 1989.

Cary, Elisabeth Luther. *The Rossettis: Dante Gabriel and Christina*. New York: G. P. Putnam's Sons, 1900.

Casteras, Susan P. "Pre-Raphaelite Challenges to Victorian Canons of Beauty." In *The Pre-Raphaelites in Context*, by Malcolm Warner, Susan P. Casteras, Lindsay Smith, Jerome McGann, Sara S. Hodson, and Shelley M. Bennett, 13–35. San Marino, CA: Henry E. Huntington Library and Art Gallery, 1992.

Chapman, Alison. "Defining the Feminine Subject: D. G. Rossetti's Manuscript Revisions to Christina Rossetti's Poetry." *Victorian Poetry* 35, no. 2 (Summer 1997): 139–56.

Chapman, Raymond. *Faith and Revolt: Studies in the Literary Influence of the Oxford Movement*. London: Weidenfeld and Nicolson, 1970.

Clifford, David, and Laurence Roussillon, eds. *Outsiders Looking In: The Rossettis, Then and Now*. London: Anthem, 2003.

Cominos, Peter. "Innocent *Femina Sensualis* in Unconscious Conflict." In *Suffer and Be Still: Women in the Victorian Age*, edited by Martha Vicinus, 155–72. Bloomington: Indiana University Press, 1972.

Conley, Susan. "Rossetti's Cold Women: Irony and Liminal Fantasy in the Death Lyrics." In *The Culture of Christina Rossetti: Female Poetics and Victorian Contexts*, edited by Mary Arseneau, Antony H. Harrison, and Lorraine Janzen Kooistra, 260–84. Athens: Ohio University Press, 1999.

Copjec, Joan. *Read My Desire: Lacan against the Historicists*. Cambridge, MA: MIT Press, 1994.

Culbertson, Philip. "Designing Men: Reading the Male Body as Text." *Journal of Textual Reasoning* 7 (1988). http://etext.virginia.edu/journals/tr/archive/volume7/index.html.

D'Amico, Diane. "Christina Rossetti: The Maturin Poems." *Victorian Poetry* 19 (1980): 117–37.

———. "'Equal before God': Christina Rossetti and the Fallen Women of Highgate Penitentiary." In *Gender and Discourse in Victorian Literature and Art*, edited by Antony H. Harrison, 67–83. DeKalb: Northern Illinois University Press, 1992.

———. "Eve, Mary and Magdalene: Christina Rossetti's Feminine Triptych." In *The Achievement of Christina Rossetti*, edited by David A. Kent, 175–91. Ithaca, NY: Cornell University Press, 1987.

Dante Alighieri. *La Vita Nuova*, translated by Dante Gabriel Rossetti. London: Ellis, 1911. In *Dante Gabriel Rossetti: Collected Writings*, edited by Jan Marsh, 79–128. Chicago: New Amsterdam Books, 2000.

———. *The Divine Comedy 1: Hell (Inferno)*. Translated by Dorothy L. Sayers. Toronto: Holt, Penguin, 1955.

———. *The Divine Comedy 2: Purgatory (Purgatorio)*. Translated by Dorothy L. Sayers. Toronto: Holt, Penguin, 1955.

———. *The Divine Comedy 3: Paradise (Paradiso)*. Translated by Dorothy L. Sayers. Toronto: Holt, Penguin, 1955.

Deleuze, Gilles, and Félix Guattari. *Anti-Oedipus: Capitalism and Schizophrenia*. 1972. Reprint, Minneapolis: University of Minnesota Press, 1983.

DiBattista, Maria. *First Love: The Affections of Modern Fiction*. Chicago: University of Chicago Press, 1991.

Ellis, Steve. *Dante and English Poetry: Shelley to T. S. Eliot*. New York: Cambridge University Press, 1978.

Evans, Dylan. *An Introductory Dictionary of Lacanian Psychoanalyis*. New York: Brunner-Routledge, 1996.

Faas, Ekbert. *Retreat into the Mind: Victorian Poetry and the Rise of Psychiatry*. Princeton, NJ: Princeton University Press, 1988.

Ferguson, George. *Signs and Symbols in Christian Art*. New York: Oxford University Press, 1961.

Foster, Shirley. "Speaking Beyond Patriarchy: The Female Voice in Emily Dickinson and Christina Rossetti." In *The Body and the Text: Hélène Cixous, Reading* and Teaching, edited by Helen Wilcox, Keith McWatters, Ann Thompson, and Linda R. Williams, 66–77. New York: St. Martin's Press, 1990.

Foucault, Michel. *The History of Sexuality.* Vol. 1, *An Introduction.* 1978. Reprint, Toronto, ON: Vintage, 1990.

Fredeman, William E. "Rossetti's 'In Memoriam': An Elegiac Reading of *The House of Life.*" *John Rylands Library Journal* 47 (1965): 298–341.

———. "A Shadow of Dante: Rossetti in the Final Years (Extracts from W. M. Rossetti's Unpublished Diaries, 1876–1882)." *Victorian Poetry* 20 (1982): 217–45.

Freud, Sigmund. *Beyond the Pleasure Principle.* 1920. Translated and edited by James Strachey. New York: Norton, 1989.

———. *Civilization and Its Discontents.* 1930. Translated and edited by James Strachey. New York: Norton, 1961.

———. *The Ego and the Id.* Translated by Joan Riviere, edited by James Strachey. New York: Norton, 1960.

———. "Fetishism." 1927. In *The Standard Edition of the Complete Psychological Works of Sigmund Freud,* vol. 7, 146–58. Translated and edited by James Strachey. London: Hogarth, 1953.

———. "Formulations Regarding the Two Principles in Mental Functioning." In *The Standard Edition of the Complete Psychological Works of Sigmund Freud,* vol. 12, 218–26. Translated and edited by James Strachey. London: Hogarth, 1958.

———. *The Interpretation of Dreams.* 1900. Translated and edited by James Strachey. New York: Avon, 1965.

———. "Leonardo da Vinci and a Memory of His Childhood." 1910. In *The Penguin Freud Library.* Vol. 14, *Art and Literature: Jensen's Gradiva, Leonardo da Vinci and Other Works,* 143–231. Translated and edited by James Strachey, Toronto: Penguin, 1985.

———. "On Narcissism: An Introduction." 1914. In *The Standard Edition of the Complete Psychological Works of Sigmund Freud.* Vol. 14, *Art and Literature: Jensen's Gradiva, Leonardo da Vinci and Other Works,* 146–58. Translated and edited by James Strachey. London: Hogarth, 1957.

———. "The Uncanny." In *The Standard Edition of the Complete Psychological Works of Sigmund Freud.* Vol. 17 (1919): 217–56. Translated and edited by James Strachey. London: Hogarth, 1955.

Frye, Northrop. *The Great Code: The Bible and Literature.* 1983. Toronto, ON: Penguin, 1990.

Garlick, Barbara. "The Frozen Fountain: Christina Rossetti, the Virgin Model, and Youthful Pre-Raphaelitism." In *Virginal Sexuality and Textuality in Victorian Literature,* edited by Lloyd Davis, 105–28. Albany: SUNY Press, 1993.

Gaunt, William. *The Pre-Raphaelite Tragedy*. 1942. London: Cardinal, 1975.
Gilbert, Sandra, and Susan Gubar. *The Madwoman in the Attic: The Woman Writer and the Nineteenth-Century Literary Imagination*. New Haven, CT: Yale University Press, 1979.
Gill, Sean. "Ecce Homo: Representations of Christ as the Model of Masculinity in Victorian Art and Lives of Jesus." In *Masculinity and Spirituality in Victorian Culture*, edited by Andrew Bradstock, Sean Gill, Anne Hogan, and Sue Morgan, 164–78. New York: St. Martin's Press, 2000.
Goldberg, Gail Lynn. "DGR's 'Revising Hand': His Illustrations for Christina Rossetti's Poems." *Victorian Poetry* 20, no. 3–4 (Autumn–Winter 1982): 145–59.
Golden, Arline. "Victorian Renascence: The Revival of the Amatory Sonnet Sequence, 1850–1900." *Genre* 7, no. 1 (1974): 133–47.
Gray, Nicolette. *Rossetti, Dante and Ourselves*. London: Faber and Faber, 1945.
Grosz, Elizabeth. *Jacques Lacan: A Feminist Introduction*. New York: Routledge, 1990.
Gurney, Stephen. "Rossetti: The Failure of Eros." *University of Hartford Studies in Literature* 14, no. 3 (1982): 101–16.
Harrison, Antony H. "Christina Rossetti and the Sage Discourse of Feminist High Anglicanism." In *Victorian Sages and Cultural Discourse*, edited by Thaïs E. Morgan, 87–104. New Brunswick, NJ: Rutgers University Press, 1990.
———. *Christina Rossetti in Context*. Chapel Hill: University of North Carolina Press, 1988.
———. "Dante Rossetti: Parody and Ideology." *Studies in English Literature* 29 (1989): 715–61.
———. "1848." In *A Companion to Victorian Literature and Culture*, edited by Herbert F. Tucker, 19–34. Malden, MA: Blackwell, 1999.
———. "Epistolary Relations: The Correspondence of Christina and Dante Gabriel Rossetti." *Journal of Pre-Raphaelite Studies* 4 (1995): 91–101.
Heath, Stephen. "Joan Riviere and the Masquerade." In *Formations of Fantasy*, edited by Victor Burgin, James Donald, and Cora Kaplan, 45–61. New York: Methuen, 1986.
Henderson, Marina. *D. G. Rossetti*. New York: St. Martin's Press, 1973.
Hobbs, Colleen. "A View from 'The Lowest Place': Christina Rossetti's Devotional Prose." *Victorian Poets* 32 (1994): 409–23.
Holt, Terence. "'Men sell not such in any town': Exchange in 'Goblin Market.'" In *Victorian Women Poets: A Critical Reader*, edited by Angela Leighton, 131–47. Cambridge, MA: Blackwell, 1996.
Honnighausen, Lothar. *The Symbolist Tradition in English Literature: A Study of Pre-Raphaelitism and the Fin de Siècle*. New York: Cambridge University Press, 1988.
Houghton, Walter E. *The Victorian Frame of Mind, 1830–1870*. New Haven, CT: Yale University Press, 1957.

Jarvie, Paul, and Robert Rosenberg. "'Willowwood' Unity and The House of Life." Pre-Raphaelite Review 1, no. 1 (1977–78): 106–19.

Johnson, Wendell Stacy. Sex and Marriage in Victorian Poetry. Ithaca, NY: Cornell University Press, 1975.

Kelvin, Norman. "Dante Gabriel and Christina Rossetti: A Pairing of Identities." Victorian Literature and Culture 32, no. 1 (2004): 239–59.

Knittel, Janna. "Knocking at Paradise: Christina Rossetti Rewrites 'The Blessed Damozel.'" Victorian Review 24, no. 1 (1998): 12–28.

Kooistra, Lorraine Janzen. "Visualizing the Fantastic Subject: Goblin Market and the Gaze." In The Culture of Christina Rossetti: Female Poetics and Victorian Contexts, edited by Mary Arseneau, Antony H. Harrison, and Lorraine Janzen Kooistra, 137–69. Athens: Ohio University Press, 1999.

Kristeva, Julia. Desire in Language. New York: Columbia University Press, 1980.

———. Powers of Horror. New York: Columbia University Press, 1982.

———. Tales of Love. New York: Columbia University Press, 1981.

Lacan, Jacques. The Four Fundamental Concepts of Psychoanalysis. New York: Norton, 1981.

———. "The Function and Field of Speech and Language in Psychoanalysis." 1953. In Ecrits: A Selection, 30–113. New York: Norton, 1977.

———. "God and the Jouissance of the Woman: A Love Letter." 1972–73. In Feminine Sexuality, by Jacques Lacan and the École Freudienne, edited by Juliet Mitchell and Jacqueline Rose, 149–61. New York: Norton, 1985.

———. "The Mirror Stage as Formative of the Function of the I." 1949. In Ecrits: A Selection, 1–7. New York: Norton, 1977.

———. The Seminar of Jacques Lacan. Book I: Freud's Papers on Technique, 1953, 1954. New York: Norton, 1991.

———. The Seminar of Jacques Lacan. Book II: The Ego in Freud's Theory and in the Technique of Psychoanalysis, 1954–1955. New York: Norton, 1991.

———. The Seminar of Jacques Lacan. Book VII: The Ethics of Psychoanalysis, 1959–1960. New York: Norton, 1992.

———. Le Seminaire. Livre XVII: L'envers de la psychanalyse, 1969–1970. Paris: Seuil, 1991.

———. "The Signification of the Phallus." 1958. In Ecrits: A Selection, 281–91. New York: Norton, 1977.

———. "Subversion of the Subject and Dialectic of Desire." In Ecrits: A Selection, 292–325. New York: Norton, 1977.

Langbaum, Robert. The Poetry of Experience: The Dramatic Monologue in Modern Literary Tradition. 1957. Chicago: University of Chicago Press, 1985.

Laplanche, Jean, and Jean-Bertrand Pontalis. "Fantasy and the Origins of Sexuality." 1964. In *Formations of Fantasy*, edited by Victor Burgin, James Donald, and Cora Kaplan, 5–34. New York: Methuen, 1986.

———. *The Language of Psycho-Analysis*. Translated by Donald Nicholson-Smith. New York: Norton, 1973.

Larg, David. *Trial by Virgins: Fragment of a Biography*. London: Peter Davis, 1933.

Linley, Margaret. "Dying to Be a Poetess: The Conundrum of Christina Rossetti." In *The Culture of Christina Rossetti: Female Poetics and Victorian Contexts*, edited by Mary Arseneau, Antony H. Harrison, and Lorraine Janzen Kooistra, 285–314. Athens: Ohio University Press, 1999.

MacCannell, Juliet Flower. *Figuring Lacan: Criticism and the Cultural Unconscious*. Lincoln: University of Nebraska Press, 1986.

MacLeod, Dianne Sachko. "Art Collecting and Victorian Middle-Class Taste." *Art History* 1, no. 3 (1987): 328–51.

———. "Dante Gabriel Rossetti and Titian." *Art Bulletin* 68 (1986): 36–39.

Marsh, Jan. *Christina Rossetti: A Writer's Life*. New York: Penguin, 1995.

———. *Dante Gabriel Rossetti: Painter and Poet*. London: Weidenfeld and Nicolson, 1999.

Marshall, Linda E. "'Abstruse the Problems!': Unity and Divisions in Christina Rossetti's *Later Life: A Double Sonnet of Sonnets*." *Victorian Poetry* 32, nos. 3–4 (1994): 299–314.

Martin, Loy. *Browning's Dramatic Monologues and the Post-Romantic Subject*. Baltimore, MD: John Hopkins University Press, 1985.

McGann, Jerome. "Christina Rossetti's Poems." In *Victorian Women Poets: A Critical Reader*, edited by Angela Leighton, 97–113. Cambridge, MA: Blackwell, 1996.

———. "Dante Gabriel Rossetti and the Betrayal of Truth." *Victorian Poetry* 26, no. 4 (1988): 339–61.

———. *Dante Gabriel Rossetti and the Game That Must Be Lost*. New Haven, CT: Yale University Press, 2000.

———, ed. *Rossetti Archive: The Complete Writings and Pictures of Dante Gabriel Rossetti; A Hypermedia Archive*. http://www.rossettiarchive.org/index.html.

McGhee, Richard D. *Marriage, Duty, and Desire in Victorian Poetry and Drama*. Lawrence: Regents Press of Kansas, 1980.

Mermin, Dorothy. *Godiva's Ride: Women of Letters in England, 1830–1880*. Bloomington: Indiana University Press, 1993.

———. "Heroic Sisterhood in 'Goblin Market.'" *Victorian Poetry* 21, no. 2 (1983): 107–18.

Miller, J. Hillis. "The Mirror's Secret: Dante Gabriel Rossetti's Double Work of Art." *Victorian Poetry* 29, no. 4 (1991): 333–59.

Miller, Lori M. "The (Re)Gendering of High Anglicanism." In *Masculinity and Spirituality in Victorian Culture*, edited by Andrew Bradstock, Sean Gill, Anne Hogan, and Sue Morgan, 27–43. New York: St. Martin's Press, 2000.

Milton, John. *John Milton: Complete Poems and Major Prose*. Edited by Merritt Y. Hughes. New York: MacMillan, 1957.

Morrill, David F. "'Twilight is not good for maidens': Uncle Polidori and the Psychodynamics of Vampirism in *Goblin Market*." *Victorian Poetry* 28, no. 1 (1990): 1–16.

Mulvey, Laura. "You Don't Know What Is Happening, Do You, Mr. Jones?" *Spare Rib* 8 (1973): 13–16.

Oppenheim, Janet. *"Shattered Nerves": Doctors, Patients, and Depression in Victorian England*. New York: Oxford University Press, 1991.

Pearce, Lynne. *Woman/Image/Text: Readings in Pre-Raphaelite Art and Literature*. Toronto: University of Toronto Press, 1991.

Pollock, Griselda. *Vision and Difference: Femininity, Feminism and the Histories of Art*. New York: Routledge, 1988.

Poovey, Mary. *Uneven Developments: The Ideological Work of Gender in Mid-Victorian England*. Chicago: University of Chicago Press, 1988.

Prickett, Stephen. *Victorian Fantasy*. Bloomington: Indiana University Press, 1979.

Ragland-Sullivan, Ellie. *Jacques Lacan and the Philosophy of Psychoanalysis*. Urbana: University of Illinois Press, 1986.

Rees, Joan. "Christina Rossetti, Poet." *Critical Quarterly* 26, no. 3 (1984): 59–72.

Reynolds, Margaret. "Speaking Unlikenesses: The Double Text in CR's 'After Death' and 'Remember Me.'" In *The Culture of Christina Rossetti: Female Poetics and Victorian Contexts*, edited by Mary Arseneau, Antony H. Harrison, and Lorraine Janzen Kooistra, 3–21. Athens: Ohio University Press, 1999.

Riede, David. *Dante Gabriel Rossetti Revisited*. Toronto, ON: Maxwell McMillan, 1992.

Rose, Jacqueline. "Introduction—II." In *Feminine Sexuality*, by Jacques Lacan and the École Freudienne, edited by Juliet Mitchell and Jacqueline Rose, 27–58. New York: Norton, 1985.

Rosenblum, Dolores. "Christina Rossetti and Poetic Sequence." In *The Achievement of Christina Rossetti*, edited by David A. Kent, 132–56. Ithaca, NY: Cornell University Press, 1987.

———. "Christina Rossetti's Religious Poetry: Watching, Looking, Keeping Vigil." *Victorian Women Poets: A Critical Reader*, edited by Angela Leighton, 114–30. Cambridge, MA: Blackwell, 1996.

Rossetti, Christina. *Christina Rossetti: Poems and Prose*. Edited by Jan Marsh. Ruland, VT: Everyman, 1994.

———. *The Complete Poems of Christina Rossetti*. Edited by Rebecca W. Crump. Baton Rouge: University of Louisiana Press, 1979.

---. *The Face of the Deep*. London: Young and Co., 1892.

---. *Selected Prose of Christina Rossetti*. Edited by David A. Kent and P. G. Stanwood. New York: St. Martin's Press, 1988.

Rossetti, Dante Gabriel. *The Complete Works of Dante Gabriel Rossetti*. Edited by William M. Rossetti. London: Ellis, 1911.

---. *Dante Gabriel Rossetti: Collected Writings*. Edited by Jan Marsh. Chicago: New Amsterdam Books, 2000.

---. *Letters of Dante Gabriel Rossetti*. Edited by Oswald Doughty and Robert Wall. Oxford: Clarendon Press, 1965.

---. "The Stealthy School of Criticism." 1871. In *The Broadview Anthology of Victorian Poetry and Poetic Theory*, edited by Thomas J. Collins and Vivian J. Rundle, 1341–45. Peterborough, ON: Broadview, 1999.

Rossetti, William Michael, ed. *Dante Gabriel Rossetti: His Family Letters with a Memoir*. London: Elvey, 1895.

Roston, Murray. *Christina Rossetti: The Poetry of Endurance*. Carbondale: Southern Illinois University Press, 1986.

---. *Victorian Contexts: Literature and the Visual Arts*. New York: New York University Press, 1997.

Roudiez, Leon S. "Introduction." In *Desire in Language*, by Julia Kristeva, edited and translated by Leon S. Roudiez, 1–20. New York: Columbia University Press, 1980.

Ruskin, John. *The Stones of Venice*. 1853. Edited by J. G. Links. New York: Da Capo Press, 2003.

Sedgwick, Eve Kosofsky. *Between Men: English Literature and Male Homosocial Desire*. New York: Columbia University Press, 1985.

Sheets, Robin. "Pornography and Art: The Case of 'Jenny.'" In *Critical Essays on Dante Gabriel Rossetti*, edited by David G. Riede, 149–68. Toronto, ON: Maxwell McMillan, 1992.

Sherbutt, Sylvia Bailey. "Revisionist Mythmaking in Christina Rossetti's 'Goblin Market': Eve's Apple and Other Questions Revised and Reconsidered." *Victorian Newsletter* 82 (1992): 40–44.

Sonstroem, David. *Rossetti and the Fair Lady*. Middleton, CT: Wesleyan University Press, 1970.

Spector, Stephen J. "Love, Unity and Desire in the Poetry of Dante Gabriel Rossetti." *ELH* 38, no. 3 (1971): 432–58.

Spitz, Ellen Handler. "A Critique of Pathography: Freud's Original Psychoanalytical Approach to Art." In *Essential Papers on Literature and Psychoanalysis*, edited by Emanuel Berman, 238–61. New York: New York University Press, 1993.

Starzyk, Lawrence J. "Victorian Artistic Recursions." *Mosaic* 20, no. 2 (1987): 57–70.

Surtees, Virginia. *The Paintings and Drawings of Dante Gabriel Rossetti (1828–1882): A Catalogue Raisonné*. Oxford: Clarendon, 1971.

Sussman, Herbert. "Industrial." In *A Companion to Victorian Literature and Culture*, edited by Herbert F. Tucker, 252–7. Malden, MA: Blackwell, 1999.

———. *Victorian Masculinities: Manhood and Masculine Poetics in Early Victorian Literature and Art*. New York: Cambridge University Press, 1995.

Taylor, Beverly. "Beatrix / Creatrix: Elizabeth Siddal as Muse and Creator." *Journal of Pre-Raphaelite Studies* 4 (1995): 29–41.

Tennyson, George B. *Victorian Devotional Poetry*. Cambridge, MA: Harvard University Press, 1981.

Trilling, Lionel. "Freud and Literature." 1940. Reprinted in *The Liberal Imagination*. New York: Viking, 1950.

Trosman, Harry. "Freud's Cultural Background." In *Freud: The Fusion of Science and Humanism: The Intellectual History of Psychoanalysis*, edited by John E. Gedo and George H. Pollock. New York: International Universities Press, 1976.

Vicinus, Martha. *Independent Women: Work and Community for Single Women, 1850–1920*. London: Virago Press, 1985.

Waugh, Evelyn. *Rossetti: His Life and Works*. London: Duckworth, 1928.

Whitla, William. "Questioning the Convention: Christina Rossetti's Sonnet Sequence 'Monna Innominata.'" In *The Achievement of Christina Rossetti*, edited by David A. Kent, 82–131. Ithaca, NY: Cornell University Press, 1987.

Wiesenthal, Christine. "Regarding Christina Rossetti's 'Reflection.'" *Victorian Poetry* 39, no. 3 (2001): 389–406.

William, Charles. *The Figure of Beatrice*. London: Faber, 1943.

Williams, Anne. *Art of Darkness: A Poetics of Gothic*. Chicago: University of Chicago Press, 1995.

Williams, Raymond. *Keywords: A Vocabulary of Culture and Society*. Revised edition. New York: Oxford University Press, 1983.

Winwar, Frances. *Poor Splendid Wings: The Rossettis and Their Circle*. Boston: Little Brown, 1933.

Wright, Elizabeth. *Psychoanalytic Criticism: Theory in Practice*. London: Methuen, 1984.

Žižek, Slavoj. *The Plague of Fantasies*. New York: Verso, 1997.

Index

Page numbers in bold type refer to definitions; those in italics refer to figures.

abject (the), 8; and beauty, 64; and the maternal era, 54–55, 175n23
Adams, James Eli, 4, 161, 129n6
Aeneid (Virgil), 71
Allen, Virginia, 183n22
Althusser, Louis, 4
Anderson, Amanda, 126
Armstrong, Isobel, 172n26
Arnold, Matthew, 182n10
Arseneau, Mary, 56, 63, 158, 170n14, 174n20
Artaud, Antonin, 172n28
Auerbach, Nina, 174n22
Austen, Jane, 51

Barthes, Roland, 108, 115
Beardsley, Aubrey, 101
Bentley, D. M. R., 125
Bernard of Clairvaux, 94
Blake, Katherine, 168n24
Blake, William, 4
Bloom, Harold, 69, 79, 103
Bodichon, Barbara Smith, 184n22
Boothby, Richard, 19
Bossche, Chris R. Vanden, 182n7
Botting, Fred, 45
Briggs, Julia, 175n34
Brontë, Charlotte, 51
Brown, Charles Brockden, 45
Brown, Ford Madox, 75–76
Bruhm, Steven, 105
Bryson, John, and Janet Camp Troxall, 177n13
Buchanan, Robert, 101, 167n15, 167n17
Bullen, J. B., 175n29
Butler, Judith, 7, 168n26, 173n15
Byron, Lord (George Gordon), 4

Carlyle, Thomas, 162
Casteras, Susan P., 79, 150
castration, **181n2**; allegories of, 42, 91; anxiety of, diagnosed in works of Dante Gabriel Rossetti, 183n22; and desire, 21, 128, 147; and fetishism, 88, 111, 128–29, 145; by the gaze, 31, 150; of the male subject, 132, 142, 164
Cavalcanti, (Guido), 93
Cayley, Charles, 14
Celine (Louis-Ferdinand), 172n28
Chapman, Alison, 168n29
Chapman, Raymond, 29
Cixous, Hélène, 7, 36
Clifford, David, and Laurence Roussillon, 168n28
Coleridge, Samuel Taylor: "Love", 135
Cominos, Peter, 158
Conley, Susan, 171n22
Copjec, Joan, 8; on desire and the symbolic law, 49; on the gaze, 120, 181n3; on the psychoanalytic subject, 4, 80; on the superego, 63–64
Cornforth, Fanny, 147
Craven, Frederick, 151
Culbertson, Philip, 181n4

D'Amico, Diane, 16, 170n16, 174n18, 185n6
Dante Alighieri, 24, 93, 103, 117, 121, 157, 162
—works: *Commedia*, 71–72, 80, 87, 123–25, 169n4; *Inferno*, 52, 59, 70, 74–76; *Paradiso*, 11, 72, 94, 120; *Purgatorio*, 80; *Vita Nuova*, 71, 76–91, 93–95, 118, 178n24
death drive (in Lacan), 21, 24–26
Deleuze, Gilles, and Félix Guattari, 182n7
desire, 130, 155; divided in the subject, 3–5, 7; divided in the works of

desire (cont.)
  Christina Rossetti and Dante Gabriel Rossetti, 1–2, 5–7; and the drives, 166n6; hysterical, **122**, 125–37, 146–50; as lack, 29, 97, 113–15, 159; and language, 76; and the Symbolic Law, 3, 41, 44–5, 124; stabilized by symbolic order, 46, 81, 84, 90, 95, 104, 108, 117, 120. *See also* love; imaginary order; symbolic order
DiBattista, Maria, 179n3
display, 135
Dixon, Thomas, 149
dreams, 57–61, 81, 84–85, 175n24
drives (the), 90, 42, 45

écriture féminine, 14, 36–37, 172n26
ego ideal, 41, 45, in Freud, 40, 71, 180n8
Ellis, Steve, 176n8, 177n18
Evans, Dylan: *Introductory Dictionary of Lacanian Psychoanalysis*, 112, 170n10, 172n3

Faas, Ekbert, 5–6
fantasy, theory of, **41–42**, 48–9, 60, 172n4
Fazio Degli Uberti, 143
Ferguson, George, 178n25
fetishism, 74, 80, 87–91, 110–14, 128, 151–52; and castration, 111; as defense against imaginary desire, 89–90, 179n32; and the drives, 111; in Freud, 87–90, 179n31; vs. *objet petit a*, 110–11; and the Other, 88
Foster, Shirley, 171n26
Foucault, Michel, 4
Fredeman, William, 180, 183n20
Freud, Sigmund: on the artist, 147; "Formulations Regarding the Two Principles in Mental Functioning," 184n24; on hysteria, 182; *Interpretation of Dreams*, 57, 71; "Uncanny," 83, 167n14. *See also under* ego ideal; fetishism; love; narcissism; psychoanalysis; repression sublimation; superego
Frye, Northrop, 58–59

Gampart, Ernest, 147, 151, 184n25
Garlick, Barbara, 168n26, 174n18m
Gaskell, Elizabeth, 178n28
Gaunt, William, 69, 149
gaze (the), **31**, **120**; and the artist, 129, 133, 139, 147, 184n24; and castration, 132; and easing of class antagonism, 147, 149–51; as gendered, 181n2; and the light, 120, 131, 138–42, 152; and the lure, 19, 133, 135–36, 144–46, 150–52; male exclusion from, 139; of the Other vs. male, 122, 181n3; and the screen, 31, 132, 140; and the showing, 143, 145
gender difference, 28, 33–37, 73, 80, 81, 135, 138, 142, 162–63, 164, 184n22
Genesis (Book of), 34
Gesta Romanorum, 132
Gilbert, Sandra, and Susan Gubar, 168n23, 171n20, 173n8, 174n17
Gill, Sean, 184n2
Goblin Market (Christina Rossetti), 5–6, 39, 158, 167n15; and familiarity with abjection, 64–65; goblins as superego, 62–64; Victorian sisterhoods in, 158
Goldberg, Gail Lynn, 168n29
Grosz, Elizabeth, 16, 36, 169n30
Guattari, Félix. *See* Deleuze, Gilles
Gubar, Susan. *See* Gilbert, Sandra
Guinicelli (Guido), 93
Gurney, Stephen, 177n12, 180n7
Guyon, Jeanne, 10, 20, 33

Hake, Thomas Gordon, 91, 146
Harrison, Antony H., 7, 10, 12, 22, 84, 169n29, 169n3, 170n14, 173n12, 185n6
Herbert, Ruth, 89–90
Hillis Miller, J., 80, 153
Hobbs, Colleen, 10, 35, 171n25
Holt, Terence, 63
homosociality, **122**, 147
Honnighausen, Lothar, 86
Houghton, Walter E., 176n5, 182n6
House of Life, The (Dante Gabriel Rossetti), 1, 9, 71–72, 74, 92, 165n2; aestheticism in, 101–2; biographical contexts of, 96, 100–101; dialogue in, 95, 97, 113–14; imaginary disarray in, 95, 97–99, 107, 117; narcissism in 105–8; *objet petit a* in, 97, 108–16; Petrarchan structure of, 95–96; sensuality of, 101–2, 123, 177n14; spiritualization of love in, 108, 113–16
—Sonnets: "Barren Spring," 115, "Birth Bond," 97–98; "Body's Beauty," 111, 145; "Broken Music," 97–99; "Day

of Love," 113–15; "Death's Songsters, 115; "Equal Troth," 113–14; "Heart's Compass," 109–10; "Heart's Hope," 103, 109, 113; "Her Gifts," 112, 116; Introductory Sonnet, 97; "Kiss," 103; "Known in Vain," 97, 99–100, 180n10; "Landmark," 99–100; "Love Letter," 103–4; "Love's Baubles," 112; "Love's Testament," 97; "Mid-Rapture," 113; "Newborn Death," 115, 121; "Nuptial Sleep," 101–2, 104; "The One Hope," 116; "Secret Parting," 104; "Severed Selves," 104; "Silent Noon," 102; "Soul's Beauty," 111; "Soul's Sphere," 156; "Through Death to Love," 97; "Transfigured Life," 97; "Vain Virtues," 120, 183n17; *Willowwood* sonnets, 16, 105–9; "Without Her," 115; "Youth's Antiphony," 113–14

Howell, Charles A., 96
Howitt, Anna, 184n22
Hunt, Holman (*The Light of the World*), 157

imaginary order, **2–3**, 9; and damnation, 71, 74–76; and degradation of the subject, 27, 52–53, 104–5; disarraying effects of, 72, 95, 97–99, 107, 117; in dreams, 16, 48, 81, 84–85, 175n24; effects on discourse, 11; and fixation on the image, 83–84, 98, 99; individualizing effects of, 73, 79–80; intimacy through, 106, 118–19; 130–31, 151–54; and mirror stage, 98; and passion, **14**–18, 76, 84, 90, 94–103, 107; and specularity, 30, 30, 78–80, 169n5; and symmetrical mirroring, 74–79. *See also* narcissism
Irigaray, Luce, 7, 36
Isaacs, Susan, 49

James, Henry, 179n33
Jarvie, Paul, and Robert Rosenberg, 180n7, 180n13
John, Book of, 11
jouissance, **9**, 48, 50–53, 62–64, 112, 145, 169n31
Julian of Norwich, 10

Kant, Immanuel, 10
Keats, John, 93, 102
Keble, John, 21

Kelvin, Norman, 168n28
Kempe, Margery, 10
Kempis, Thomas à, 10
Kingsley, Charles, 163
Kooistra, Lorraine Janzen, 39, 174n16
Kristeva, Julia: on art, 91, 140; on Dante, 72; on love, 94, 119–20, 144; 151; on semiotic order and the chora, 37, 61, 99, 172n28; on symbolism, 86; on writing, 123, 172n28. *See also* abject; *under* love; repression

Lacan, Jacques: and division of the subject, 2; and Freud, 2; optical schema for the theory of narcissism, 106, 107; *Seminar VII*, 26. *See also* castration; desire; display; drives; ego ideal; fantasy; gaze; imaginary order; jouissance; love; masquerade; narcissism; *objet petit a*; Other; phallus; psychoanalysis; real; subject; sublimation; superego; symbolic law; symbolic order; Thing
Laplanche, Jean, and Pontalis, Jean-Bertrand, 41–42, 58, 172n4
Larg, David: *Trial By Virgins*, 94
Later Life (Christina Rossetti), 1, 14, 26, 156; and Christian discourses, 31–33; as deconstruction of desire, 28–30; and the gaze, 30–31
Linley, Margaret, 173n8
love, 182n7; courtly, 26–28, 77–78, 93–95, 137, 143, 144, 160, 185n7; critique of in Christina Rossetti, 13–18, 27; as dialectic between imaginary and symbolic orders (Lacan), 91; divine (Kristeva), 14; in Freud, 96; as redemptive in Dante Gabriel Rossetti, 72–73, 94–96, 116–17, 126, 130–31, 151–54, 179n32; spirituo-erotic (Kristeva), 10–14, 18–19, 169n5, 158; as trauma, 72–73, 176n9

Macleod, Dianne Sachko, 91, 181n2, 184n26
Marsh, Jan, 14, 33, 37, 50, 57, 59–60, 65, 71, 96–97, 125, 138, 149, 167n15, 172nn6–7, 178n28, 180nn9–12, 184n22
Martin, Loy, 2
masquerade (the), 135

Matthew, Book of, 40,
Maude (Christina Rossetti), 42–50, 57, 168n23; death drive in, 44–47; evasion of normative sexuality in, 46–49; moral masochism in, 43–44
McGann, Jerome, 6, 70–1, 146, 151, 165n2, 183n20, 184n27
Mermin, Dorothy, 173n8
Miller, J. Hillis, 80, 106, 167n22, 180n13, 183n22
Mitchell, John, 151
Morrill, David F., 40, 57, 174n18
Morris, Jane, 90, 96–97, 177n13, 179n33, 180n12
Morris, William, 90, 101
Mulvey, Laura, 7, 88, 179n31

narcissism, 9; and the abject (Kristeva), 48, 50, 175n28; and death, 47–49; diagnosed in Dante Gabriel Rossetti's works, 98, 105–8, 114, 153, 180n13; in Freud, 71, 105, 176n9, 180n8, 184n23; and the maternal era (Kristeva), 53–55, 61, 98, 107; optical schema for the theory of narcissism (Lacan), 106, 107; primary and secondary, 72; and the superego, 46–47; and symmetrical mirroring, 74–79, 98, 101–4, 113. *See also* imaginary order

objet petit a, 97, **108**, 108–16, 154
Oppenheim, Janet, 167n18
Other (the): beyond language, 23; castrating, 128, 134–35, 145–47; in contrast with the other, 3; desire of, 121, 129–30, 135, 154; direct solicitation of in Christina Rossetti, 20, 159; gaze of, 76, 122–23, 131–33, 140–45, 152–54; inexorability of in Dante Gabriel Rossetti, 124, 132–35, 142, 183n16, 183n17; secular, 129–30, 142, 144–51; unresponsiveness of in Christina Rossetti, 20
Oxford Movement. *See* Tractarianism

Patmore, Coventry: "The Angel in the House," 163
Pearce, Lynne, 88, 178n28
Petrarch, 26; *Canzoniere*, 95
phallus (the), 27–28, 35, 128, 135
Plato, 112

Polidori, John, 5, 40, 174n18
Pollock, Griselda, 88, 121, 178n28, 183n22
Poovey, Mary, 162
Pre-Raphaelite Brotherhood, 8, 73
Pre-Raphaelitism, 96, 150, 155, 161, 179n33
psychoanalysis (clinical): in Freud, 29, 67–68, 155; in Lacan, 97
psychoanalytic theory: and cultural materialism, 4; and Christian discourses, 4–5; 21, 58–60, 63; and romanticism, 5, 166n12; and utilitarianism, 4, 63; and Victorian art, 3–7
psychobiography, 166n11
Pusey, Edward, Bouverie, 163

Rae, George, 181
real (the), 9, 33, 166n6
repetition compulsion, 21, 171n20
repression, 39–40, 158, 182n7; in Freud, 25, 71; primary and secondary (Kristeva), 48, 53–56, 175n23, 182n7
Revelation, Book of, 24, 39, 43, 58–61, 64
Reynolds, Margaret, 168n26, 172n26
Riede, David, 98, 146, 183n22
Romans, Book of, 125
Rose, Jacqueline, 36, 172n27
Rosenberg, Robert. *See* Jarvie, Paul
Rosenblum, Dolores, 170n12, 171n20
Rossetti, Christina, 103, 158; apocalyptic vision in, 14, 24–26, 34–37, 39, 43, 58; asceticism in, 18, 26; and Christian discourses, 29, 31–37, 59; and Christian transcendence, 19, 22–26, 28–30, 49–50; and Dante, 69, 176n3; and Dante Gabriel Rossetti, 16, 24, 100, 174n20, 183n21; and death, 24–26; demonic figures in, 38–43, 53–58, 62–63, 66–68; fantasy writing in, 42–43, 57–60, 65–68; gothicism in, 5, 38–46, 50–57, 62, 107; and medieval mysticism, 10–12; minimalism in, 22–24; obstructed scopic desire in, 38–39, 55–56; psychoanalytical criticism of, 7; repetition in, 21–22, 24; seduction narratives in, 42, 52, 58; spirituo-eroticism in, 10–12, 18–20; Tractarian influence on, 21, 29
—Works: "Amor Mundi," 18; "Better Resurrection," 10, 19; "Coast Night-

mare," 40, 54–56; "Chilly Night," 54–55; "Confluents," 11, 18; "Echo from Willowood," 16; *Face of the Deep*, 14, 34–35; "Eve," 39; "Hour and the Ghost," 39, 52; "If I Had Words," 23; "In an Artist's Studio," 183n21; "Love from the North," 52; "Lowest Place," 20–21; *Monna Innominata*, 14, 26–28, 94; "My Dream," 39–40, 57, 60–62, "The Prince's Progress," 100; "Shut Out," 38–39, 42, 66; "So I Grew Half Delirious and Quite Sick," 57–62; "Somewhere or Other," 24–25; "Song," 24; *Speaking Likenesses*: 39, 65–67; "Three Nuns," 47–49, 173n12, 173n13; "Triad," 8, 17–18; "Twice," 14; "Weary in Well-Doing," 19; "Who Shall Deliver Me," 40; "Winter My Secret," 173n13

See also *Goblin Market*; *Later Life*; *Maude*

Rossetti, Dante Gabriel: agnosticism in, 70, 117, 125, 138, 146, 183n16; Art Catholic period, 70, 121–23, 142, 145–46, 154; and Dante Alighieri, 69–92, 93–94, 103, 117, 124, 176n2; neuroticism of, 71–72, 125, 162; and the inaccessible love object, 77, 90–91; middle-class clientele of, 122–23, 146–51, 154, 183n20; psychoanalytical criticism of, 9; recursiveness in, 83–84; shift from poetry to painting, 92, 96–97, 129, 180n9; symbolism in, 85, 116, 133, 140; Venetian period, 91, 121–23, 142–46, 147–51; and Victorian aesthetic canons, 79–80, 87

—Works: "Altar-Flame," 94; *Beata Beatrix*, 118–22, 144; *Beatrice Meeting Dante at a Marriage Feast, Denies Him Her Salutation*, 78, 77; *Belcolore*, 147; "Blessed Damozel," 24, 94, 123–26, 131, 134, 151, 162–63; *Blue Bower*, 149; *Boat of Love*, 184n25; *Bocca Baciata*, 122, 147; *Bonifazio's Mistress*, 143–44, 147; *Dante's Dream at the Time of the Death of Beatrice* (1856), 85, 84–85; *Dante's Dream at the Time of the Death of Beatrice* (1871), 86, 85–89, 180n9; "Dantis Tenebrae," 5, 70–71; *La Donna della Finestra*, 146; *Early Italian Poets from Ciullo d'Alcamo to Dante Alighieri*, 93; *Ecce Ancilla Domini!* 138–39, 141, 143; *Fair Rosamund*, 142; *Fazio's Mistress*, 143, 143, 149; *Fight for a Woman*, 184n25; *First Anniversary of the Death of Beatrice* (1849), 82, 81–83, 98; *First Anniversary of the Death of Beatrice* (1853), 83, 83–84; *Genevieve*, 135–37, 136; *Girlhood of Mary Virgin*, 138–39, 139, 183n19; "Hand and Soul," 160–61; *Helen of Troy*, 142, 145; "Jenny," 2, 5–6, 123, 126–31, 151–52, 162; *Lady Lilith*, 111, 145–46, 183n22; *Mary Magdalene at the Door of Simon the Pharisee*, 123, 152–54, 153; "Mary's Girlhood," 183n19; *The Merciless Lady*, 147; *Monna Pomona*, 145; *Morning Music*, 145; *Paolo and Francesca da Rimini*, 75, 74–6, 79–80, 84, 101, 119, 174n20; *La Pia de Tolomei*, 146; "Portrait," 121; *Salutation of Beatrice*, 79, 77–81; *Sibylla Palmifera*, 111; "Staff and Scrip," 123, 132–35; "St. Agnes Intercession," 144; *Venus Verticordia*, 145; *Woman Combing Her Hair*, 145

—Volumes: *Ballads and Sonnets* (1881), 165n2; *Poems* (1870), 165n2; *Sonnets by Dante Gabriel Rossetti* (notebook), 179n4

—Translations: *Early Italian Poets from Ciullo d'Alcamo to Dante Alighieri*, 93; *La Vita Nuova* (Dante Alighieri), 93

Rossetti, Frances, 5
Rossetti, Gabriele, 5, 69, 101, 138, 176n2; *Il mistero dell'amor platonica del medio evo*, 93
Rossetti, William Michael, 93, 116, 127, 172n6, 173n9, 183n16
Rossetti family, 5, 93
Roston, Murray, 127
Roussillon, Laurence. See Clifford, David
Ruskin, John, 174n21

Sayers, Dorothy L., 71, 76, 169n4, 175n28
Scott, Walter, 94
Sedgwick, Eve, 122, 181n4
Sherbutt, Sylvia Bailey, 174n22,
Siddal, Elizabeth (Rossetti), 89, 96, 98, 101, 177n13
Smiles, Samuel: *Self-Help*, 175n33
Song of Solomon, 18
Spector, Stephen J., 106, 114, 180n7
Spitz, Ellen Handler, 7
Starzyk, Lawrence, J., 83
Stilnovisti poets, 94

subject (the): as castrated, 132, 181n2, 182n15; Christian, 2, 4; female, 26–28; male, 73, 125–29, 138–42, 161–62, 182n7; psychoanalytic, 1–2, 4; Romantic, 4

sublimation: through art, 157, 71–72; through courtly love, 27, 94–95, 160–62; in Freud, **12**, 19, 28–29, 31, 71, 157, 170n9; through language, 13, 20–24, 32–33, 115–17; through symbolism, 86

superego, 41, in Freud, **40**; and jouissance, 62–64, 134; and narcissism, 46–47; and narrative, 68; and the symbolic law, 41, 45, 51, 63

Surtees, Virginia, 84, 89, 142, 149, 178n25

Sussman, Herbert, 122, 139, 161, 178n20

Swinburne, Algernon, 167n15

symbolic order: **2–3**, 155, Dantean, 80; and language, 91; and prohibition, 76; subjection through the gaze, 121. *See also under* desire; superego

Taylor, Beverley, 177n13
Taylor, Jenny Bourne, 167
Tennyson, Alfred, Lord, 162
Tennyson, George B., 21
Thing (the), **12**, 156–58

Titian (Tiziano Vecelli), 149
Tractarianism, 21, 29, 158
Trilling, Lionel, 166n12
Trosman, Harry, 167n12
Troxall, Janet Camp. *See* Bryson, John

Vicinus, Martha, 159, 185n3
Victorian period: aesthetic culture in, 150–51; Anglican sisterhoods in, 159; Dante, reception of, 93; feminist movement in, 33, 163–64; masculinity, anxieties regarding in, 161–63; materialism of, 161–62; mental sciences, 6; sonnet, revival in, 93; sublimation opportunities in, 157–58; woman, idealization of, 126, 137, 142

Waugh, Evelyn, 118
Wiesenthal, Christine, 167n22, 168n26, 173n15
Williams, Anne, 50, 53
Williams, Charles, 74, 150
Williams, Isaac, 21
Wright, Elizabeth, 166n11

Žižek, Slavoj, 8, 74, 87–88, 110, 128, 142, 179n30, 181n16